**Temple Israel Library**
**Minneapolis, Minn.**

Please sign your full name on the above card.

Return books promptly to the Library or Temple Office.

Fines will be charged for overdue books or for damage or loss of same.

DEMCO

# The
# Torah
# Revealed

## Talmudic Masters
## Unveil the Secrets
## of the Bible

**Avraham Yaakov Finkel**

AN ARTHUR KURZWEIL BOOK

JOSSEY-BASS
A Wiley Imprint
www.josseybass.com

Published by Jossey-Bass
A Wiley Imprint
989 Market Street, San Francisco, CA 94103-1741   www.josseybass.com

Jossey-Bass books and products are available through most bookstores.
To contact Jossey-Bass directly call our Customer Care Department
within the U.S. at 800-956-7739, outside the U.S. at 317-572-3986 or
fax 317-572-4002.

Jossey-Bass also publishes its books in a variety of electronic formats. Some
content that appears in print may not be available in electronic books.

**Library of Congress Cataloging-in-Publication Data**
Finkel, Avraham Yaakov.
The Torah revealed: Talmudic masters unveil the secrets of the Bible
/ Avraham Yaakov Finkel.—1st ed.
    p. cm.
"An Arthur Kurzweil book."
Includes bibliographical references and index.
ISBN 0–7879–6920–6
  1. Bible. O.T. Pentateuch—Criticism, interpretation, etc.  2. Talmud.
3. Rabbinical literature.  4. Midrash.  5. Hasidim—Legends.  6. Ethics,
Jewish. I. Title.
BS1225.52.F56 2004
222'.107—dc22
2003019410

Printed in the United States of America
FIRST EDITION
*HB Printing*   10 9 8 7 6 5 4 3 2 1

# Contents

---
### NUMBERS
---

*To my children*
*Moshe and Brenda Finkel*
*Berish and Elisheva Weinberg*
*Moshe and Judy Klein*
*Chaim and Naomi Finkel*
*my grandchildren and great-grandchildren*
*who are a source of great nachas and inspiration,*
*with love*

# Introduction

In his *Introduction to the Mishnah*, Maimonides tells us that when Moses went up Mount Sinai to receive the Ten Commandments, God taught him the entire Torah. In addition, God gave Moses orally a detailed explanation of every mitzvah. Moses recorded the laws on a scroll—*Torah shebiktav*, the Written Torah—which was eternally fixed and unchanging. He then verbally transmitted the explanations of the laws to the people. This vast body of knowledge is known as *Torah sheb'al peh*, the Oral Torah. It had to be memorized and was passed down from father to son, from master to disciple. Thus, an unbroken chain of tradition came into being, a heritage spanning the generations, a timeless legacy reaching back to Sinai.

For example, the Torah says, "You must live in *sukkot* [thatched huts] for seven days" (Leviticus 23:42). But it does not mention the specifics of the *sukkah*, its walls, and the material to be used for its roof. These details were given orally to Moses along with the pertinent scriptural verses.

Another example: The Torah says that the Jews should "make zizith on the corners of their garments" (Numbers 20:38). But how are we to make the zizith? How many threads and how many knots? How should they be attached? The Torah does not say. God gave these details to Moses by word of mouth.

Another example: The Torah says, "You must love your neighbor as you love yourself" (Leviticus 19:18). But what are the ramifications of this commandment? These are discussed in the Talmud.

Another example: The Torah says about preparing kosher meat, "You may slaughter . . . as I have commanded you" (Deuteronomy 12:21). But there is no commandment anywhere in the Torah regarding the specifics of *shechitah* (ritual slaughtering) of animals and birds, how it is to be performed, and on what part of the animal the cut is to be made. So the phrase "as I have commanded you" must undoubtedly refer to another source of law: the unwritten Oral Law.

Rabbi Samson Raphael Hirsch compares the relationship between the Written and Oral Torah to the short notes a student takes while listening to a lecture on a complex scientific subject. In the analogy, the student's notes exemplify the Written Torah, whereas the lecturer's discourse represents the Oral Torah. For students who have heard the whole lecture, the short notes are sufficient to refresh their memories on all the fine points of the master's lecture. For these students, a word, a question mark, an exclamation point, or an underlined phrase call to mind an entire train of thought. For students who have not heard the lecture, such notes are useless. If they reconstruct the lecture from these notes, they are bound to get a total distortion. Words and punctuation marks that help the student who heard the lecture recall the wisdom that has been taught are so much gibberish to the outsider. The one who has not attended the lecture sneers at the truths that the student reproduces from his notes.

ൟ ൟ ൟ

The Torah was given into the hands of those who were already familiar with the Law. It was to be a means of reviving the knowledge they had committed to memory. The Torah was meant to be a book to which the student could go for references to the traditional actual laws, so that the written verses would make it easy for him to recall the knowledge he had received orally.

The following verse hints at the idea: "God said to Moses, 'Come up to Me to the mountain and remain there. I shall give you the stone tablets, the Torah and the mitzvah that I have written for the people's instruction'" (Exodus 24:12). R. Shimon ben Lakish in tractate *Berachot* 5a expounds: "The Torah" refers to the Written Law, "and the mitzvah" refers to its interpretation, the Oral Law.

You could say that the Written Torah is only a set of notes that help the teacher impart verbally the real lesson that the Oral Torah contains. Thus, the Written and the Oral Torah are inseparably linked with one another. Without the interpretation of the Oral Torah, the laws of the Written Torah are incomprehensible and cannot be applied. Deviant sects, such as the Sadducees and Karaites, who denied the validity of the Oral Torah, could not survive and have faded into oblivion.

The oral transmission continued until the growing might of the Roman Empire and the tribulations and dispersion of the Jewish people that followed in its wake threatened the survival of the unbroken chain of tradition. Recognizing the danger, R. Yehudah Hanasi—also called Rabbeinu Hakadosh or Rebbi—took it upon himself to compile the teachings of the Oral Torah and record them in the Mishnah as we know it. The Mishnah became the framework of the Talmud, also called Gemara, which expounds the very compact text of the Mishnah. Thus, Mishnah and Talmud merged into one work, and it is this work that has kept the spirit of Judaism alive throughout the centuries of dispersion and persecution.

ᴔ ᴔ ᴔ

The aim of the present work is to offer you a translation of an extensive selection of verses of the Written Torah together with their interpretations as found in the Oral Torah. The majority of the verses I selected deal with ethical and moral themes. I have rendered the material in conventional, easy-to-understand English. The commentaries are culled from talmudic, rabbinic, and midrashic sources, all clearly identified. Occasionally, I added notes for further clarification. These notes are either my own or excerpts from commentaries on the talmudic or midrashic selections.

The Torah text is divided into sections or portions. At the Sabbath service, the weekly portion is read from a handwritten scroll, so that over the course of one year the entire Torah is read. The weekly portions are identified at the beginning of each chapter by the key Hebrew word or phrase in the first verse, for example *Bereishit, Noach, Lech lecha, Varyeira,* and so on.

Studying the Written Torah in conjunction with its oral component gives you a taste of Torah in its purest form. You are learning Torah as it was transmitted by God to Moses at Sinai and as it is studied to this day by a vast number of students and laypeople in yeshivas and study halls throughout the world.

It is my hope that this volume will bring you the joy of *limud haTorah* (Torah study) by giving you a better understanding of the underlying meaning of the Torah passages. I hope that it will spark a deeper appreciation of the wisdom of the talmudic Sages and inspire you to explore the sources in greater depth.

*December 2003*                    Avraham Yaakov Finkel
*Brooklyn, New York*

# Acknowledgments

*How can I repay Hashem for all His bounty to me?*
PSALMS 116:2

First and foremost, I am grateful to Hashem for enabling me to complete this volume.

I wish to express my thanks to the astute Alan Rinzler, executive editor at Jossey-Bass/Wiley, for taking on the publication of this book and offering valuable advice and suggestions.

I thank Arthur Kurzweil, the well-known personality in the literary world, for proposing that I write this book and encouraging me along the way.

A special word of gratitude is due to Andrea Flint, production editor, for piloting this project from manuscript to finished project with competence and grace, and thanks also to Seth Schwartz, editorial assistant.

Many thanks to the talented Geneviève Duboscq, for meticulously and painstakingly copyediting the manuscript.

I appreciate the efforts of Sachie E. Jones, marketing assistant, in publicizing the book.

I am grateful to Paula Goldstein for designing the artistic book cover.

I want to thank my children, grandchildren, and great-grandchildren for being such a great source of genuine *nachas* and for showing such a lively interest in the progress of the work.

Most important, I want to express my gratitude to my dear wife, Suri, for her love, patience, and perceptive advice. Thanks for bearing with me when I am sitting glued to my computer until late into the night. May Hashem grant us *nachas, simchahs,* and good health.

# Genesis

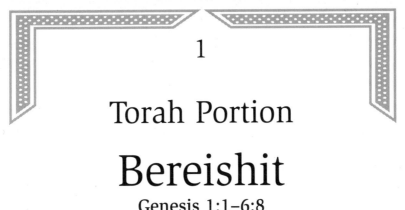

1

# Torah Portion

# Bereishit
### Genesis 1:1–6:8

## CREATION

**(1:1) In the beginning God created heaven and earth.**

✹ *The Jerusalem Talmud Teaches*
*[Bereishit] in the beginning* Why does the account of Creation begin with the letter *bet* of *bereishit*? Shouldn't it start with an *alef,* the first letter of the *alef bet?* Because the *bet* is the initial letter of the word *berachah,* "blessing," whereas the *alef* is the first letter of *arirah,* "curse." God said: I will not create the world with an *alef,* so that people should not say: How can you expect the world to endure if it was created with a letter that brings to mind *arirah,* "curse." Instead, I will create the world with the letter *bet* that suggests *berachah,* "blessing," and I wish that it will endure (Jerusalem Talmud, *Chagigah* 2:5).

✸ *The Talmud Teaches*
*In the beginning God created* It happened that King Ptolemy of Egypt gathered seventy-two sages and placed them in seventy-two chambers without telling them why he had brought them together. He went to each one, telling him: Translate for me the Torah of your master Moses into Greek. God then prompted each of them so that they all reached the same idea about how to translate a number of passages in the Torah whose literal translation King Ptolemy might misconstrue. And so they all rendered for him in Greek, "God created in the

beginning" instead of the literal translation, "In the beginning created God," for Ptolemy might misinterpret this to mean that God was created by a being named "In the beginning" (*Megillah* 9a).

NOTE: This Greek translation of the Bible is known as the Septuagint, the Translation of the Seventy.

**Heaven and earth**  What is the origin of the word *shamayim*, "heaven"? R. Yose b. R. Chanina said: It is a contraction of *sham mayim*, "there is water in that place." Alternatively, it was taught: *Shamayim* is a combination of *esh* and *mayim*, "fire and water." This teaches us that God brought fire and water together and mixed them, making the sky out of them (*Chagigah* 12a).

NOTE: The divine attributes of justice and mercy are compared to fire and water. Thus, the mixing of fire and water implies that God tempered justice with mercy in ruling the world (*Bereishit Rabbah* 12).

**(1:2) The earth was without form and empty, with darkness on the face of the depths, and the Divine Presence hovered on the surface of the water.**

### ✖ *The Talmud Teaches*
**The earth was without form and empty**  Let's see: The Torah begins by mentioning first heaven: *"God created heaven and earth."* Why then does it continue by telling us first the details about the unfolding creation of the earth? The yeshiva of R. Yishmael taught: You can compare it to a human king who said to his servants: Come to my palace door early in the morning. When the king got up, he found women and men gathered at the palace door, eager to serve him. Whom does he praise? He praises the people who do not usually rise early but who nevertheless got up early to serve him (*Chagigah* 12b).

NOTE: Because heaven by its spiritual quality is closer to God than the physical earth, we would expect heaven to react more zealously to God's command than earth. Yet in spite of its crass physicality, the earth responded just as enthusiastically to God's call as heaven did. That is why the earth is praiseworthy and its development is mentioned first.

**(1:3) God said, "There shall be light," and light came into existence.**

✳ *The Talmud Teaches*
**There shall be light** This teaches us that light was created on the first day. The Gemara asks: But was light then created on the first day? Surely, it says "God placed them—the sun, the moon, and the stars—in the heavenly sky to shine on the earth" (1:17)! And this happened on the *fourth* day of Creation! The Sages explain: The luminaries were created on the first day, but they were not hung up in the sky until the fourth day (*Chagigah* 12a).

**(1:4) God saw that the light was good, and God divided between the light and the darkness.**

✳ *The Talmud Teaches*
**That the light was good** R. Elazar said: The light that God created on the first day was a kind of light by which a person could see from one side of the world to the other, meaning that with this light, he could fathom the impenetrable mysteries of the universe. But when God saw the generation of the Flood and the generation of the Dispersion (the generation that rebelled against God by building the Tower of Babel) and saw how corrupt and unworthy of this sublime light they were, He took this light, hiding it from them and saving it for the righteous in the time to come, for it says "God saw that the light was *tov*, 'good,'" and the word *tov* refers to the righteous, for it says "Tell each righteous man that his deeds are *tov*, 'good'" (Isaiah 3:10) (*Chagigah* 12a).

NOTE: This primordial light is hidden in the Torah, where its radiance is enjoyed by those who study it.

**(1:6) God said, "There shall be a firmament in the middle of the water, and it shall separate water from water."**

### ❊ The Talmud Teaches

*And it shall separate water from water* And how big is the gap between water and water? R. Acha b. Yaakov said: As thin as a hair's breadth (*Chagigah* 15a).

NOTE: Man divides things by making a rough estimate. Only God measures with absolute precision.

**(1:8) It was evening and it was morning, a second day.**

### ❊ The Talmud Teaches

*A second day* R. Bana'ah, the son of R. Ulla, said: Why doesn't it say, "God saw that it was good" on the second day of Creation, as it does on all other days? Because the fire of Gehinnom was created on the second day of Creation (*Pesachim* 54a).

NOTE: Rashi suggests that the reason for the omission of "it was good" on the second day is because the creation of the water was not yet fully completed. And an unfinished product is not yet "good." On the third day, when it was completed, the phrase "it was good" appears twice, to make up for it.

**(1:11) God said, "The earth shall sprout vegetation: seed-bearing plants and fruit trees that produce their own kind of fruit with seeds shall be on the earth."**

### ❊ The Talmud Teaches

*The earth shall . . . sprout* R. Eliezer says: From where do we know that the world was created in the month of Tishri? Because it says "God said, 'The earth shall sprout vegetation: seed-bearing plants and fruit trees.'" And in the month of Tishri (in the fall of the year) the earth sprouts grass, and the trees are full of fruit (*Rosh Hashanah* 11a).

*Fruit trees that produce their own kind of fruit* R. Chanina b. Papa expounded: When God commanded the trees to produce their own kind of fruit, the herbs drew a logical inference: If God wished to have vegetation grow haphazardly and intermingle promiscuously, why did He tell the trees to "produce their own kind of fruit"? Furthermore, common sense tells you:

Regarding trees that by nature do not grow crammed together, because their branches keep them spaced apart, God commanded that they produce their own kind of fruit, how much more so does this apply to herbs that grow packed tightly, exposing them to the danger of mixing with other species! Immediately, each plant produced its own kind of fruit. Seeing this, the angels declared, "'May the glory of God endure forever, may God rejoice in His works' (Psalms 104:31), for all species scrupulously obey His command and do not intermingle, even though, unlike the herbs, they were not explicitly told not to mix!" (*Chullin* 60a).

**(1:12) The earth brought forth vegetation, plants bearing their own kinds of seeds, and trees producing fruits containing their own kinds of seeds.**

※ *The Talmud Teaches*
*The earth brought forth vegetation*  R. Assi pointed out a contradiction between verses: One verse says that on the third day "The earth brought forth vegetation," yet it says that on the sixth day, "all the grasses of the field had not yet sprouted" (2:5). How could they emerge from the earth on the third day, when on the sixth day they had not yet sprouted? This teaches us that the grasses began to grow but stopped just as they were about to break through the soil. They stayed below the surface, unable to sprout, until Adam prayed for rain for them; and when the rain fell, they shot up. This teaches us that God yearns for the prayers of the righteous. He withholds favor so that the righteous will pray to Him for His blessing (*Chullin* 60b).

**(1:16) God made the two large luminaries, the greater luminary to rule the day, and the smaller luminary to rule the night. He also made the stars.**

※ *The Talmud Teaches*
*The two large luminaries*  R. Shimon b. Pazzi pointed out a contradiction between two verses: One verse says, "God made the two large luminaries," implying that the sun and the moon were of equal size, and the verse continues, "the greater luminary . . . and the smaller luminary," suggesting that the sun is

larger than the moon. This is what happened: Originally, the sun and the moon were the same size. The moon then said to God, "Master of the universe! Is it possible for two kings to wear the same crown? I should be larger than the sun!" God answered, "Go and make yourself smaller!" as punishment for its arrogance. This explains the inconsistency between the two verses (*Chullin* 60b).

**(1:20) God said, "The water shall teem with swarms of living creatures, and birds that fly above the earth across the expanse of the sky."**

### ❋ The Talmud Teaches

**The water shall teem**  One verse says, "The waters shall teem with swarms of living creatures, and birds that fly," which suggests that the birds were created out of the water; but another verse says, "God had formed all the wild beasts and all the birds of sky out of the ground" (2:19), which implies that the birds were created out of the earth. How can it be that they were created both from water and earth? R. Yochanan b. Zakkai explained: They were created out of the primordial mud, which is a mixture of earth and water. That's why birds have characteristics in common with both animals and fish (*Chullin* 17b).

**(1:26) God said, "Let us make man with our image and our likeness. Let him dominate the fish of the sea, the birds of the sky, the livestock animals, and the whole earth—and every creeping thing that creeps on the earth."**

### ❋ The Talmud Teaches

**Let us make man**  R. Yochanan said: In all the verses which the *minim* (heretics or early Christians) have used as backing for their heresy [for example, verses where God is referred to in the plural], the rebuttal of their argument can be found close by. They used the verse, "Let us make man with our image and our likeness" to prove their misguided belief in multiple deities. But immediately following this verse, it says "God created man in His image" in the singular (1:27) (*Sanhedrin* 38b).

NOTE: The plural "Let us" is meant in the sense of the royal *we,* with which human sovereigns proclaim their will to their subjects (R. Samson Raphael Hirsch). *Targum Yonatan* explains "Let us make man" as God addressing the ministering angels who had been created on the second day of Creation.

**(1:27) So God created man in His image, in the image of God He created him; male and female He created them.**

### ✳ *The Talmud Teaches*
***In His image*** This teaches us that Adam was born circumcised. Because he was created in the image of God, he was perfect, lacking nothing, which means that he was circumcised (*Avot d'Rabbi Natan,* Chapter 2).

***He created him*** R. Yehudah pointed out an inconsistency: It says "In the image of God He created *him*"; and the verse continues, "male and female He created *them.*" How can this be reconciled? He resolved it by saying: Originally, God had in mind to create two human beings—man and woman—but in the end, only one man was created; and the woman was formed by God from man (*Ketubot* 8a).

NOTE: The implication is that both sexes were created equal and directly by God and in equal likeness to Him (R. Samson Raphael Hirsch).

***Male and female*** R. Yitzchak said further: When a male, *zachar,* is born, his "loaf of bread," that is, his livelihood, comes with him, for *zachar* can be seen as a contraction of *zeh kar,* "this is a meal." A female, *nekevah,* comes empty-handed, *nekiah.* Unless she demands her food, nothing is given to her, for it says "Name your price, *nakvah,* and I will give it" (Genesis 30:28) (*Niddah* 31b).

NOTE: All living creatures—humans, animals, and plants—were created in both sexes, the male giving and the female receiving.

**(1:28) God blessed them and God said to them, "Be fruitful and increase, fill the earth and conquer it; and rule over the fish of the sea, the birds of the sky, and every living thing that moves on the earth."**

## ✳ The Talmud Teaches

**And conquer it** Only man, not woman, is commanded to get married. For it says "And conquer it," which applies only to the male, for it is the nature of a man to conquer, but it is not the nature of a woman to conquer (*Yevamot* 65b).

**(1:29) God said, "Behold, I have given you every seedbearing plant on the face of the earth, and every tree that has seedbearing fruit. It shall be to you for food."**

## ✳ The Talmud Teaches

**It shall be to you for food** Rav Yehudah said: Adam was not permitted to eat meat, for it says "Every plant shall be to you for food, and for every beast of the earth," meaning, the plants have been given to you and to the beasts of the earth to eat, but the beasts of the earth have not been given to you for food. The Gemara asks: But it says "Rule over . . . every beast that walks on the earth"! (1:28). Surely, this means that they should serve as food? The Gemara answers: No, "rule over every beast" means making the animals work for you (*Sanhedrin* 59b).

**(1:31) God saw all that He had made, and behold, it was very good. It was evening and it was morning, the sixth day.**

## ✳ The Talmud Teaches

**The sixth day [hashishi]** What is meant by the extra *hei* of ha*shishi*, "the sixth day"? You will notice that the other days of Creation are described simply as "a third, a fourth, a fifth day," without the article *ha,* "*the* third day." The article *ha* comes to teach us that God stipulated with the works of Creation, telling them: If Israel accepts the Torah, you will continue to exist; if not, I will turn you back to primeval emptiness and void (*Shabbat* 88a).

NOTE: On the sixth day, when God completed His creation, it says "*Yom* ha*shishi, the* sixth day," alluding to the sixth day of Sivan, the day on which the Torah was given. The verse is thus to be understood as "It was evening and it was morning"; and the universe will continue to exist only because of the sixth day of Sivan, the day the Torah will be given at Mount Sinai.

**(2:1) Heaven and earth and all their array were finished.**

❋ *The Talmud Teaches*
*And all their array* R. Yehoshua b. Levi said: All creatures were
brought into being full-grown, they gave their consent to being
created, and they were created with their genetic pattern. For it
says "Heaven and earth and all their array *[tzeva'am]* were finished." Don't read *tzeva'am* but *tzivyonam*, "their genetic pattern" (*Rosh Hashanah* 11a).

## GAN EDEN: THE GARDEN OF EDEN

**(2:4) These are the products of heaven and earth when they
were created, on the day that God made earth and heaven.**

❋ *The Talmud Teaches*
*the products of heaven and earth* R. Eliezer the Great said: All
things of heaven, that is, the sun, moon, and stars, were made
from heaven; and the products of the earth were made from the
substance of the earth, meaning, heaven and earth are the basic
elements from which all creations of the world were made
(*Yoma* 54b).

❋ *The Jerusalem Talmud Teaches*
*earth and heaven* Throughout Scripture, heaven always comes
before earth; only here does earth precede heaven. This teaches
you that heaven and earth are equivalent (Jerusalem Talmud,
*Chagigah* 2:1).

**(2:6) A mist rose up from the earth, and it watered the whole
surface of the ground.**

❋ *The Talmud Teaches*
*A mist rose up* R. Eliezer said: The whole world draws its
water supply from the ocean, as it says "A mist rose up from the
earth, and it watered the whole surface of the ground." Countered R. Yehoshua: But isn't the water of the ocean salty, and
rain is sweet? He replied: The water of the ocean is sweetened
by the clouds (*Taanit* 9b).

NOTE: This is an apt description of the distillation process, which separates salt from ocean water by the heat of the sun. The rising vapors condense in the cool upper atmosphere where they form clouds that release the rain.

### ▒ *The Jerusalem Talmud Teaches*
**A mist rose up**  The next verse reads, "Then God formed man out of the dust of the ground," like a woman who kneads her dough with water, after which she separates challah from it.

This teaches us that Adam is called "the challah of the world." Now, Eve was the one that caused Adam's death by making him eat from the forbidden fruit; that is why women have to observe the mitzvah of separating the challah from the dough to atone for Eve's sin (Jerusalem Talmud, *Shabbat* 2:6).

NOTE: A small piece of dough, called challah, must be separated as a tithe from each batch of dough (see Numbers 15:21).

**(2:15) God took the man and placed him in the Garden of Eden, to work it and to guard it.**

### ※ *The Talmud Teaches*
**to work it and to guard it**  R. Shimon b. Elazar said: This shows you how great work is, for even Adam ate nothing before he worked, as it says "God placed him in the Garden of Eden, to work it and to guard it"; and only then does it say in the next verse "Of every tree in the garden you may freely eat" (2:16). The underlying idea is: Man should not enjoy the goodness of the earth without contributing something to its advancement (*Avot d'Rabbi Natan*, Chapter 11).

**(2:16) The Lord God gave man a commandment, saying, "Of every tree in the garden you may freely eat."**

### ※ *The Talmud Teaches*
**The Lord God gave man a commandment**  Our Rabbis taught: Seven commandments were given to the descendants of Noah, that is, all mankind, namely: the duty to set up courts and bring offenders to justice; and the prohibitions against cursing God, worshiping false gods, sexual immorality, murder, stealing, and eating the limb of an animal before it is killed.

These seven laws are derived from the verse, "God gave man a commandment, saying, 'Of every tree in the garden you may freely eat.'" This commandment was given to Adam and therefore to all mankind. The Talmud derives the Seven Laws as follows:

> "He gave man a commandment" alludes to the requirement of establishing courts, for *commandment* is associated with justice.
>
> "The Lord" suggests the prohibition against blasphemy.
>
> "God" hints at the prohibition against idol worship.
>
> "Man" alludes to murder, and so it says "Whoever sheds the blood of man, by man shall his blood be shed" (Genesis 9:6).
>
> "Saying" refers to adultery, and so it says "Saying: If a man divorces his wife, and she goes from him and became another man's" (Jeremiah 3:1).

NOTE: In the Torah, the word *saying* denotes the transmission of a commandment from one generation to the next. This is possible only if children find fathers and mothers who transmit the laws to them. Therefore, *saying* implies family life that blossoms in sexual purity, free of adultery (R. Samson Raphael Hirsch).

> "From every tree in the garden," but not by stealing. [Rashi explains: Because Adam needed permission to eat from the trees, we gather that without permission it is forbidden to take things that belong to someone else.]
>
> "You may freely eat," implying: but not a limb cut from a living animal (*Sanhedrin* 56b).

## ADAM AND EVE

**(2:18) God said, "It is not good for man to be alone. I will make a compatible helper for him."**

### ※ *The Talmud Teaches*
*I will make a compatible helper for him* R. Yose met Elijah and asked him: It says "I will make a compatible helper for him." In what way does a wife help her husband? Replied Elijah: If a man brings wheat, does he chew the wheat? His wife

grinds and bakes it for him. If he brings flax, can he wear the flax? His wife spins the flax and turns the cloth into a garment. Doesn't this prove that a wife brightens her husband's eyes and puts him on his feet (*Yevamot* 63a)?

NOTE: R. Yose's question holds a veiled reproach, as if to say: God did man no favor by giving him a wife. By bringing sin into the world, she did more harm than good, for now man has to work hard to earn a living. Elijah showed him that even if crops would grow by themselves, as they did in Gan Eden, man still needs a wife to prepare his food and make his clothes.

***a compatible helper*** In Hebrew, this phrase reads, *ezer kenegdo.* But the word *kenegdo* literally means "against him." Therefore, R. Elazar translates the passage as "I will make him a helper against him." But how can she be his helper and at the same time be against him? If he merits it, his wife is a help to him; if he does not merit it, she opposes him (*Yevamot* 63a).

**(2:22) God built the rib that he took from the man into a woman, and He brought her to the man.**

### *The Talmud Teaches*

***God built the rib*** R. Chisda said: What is meant by the words, "God built *[vayiven]* the rib that he had taken from the man into a woman"? This teaches us that God endowed the woman with more understanding *[binah]* than the man (*Niddah* 45b).

NOTE: The word *binah* is seen as cognate with *vayiven.* Thus, "God built," *vayiven,* is understood to imply that He granted the woman more *binah,* "understanding."

**(2:23) The man said, "This time it is bone from my bones and flesh from my flesh. She shall be called Woman Ishah because she was taken from man Ish."**

### *The Talmud Teaches*

***. . . This time*** R. Elazar said: What is meant by, "This time it is bone from my . . . bones"? It teaches us that, searching for a mate, Adam had sexual intercourse with every animal, but he was not satisfied until he had intercourse with Eve, and then he said, . . ."This time" (*Yevamot* 63a).

**(2:24) A man shall therefore leave his father and mother and be united with his wife, and they shall become one flesh.**

### ※ The Talmud Teaches

**And be united with his wife** but not with a male. "*With his wife*" but not with his neighbor's wife (*Yevamot* 63a).

## THE SIN

**(3:1) The serpent was the shrewdest of all the wild beasts that God had made. [The serpent] asked the woman, "Did God really say that you may not eat from any of the trees of the garden?"**

### ※ The Jerusalem Talmud Teaches

**The serpent was the shrewdest** What was his shrewdness? The serpent said: I know full well that God said to Adam and Eve, "On the day you eat from the Tree of Knowledge, you will definitely die" (2:17). I am going to dupe them and make them eat from the Tree. They will then be punished with death, and I will inherit the world and have it all to myself (Jerusalem Talmud, *Kiddushin* 4:5).

**(3:3) The woman replied to the serpent, "But of the fruit that is in the middle of the garden, God said, 'Do not eat it, and do not even touch it, or else you will die.'"**

### ※ The Talmud Teaches

**Do not even touch it** God had commanded them only not to *eat* the fruit of the tree, but Eve added to the prohibition. By adding to the command, she diminished it. Chizkiah said: From where do we know that he who adds to the word of God takes away from it? From the verse "God said, 'Do not eat it, and do not even touch it'" (*Sanhedrin* 29a).

NOTE: Rashi, quoting the Midrash, comments: The serpent pushed Eve against the tree and said, "See, you did not die by touching it, and neither will you die from eating it." Thus, the serpent convinced her that God's death threat was merely to intimidate them not to eat but that they would not really die. Thus, by adding to the word of God, she suffered loss.

**(3:7) The eyes of both of them were opened, and they realized that they were naked. They sewed together fig leaves and made themselves aprons.**

✳ *The Talmud Teaches*
**They made themselves aprons**  R. Nechemiah said: The tree from which Adam and Eve ate was a fig tree, so that the thing with which they sinned, the fig, became the means through which the damage was repaired, for it says "They sewed together fig leaves" (*Sanhedrin* 70b).

**(3:9) God called out to the man, and He said, "Where are you?"**

✳ *The Talmud Teaches*
**God called out**  A person should never enter his friend's house unannounced. You can learn proper manners from God, for God was standing at the entrance of the garden and announced Himself, as it says "God called out to the man" (*Derech Eretz,* Chapter 5).

**(3:11) God asked, "Who told you that you are naked? Did you eat from the tree which I commanded you not to eat?"**

✳ *The Talmud Teaches*
**Did you eat [hamin] from the tree**  Where do we find an allusion to Haman in the Torah? In the verse, "Did you eat *[hamin]* from the tree which I commanded you not to eat?" And *hamin* sounds like Haman (*Chullin* 139b).

NOTE: R. Aharon Kotler explains the underlying thought: Adam, who had everything in the world, wanted the one thing that was forbidden to him. So too Haman, who was revered by the entire Persian nation, craved the bowing down of one lone individual, Mordechai (Mishnat Rabbi Aharon, vol. 3, essay entitled "Purim").

**(3:12) The man replied, "The woman that You gave to be with me—she gave me what I ate from the tree."**

### *The Talmud Teaches*

***The woman that You gave to be with me*** The Rabbis taught: Adam was ungrateful. Instead of thanking God for giving him a wife, he implied that God was to blame for his transgression, because He gave him the wife that made him sin (*Avodah Zarah* 5b).

**(3:14) God said to the serpent, "Because you did this, cursed are you more than all the cattle and all the wild beasts. On your belly you shall crawl, and dust shall you eat, all the days of your life."**

### *The Talmud Teaches*

***God said to the serpent*** From where do we know that we do not try to find a defense for a person who entices others to worship idols? From the story of the serpent in the Garden of Eden. The serpent could have pleaded, "When the master's command contradicts the command of his student, whose command should you obey? Surely, the master's command! So too although I enticed Eve, she should have obeyed the command of God and rejected my temptation. Therefore, don't blame me for Eve's sin." But this defense was not accepted—proof that the legal plea of a seducer to sin is rejected (*Sanhedrin* 29a).

***Cursed are you*** The Rabbis taught: Whoever sets his eyes on something that does not belong to him will not obtain what he desires, and what he has is taken away from him. This concept is found with the serpent in the Garden of Eden, which craved something that was out of bounds for it: It lusted after Eve. And so the thing it wanted, it did not get; and what it had was taken away from it. What did the serpent have that was taken away? God said: Originally, I declared that the serpent should be the king of all animals, but now "Cursed are you more than all the cattle and all the wild beasts." I declared that the serpent should walk with an erect posture, but now "On your belly you shall crawl." I said that it should eat the same food as man eats, but now it has to eat dust. The serpent had planned to kill Adam and marry Eve; but now, God said, "I will plant hatred between you and the woman, and between your offspring and her offspring" (3:15) (*Sotah* 9b).

**(3:16) To the woman He said, "I will greatly increase your anguish and your childbearing. It will be with anguish that you will give birth to children. Your passion will be to your husband, and he will dominate you."**

✳ *The Talmud Teaches*
*Your anguish and your childbearing* "Your anguish" refers to the pain of raising children. "Your childbearing" refers to the discomfort of pregnancy (*Eruvin* 100b).

R. Yochanan said: It is twice as distressful for a man to earn his livelihood as it is for a woman to give birth. For about a woman in childbirth, it says "It will be with pain *[be'etzev]* that you will give birth to children"; whereas in relation to earning a livelihood, it says "In anguish *[be'itzavon]* shall you eat of the ground" (3:17); *itzavon* denotes a more intense pain than *etzev* (*Pesachim* 118a).

NOTE: Etz Yosef comments: The pain of childbirth is short and mixed with joy; the hardship of earning a living is a constant and joyless burden.

**He will dominate you** This teaches that although the wife solicits with her heart, the husband does so with the mouth. This quality of modesty is a noble character trait of women (Eruvin 100b).

NOTE: R. Samson Raphael Hirsch comments: After the sin, when earning the livelihood required hard labor, women became dependent on the physically stronger men. Obedience to the Torah, however, restores her to her former and proper status as the "crown of her husband" (Proverbs 12:4).

**(3:18) The earth will bring forth thorns and thistles for you, and you will eat the grass of the field.**

✳ *The Talmud Teaches*
**Thorns and thistles** R. Yehoshua b. Levi said: When God said

to Adam, "The earth will bring forth thorns and thistles for you, and you will eat the grass of the field," tears flowed from his eyes. He said to God, "Master of the universe! Will I and my donkey eat from the same trough! Will we be eating the same food?" But as soon as God said to him, "By the sweat of your brow will you eat bread" (3:19) and not grass, he was relieved (*Pesachim* 118a).

**(3:21) God made garments of skin for Adam and his wife, and He clothed them.**

### ✳ *The Talmud Teaches*
**Garments of skin**  Rav and Shmuel offer different interpretations of this phrase. One said: It means that the garments were made from material that grows on the skin, meaning wool. The other said: It was material that feels pleasant to the skin, meaning linen, which is worn close to the skin (*Sotah* 14a).

NOTE: Maharsha comments: "Garments of skin" could not mean leather, because at that time no animal had been killed yet.

**and He clothed them**  This teaches us that God clothes the naked, and we should emulate Him by donating clothes to the poor.
       R. Simla'i expounded: The Torah begins with an act of kindness and ends with an act of kindness. It begins with an act of kindness, for it says "God made garments of skin for Adam and his wife, and He clothed them." It ends with an act of kindness, for it says "God buried Moses in the valley" (Deuteronomy 34:6) (*Sotah* 14a).

NOTE: Both giving clothes to the needy and burying the deceased are acts of kindness designed to keep the human body from being disgraced in life and in death.

## CAIN AND ABEL

**(4:7) God said to Cain, "Surely if you improve yourself you will be forgiven, but if you do not improve yourself, sin is lying in wait at the door. It lusts after you, but you can dominate it."**

## ※ *The Talmud Teaches*

***Surely if you improve yourself you will be forgiven*** God said to the Jewish people: I created the *yetzer hara,* "the evil impulse," and I created the Torah as its antidote. If you study the Torah, you will not fall prey to the *yetzer hara,* for it says "Surely if you improve yourself and study the Torah, you will be able to subdue your evil impulse." But if you do not study the Torah, you will be trapped by the *yetzer hara,* for it says "Sin, that is, the *yetzer hara,* is lying in wait at the door." And that's not all, but the *yetzer hara* spends all his energy on making you sin, for it says "It lusts after you." But if you want, you can overpower it by learning Torah, as it says "But you can overcome it" (*Kiddushin* 30b).

***Sin is lying in wait at the door*** Rebbi said: Antoninus taught me something, and Scripture supports him: The evil impulse holds sway over man from the time he comes into the world, not in his embryonic stage, for it says "Sin is lying in wait at the door," from the moment he is born (*Sanhedrin* 91b).

NOTE: Antoninus was the Roman emperor Marcus Aurelius Antoninus, who ruled from 161–180 C.E. In the course of his travels, he visited Judea. There he met Rebbi with whom he formed a lifelong friendship, which was of great benefit to the Jewish people. Antoninus engaged Rebbi in many discussions of religious and philosophical matters. Rebbi is the affectionate name of the illustrious Rabbi Yehudah Hanasi (the Prince), the compiler of the Mishnah.

R. Simla'i expounded: While the embryo is in its mother's womb, it is taught the entire Torah. As soon as it enters the world, an angel comes and taps it lightly on its mouth, and it forgets all the Torah completely, for it says *"Sin is lying in wait at the door"* (*Niddah* 30b).

NOTE: The word *sin* implies loss and deficiency, alluding to the loss of the Torah knowledge the embryo suffers.

**(4:10) God said, "What have you done? The voice of your brother's blood is screaming to me from the ground."**

✳️ *The Talmud Teaches*
**The voice of your brother's blood [demei]** It does not say, "The voice of your brother's blood *[dam]*" but "The voice of your brother's *bloods,*" in the plural, which suggests "his blood and the blood of his offspring." This teaches us that capital cases are not like monetary cases. In monetary cases, if a witness gives false testimony, it is sinful; but he can make monetary restitution to the person who suffered a loss because of the false testimony, and the false witness's sin is thereby forgiven. But in capital cases, the false witness cannot make amends. He is held responsible for the blood of the person who was executed on the basis of his false testimony and for the blood of the descendants the victim could have had until the end of time.

Rav Yehudah, the son of R. Chiya, said: The plural of "bloods" teaches that Cain stabbed his brother many times because he did not know the fatal spot where the soul leaves the body, until he stabbed him in the throat, and that killed him (*Sanhedrin* 37a).

**(4:13) Cain said: "Is my sin too great to bear?"**

✳️ *The Talmud Teaches*
**Is my sin too great to bear?** Cain came with craftiness when he said, "Is my sin too great to bear?" Cain said to God: Master of the universe! Is my sin greater than that of the six hundred thousand Jews who will sin against You in the future, and whom You will nevertheless forgive? (*Sanhedrin* 101b).

NOTE: Rashi explains how Cain was crafty: Rather than pray for forgiveness, he used an irrefutable argument. Maharsha comments: God forgave the children of Israel, who numbered six hundred thousand, for the sin of the golden calf and for the sin of the spies. Cain argued that certainly the sin of an entire nation is greater than that of a single individual.

## THE GENERATIONS OF MANKIND

**(5:1) This is the book of the descendants of Adam: On the day that God created man, He made him in the likeness of God.**

## ※ *The Talmud Teaches*

*This is the book of the descendants of Adam* Resh Lakish said: Did Adam really have a book? The passage comes to tell us that the Holy One, blessed be He, showed Adam every future generation with its teachers, its sages, and its leaders (*Avodah Zarah* 5a).

**(5:2) He created them male and female. He blessed them and named them Man, Adam, on the day that they were created.**

## ※ *The Talmud Teaches*

*He created them male and female* R. Abbahu pointed out a contradiction between two verses. It says "He created them male and female," implying that from the start God created both a male and a female. But it also says "God made man with His own image" (9:6), only a male. How can these verses be reconciled? At first, His intention was to create two, but in the end only one was created, from which He later formed two (*Berachot* 61a).

*He named them Man* R. Elazar said: A man who does not have a wife is not considered a man, for it says "He created them male and female, and He named them Man." Only when man was united with woman were they called Adam, "man" (*Yevamot* 63a).

**(6:2) The sons of the rulers saw that the daughters of man were good, and they took themselves wives from whomever they chose.**

## ※ *The Talmud Teaches*

*The sons of the rulers saw* R. Yose said: The people of the generation of the Flood became arrogant only as a result of the freedom they exercised with the eyeball, which resembles water.

Looking at their great prosperity, they developed haughtiness, which in turn led them to lust after whatever they set their eyes on. Therefore, God punished them with water, which resembles the eye, as it says "All the fountains of the great deep

burst forth and the windows of heaven were opened" (6:5)
(*Sanhedrin* 108a)

NOTE: Rashi explains: Fountains resemble the eyeball, which is
moist and produces tears. The ocean that surrounds dry land
resembles the white of the eye surrounding the pupil. Because
the people of that generation opened their eyes too widely, cov-
eting whatever they saw, God punished them by causing water
to cover the earth, hiding it from sight.

# 2

# Torah Portion

# Noah
### Genesis 6:9–11:32

## THE FLOOD

**(6:9) These are the offspring of Noah—Noah was a righteous man, faultless in his generation. Noah walked with God.**

✳ *The Talmud Teaches*
*A righteous man, faultless in his generation* This was said in Noah's absence. But further on, when God is speaking to Noah directly, He says, "I have seen that you are righteous before Me in this generation" (7:1), praising him only for his righteousness, whereas in Noah's absence he is praised fully, for being both righteous and faultless. Why the diminished praise in his presence?

R. Yirmeyah b. Elazar said: Only part of a person's praise should be said in his presence, but all of his praise should be said in his absence (*Eruvin* 18b).

NOTE: Rashi explains: Praising him fully to his face may be interpreted as flattery.

*in his generation* R. Yochanan said: In his generation of very wicked people, he was considered perfectly righteous, but he would not have been considered perfectly righteous in other generations that were not as wicked. But Resh Lakish said: If in his wicked generation he was able to be righteous, he surely would have been righteous if he had lived in a generation of righteous people (*Sanhedrin* 108a).

**(6:12) God saw the world, and it was corrupted. All flesh had perverted its way on earth.**

※ *The Talmud Teaches*
*All flesh* R. Yochanan said: The expression "all flesh" teaches us that they mated domesticated animals with wild animals, wild animals with domesticated animals, and all types of animals with humans, and humans with all types of animals (*Sanhedrin* 108a).

**(6:13) God said to Noah, "The end of all flesh has come before Me. The world is filled with robbery on account of them, and I will therefore destroy them from the earth."**

※ *The Talmud Teaches*
*The world is filled with robbery* R. Yochanan said: Come and see how far-reaching are the consequences of robbery. For the people of the generation of the Flood transgressed all seven Noahide laws that were given to all mankind, yet the decree of their punishment was not sealed until they engaged in robbery. For it says "The world is filled with robbery, and I will therefore destroy them from the earth" (*Sanhedrin* 108a).

NOTE: The seven Noahide laws are the following: The prohibition against murder, idol worship, immorality, cutting a limb off a live animal, robbery, blasphemy, and the command to administer justice.

**(6:16) Make a skylight for the ark. Make it slanted, so that it is one cubit wide on top. Place the ark's door on its side. Make a first, second, and third deck.**

※ *The Talmud Teaches*
*a first, second, and third deck* The third deck was for refuse, the second deck for animals, and the upper deck for people (*Sanhedrin* 108a).

**(6:17) I Myself am bringing the Flood-waters on the earth to destroy from under the heavens all flesh having in it a breath of life. All that is on land will die.**

### ✳ *The Talmud Teaches*
*I Myself am bringing the Flood-waters* The people of the generation of the Flood became arrogant only because of the bounty that God lavished on them. They said, "Do we need the Almighty for anything other than a drop of rain? Why, we don't even need Him for that! We have rivers and streams from which to supply ourselves." Said God, "With the very bounty that I lavished on them they provoke Me. With that very bounty I shall punish them!" As it says "I Myself am bringing the Flood-waters" (*Sanhedrin* 108a).

**(7:8) The clean animals and the animals that were not clean, the birds and all that walked the earth.**

### ✳ *The Talmud Teaches*
*The animals that were not clean* R. Yehoshua b. Levi said: A person should not utter coarse language, for the Torah uses eight letters more than necessary in an effort to avoid using the uncouth term *temei'ah*, "unclean." For it says God said to Noah, "Of every animal that is not clean, take two" (7:2). The Torah uses the phrase *asher einenah tehorah*, "that is not clean," in order to avoid using the distasteful word *temei'ah*, "unclean." In the process, the Torah added eight Hebrew letters (*Pesachim* 3a).

**(7:10) Seven days passed, and the waters of the Flood were on the earth.**

### ✳ *The Talmud Teaches*
*Seven days passed* What was the nature of the seven-day period that preceded the Flood? Rav said: These were the seven days of mourning for Methuselah, who had just died. This comes to teach you that eulogies for the righteous prevent a preordained punishment from happening because people are moved by eulogies to do *teshuvah* (repentance).

An alternative explanation: the phrase "seven days passed" teaches that before the Flood, God gave them to take a semblance of the reward awaiting the righteous in the world to come, so that they would realize what goodness they were deprived of through their sinful ways (*Sanhedrin* 108b).

**(7:22) Everything on dry land whose life was sustained by breathing died.**

### ⚹ *The Talmud Teaches*
*Everything on dry land* R. Chisda said: The decree of destruction was not issued against the fish in the sea, because it says "Everything on dry land . . . died" but not the fish in the sea (*Zevachim* 113b).

NOTE: Unlike land animals, which mated with other species, the fish did not intermingle with other breeds of fish and "did not pervert their way." Therefore, they were not punished.

**(8:7) Noah sent out the raven, and it departed. It went back and forth until the water had dried up from the surface of the earth.**

### ⚹ *The Talmud Teaches*
*He sent out the raven* Resh Lakish said: When Noah sent out the raven, it retorted with a winning argument. It said to Noah, "Your Master, God, hates me, and you, Noah, hate me, too. Your Master hates me, for He instructed you to take into the ark seven of each species of the clean animals but only two of each species of unclean animals. I am counted among the unclean animals." Continued the raven, "You too hate me, for when you needed a bird to send out on a dangerous mission, you let stay the species of which there are seven, and you chose me, one of a species of which there are only two! If I die of heat or cold, won't the result be that the world will be missing one species entirely? For if I perish, there will be no male left to reproduce the species" (*Sanhedrin* 108b).

**(8:11) The dove returned to him toward evening, and there was a freshly picked olive leaf in its beak. Noah then knew that the water had subsided from the earth.**

### ✳ *The Talmud Teaches*

**and there was a freshly picked olive leaf in its beak** R. Yir-meyah said: The dove said to God: Master of the universe! I'd rather my food be bitter like an olive but from God's hand than sweet as honey but dependent on man (*Eruvin* 18b).

NOTE: Noah provided all the dove's needs, but the olive leaf comes directly from God.

**(8:19) Every beast, every creeping thing, and every bird— all that walk the land—left the ark by families.**

### ✳ *The Talmud Teaches*

**they left the ark by families** Eliezer, Abraham's servant, once said to Noah's son, Shem: It says "They left the ark by families," which implies that each species was cared for individually in the ark. How were you able to feed all these animals? Replied Shem: Indeed, we did suffer great distress in the ark. Any creature that was used to being fed by day, we fed by day, and any creature that was used to being fed by night, we fed by night; thus, we were kept busy around the clock (*Sanhedrin* 108b).

## AFTER THE FLOOD

**(8:21) God smelled the pleasing fragrance of the sacrifice, and God said, "Never again will I doom the soil because of man, for the inclination of man's heart is evil from his youth. I will never strike down all life, as I have just done."**

### ✳ *The Talmud Teaches*

**God smelled the pleasing fragrance** R. Chanina said: A person who can be placated when he is drinking wine has one of the qualities of his Creator. For it says when Noah came out of the ark and offered sacrifices, "God smelled the pleasing fragrance, and He said, 'Never again will I doom the earth because of man,'" which proves that God was appeased when He smelled the pleasing fragrance of the sacrifice (*Eruvin* 65a).

NOTE: The senses of smell and taste are closely related. R. Chanina praises a person who has a forgiving nature, and wine puts a person in an amiable mood.

**(9:2) The fear and dread of you shall be instilled in all the wild beasts of the earth, and all the birds of the . . . sky.**

✳ *The Talmud Teaches*
*The fear and dread of you* R. Shimon b. Elazar said: A day-old infant need not be guarded against cats and mice, but the dead giant Og, king of Bashan, must be guarded against cats and mice. For it says "The fear and dread of you shall be instilled in all the wild beasts." As long as a person is alive, he inspires fear in animals; once he is dead, they no longer are afraid of him (*Shabbat* 151b).

**(9:5) However, of the blood of your own lives will I demand an account; I will demand such an account from the hand of every beast. From the hand of man—even from a man's own brother—I will demand an account of every human life.**

✳ *The Talmud Teaches*
*Of the blood of your own lives will I demand an account* R. Elazar says: This means, I will demand an account of the blood, even if it was shed by yourselves. From here we know that a person is forbidden to commit suicide (*Bava Kamma* 91b).

**(9:6) He who spills human blood shall have his own blood spilled by man, for God made man with His own image.**

✳ *The Talmud Teaches*
*He who spills human blood* The literal translation is: "He who spills man's blood *within man*, that is, within him, shall have his own blood spilled by man." R. Yishmael said: What is a man within another man? A fetus in his mother's womb. From here, we know that a non-Jew is executed for the murder of an embryo, because this law was given to Noah and his descendants, that is, all humankind (*Sanhedrin* 57b).

**(9:7) Now be fruitful and multiply, teem all over the earth and multiply on it.**

✳ *The Talmud Teaches*
*Now be fruitful and multiply* Ben Azzai said: Any Jew who does not get married and have children is considered as if he

spills blood and diminishes the divine image. For it says "He who spills blood shall have his own blood spilled by man"; and in the next verse, it says "Now be fruitful and multiply" (*Yevamot* 63b).

## NOAH PLANTS A VINEYARD

**(9:20) Noah began to be a man of the soil, and he planted a vineyard.**

### ※ *The Talmud Teaches*
*a man of the soil*  What is meant by "a man of the soil"? God said to Noah, "Noah, shouldn't you have learned a lesson from Adam, who was created from the soil and whose transgression was caused by wine?" This is in line with the view that the forbidden tree from which Adam ate was a vine (*Sanhedrin* 70a).

**(9:25) Noah said, "Cursed is Canaan! He shall be a slave's slave to his brothers!"**

### ※ *The Talmud Teaches*
*He shall be a slave's slave to his brothers*  When the Africans came to contend with the Jews before Alexander the Macedonian who had conquered Eretz Yisrael (the Land of Israel), they said to him, "The land of Canaan is rightfully ours, for it says in the Torah that the Jews should conquer 'The land of Canaan according to its borders' [Numbers 34:2]. And Canaan was our ancestor; so they took it from us." Retorted Geviha ben Pesisa, It says in the Torah: "Noah said: 'Cursed is Canaan! He shall be a slave's slave to his brothers, Shem and Japheth.'" And the Jews are Semites, descendants of Shem. Now, if a slave acquires property, to whom does the slave and the property belong? Of course, to the master! Because your ancestor was the slave of Shem, the land of Canaan belongs to us, the descendants of Shem (*Sanhedrin* 91a).

## THE TOWER OF BABEL

**(11:5) They said, "Come let us build ourselves a city and a tower with its top in the heavens, and let us make a name**

for ourselves, so that we will not be scattered across the whole earth."

### ※ *The Talmud Teaches*
*Come let us build ourselves a city* R. Yirmeyah b. Elazar said: They split into three groups: One group said, "Let us climb to the top of the tower and live there"; another group said, "Let us climb to the top of the tower and worship idols"; and the third group said, "Let us climb to the top of the tower and wage war against God." They were punished measure for measure. The group that said, "Let us climb up and live there," God dispersed them around the world. The group that said, "Let us climb up and make war against God" became apes and turned into all kind of demons that do not have the intelligence needed to wage war. And regarding the group that said, "Let us climb up and worship idols," the Torah says "This was the place where God confused the world's languages" (11:9), so that they could no longer communicate with each other and carry out their plan (*Sanhedrin* 109a).

*and let us make a name for ourselves* God said to Israel, "I love you, because even when I confer greatness on you, you humbled yourselves before Me, as Abraham did when he said, 'I am mere dust and ashes' (Genesis 18:27). But the heathens react differently. I bestowed greatness on Nimrod, and he said, 'Come let us build a city and make a name for ourselves'" (*Chullin* 89a).

**(11:30) Sarai was barren; she had no children.**

### ※ *The Talmud Teaches*
*she had no children* R. Nachman said: Our mother Sarah had a physical defect that prevented her from having children, for it says "Sarai was barren; she had no children." Why the redundant "She had no children"? She did not even have a womb (*Yevamot* 64a).

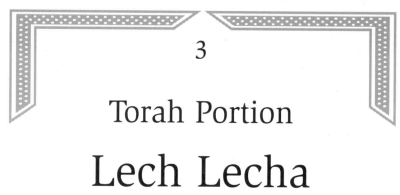

# 3

## Torah Portion

# Lech Lecha
### Genesis 12:1–17:27

## ABRAHAM'S CALL AND WANDERINGS

**(12:1) God said to Abram, "Go away from your land, from your birthplace, and from your father's house, to the land that I will show you."**

NOTE: Originally, his name was Abram. At his circumcision, God changed his name to Abraham; and the name Sarai was changed to Sarah (17:5).

✳ *The Talmud Teaches*
*Go away from your land* Some say that changing your place of residence helps to have an evil decree cancelled. For it says "God said to Abram, 'Go away from your land,'" and in the next verse it says "I will make you into a great nation" (*Yevamot* 64a).

NOTE: Abraham and Sarah were both destined to be infertile, but God rescinded His decree and promised that they would become a great nation.

**(12:5) Abram took his wife Sarai, his nephew Lot, and all their belongings, as well as the people they had made in Haran, and they left, heading toward Canaan; and they came to Canaan.**

### ✳ *The Talmud Teaches*
**The souls they had made** Resh Lakish said: Whoever teaches his neighbor's son Torah is regarded by Scripture as if he "made" that son, as it says "and the people they had made in Haran" by converting them to the belief in one God (*Sanhedrin* 99b).

**(12:16) Pharaoh treated Abram well because of Sarai, and Abram thus acquired sheep, cattle, donkeys, male and female slaves, she-donkeys, and camels.**

### ✳ *The Talmud Teaches*
**He treated Abram well because of her** R. Chelbo said: A person should always be careful to accord his wife the honor due to her, because blessings come to a man's home only on account of his wife, for it says "He treated Abram well because of her" (*Bava Metzia* 59a).

NOTE: Maharsha explains: The blessings really came from God. Pharaoh was merely the instrument through whom God bestowed blessings on Abraham because of Sarah (*Bava Metzia* 59a).

**(12:20) So Pharaoh gave men orders concerning [Abram], and they escorted him and his wife and all that was his.**

### ✳ *The Talmud Teaches*
**So Pharaoh gave men orders concerning Abram, and they escorted him** R. Yehoshua b. Levi said: Because of the four steps that Pharaoh accompanied Abraham, as it says "Pharaoh gave men orders, and they escorted him," he was allowed to enslave Abraham's children for four hundred years. For if you order an agent to escort someone, it is considered as if you yourself escorted him (*Sotah* 46b).

NOTE: Maharsha explains: The Jews' four-hundred-year bondage was not decreed because Pharaoh escorted Abraham. It was ordained at the covenant between the halves, when God said to Abraham, "Your descendants will be foreigners in a land that is not theirs for four hundred years. They will be enslaved and oppressed" (15:13). But God did not specify in which land. For escorting Abraham, Pharaoh merited that Israel should be enslaved in the land of Egypt and not in a different country.

**(13:13) But the people of Sodom were very wicked, and sinful against God.**

### ❈ *The Talmud Teaches*
*Very wicked, and . . . sinful* The people of Sodom have no share in the world to come, for it says "But the people of Sodom were very wicked, and sinful against God": wicked in this world and sinful in the world to come (*Sanhedrin* 107b).

NOTE: Their wickedness wiped them out in this world, and their sinfulness barred them from entering the world to come.

**(13:17) God said to Abram, "Rise, walk the land, through its length and breadth, for I will give it all to you."**

### ❈ *The Talmud Teaches*
*Rise, walk the land* When Moses complained to God, "Why do You mistreat Your people" (Exodus 5:22), the Holy One, blessed be He, said to Moses: Alas for the patriarchs who are gone and no more to be found; meaning: I miss the patriarchs. I appeared many times to the patriarchs, promising them Eretz Yisrael; yet though they did not see the fulfillment of these promises, they did not question the justice of My ways. I said to Abraham, "Rise, walk the land, for I will give it to you." Subsequently, he looked for a spot to bury his wife and could not find one until he purchased land for the exorbitant price of four hundred silver shekels (23:16); still, although that land had been promised him, he did not question My ways (*Sanhedrin* 111a).

**(14:14) When Abram heard that his kinsman had been taken captive, he armed his students who had been born in his house—three hundred and eighteen—and he pursued the four kings as far as Dan.**

## ※ *The Talmud Teaches*

*He armed [vayarek] his students* Rav said: The word *vayarek*—derived from *reik,* "empty"—implies that he emptied them of their Torah knowledge, making them neglect their Torah studies by pressing them into military service.

R. Abbahu said: Why was Abraham punished that his descendants were enslaved in Egypt for 210 years? Because he pressed Torah scholars into military service to fight the war against the four kings, thereby keeping them from learning Torah (*Nedarim* 32a).

**(14:21) The king of Sodom said to Abram, "Give me the people; you can keep the goods."**

## ※ *The Talmud Teaches*

*Give me the people* R. Yochanan said: Why was Abraham our Father punished that his descendants were enslaved in Egypt for 210 years? Because he prevented people from entering under the wings of the Shechinah, that is, from believing in God. For it says that after his victory over the four kings, Abraham returned all the captured property, whereupon, "The king of Sodom said to Abram, 'Give me back the people. You can keep the goods'" (*Nedarim* 32a).

NOTE: Abraham was punished because he should have insisted on taking the people with him in order to teach them to believe in God.

**(14:23) Abram swore, "Not a thread nor a shoelace! I will not take anything that is yours! You should not be able to say, 'It was I who made Abram rich.'"**

## ※ *The Talmud Teaches*

*Not a thread nor a shoelace!* Rava expounded: As a reward for saying to the king of Sodom, "Not a thread nor a shoelace! I will not take anything that is yours," Abraham's descendants were given two mitzvoth, namely, the blue thread of the zizith and the straps of the tefillin (*Sotah* 17a).

NOTE: By declining the spoils of a war that he had won miraculously, Abraham demonstrated that he attributed the victory to God and not to his own military prowess.

## GOD REASSURES ABRAHAM

**(15:5) God then took Abram outside and said, "Look at the sky and count the stars. See if you can count them."**

✳ *The Talmud Teaches*
*God then took him outside*  What is meant by "God then took him outside?" R. Yehudah said: Abraham said to the Holy One, blessed be He, "Looking at my horoscope, I see there that I am not destined to beget a son." Replied God, "Step 'outside' your astrology. Israel is not governed by the planets" (*Shabbat* 156a).

NOTE: If the stars portend misfortune for Israel, their fate is reversed through mitzvoth, prayer, and good deeds.

**(15:18) On that day, God made a covenant with Abram, saying "To your descendants I have given this land, from the Egyptian River to the great river, the Euphrates."**

✳ *The Jerusalem Talmud Teaches*
*To your descendants I have given this land*  R. Huna said: It does not say, "To your descendants I *will* give this land" but "To your descendants I *have* given this land"—I already gave it to them—as of now—they took possession of the land long before they entered it (Jerusalem Talmud, *Challah* 2:1).

**(16:8) The angel said, "Hagar, maid of Sarai! From where are you coming, and where are you going?" "I am running away from my mistress, Sarai," she replied.**

✳ *The Talmud Teaches*
*I am running away from my mistress, Sarai*  Rava said to Rabbah b. Mari: From where do we derive the rabbinic saying: "If your neighbor calls you a donkey, put a saddle on your back"? Meaning, agree with his insult. Don't argue with him trying to

convince him otherwise. Because the angel said, "Hagar, maid of Sarai! From where are you coming?" The angel disdainfully called her "maid of Sarai," and she replied, "I am running away from my *mistress* Sarai," candidly admitting that Sarah was her mistress (*Bava Kamma* 92b).

## THE COVENANT OF *MILAH* AND NEW NAMES

**(17:1) When Abram was ninety-nine years old, God appeared to Abram and said to him, "I am God Almighty. Walk before Me and be perfect."**

### ※ *The Talmud Teaches*
**and be perfect** The mitzvah of *milah* (ritual circumcision) is great indeed, for no one was more eager to fulfill the mitzvoth than Abraham; yet he was called perfect only because of the *milah*. For it says "Walk before Me and be perfect," and this is followed by, "I will make a covenant *[brit]* between Me and you."

Rav Yehudah said: When the Holy One, blessed be He, said to our father Abraham, "Walk before Me and be perfect," he was overcome with trembling. He thought, "Perhaps there still is something shameful in me!" because before this point, God had never said to him that he would be perfect. But when God added, "I will make a covenant between you and Me," his misgivings were eased. He realized that the imperfection was not in himself, but in the lack of the *brit milah* (*Nedarim* 32a).

**(17:5) No longer shall you be called Abram. Your name shall become Abraham, for I have set you up as a father of a multitude of nations.**

### ※ *The Talmud Teaches*
**Your name shall become Abraham** R. Ammi b. Abba said: First, his name was Abram, with the numeric value of 243; then, it was changed to Abraham with the numeric value of 248. At first, God placed 243 limbs under his control and later 248 limbs, which is the number of all the parts of the human body, the additional five are the two eyes, two ears, and the male organ (*Nedarim* 32b).

NOTE: Seeing and hearing lewd things entice a person to immorality. Through *milah*, a Jew is given mastery over his eyes and his ears and over the organ of sexual desire (*Nedarim* 32b).

**(17:7) I will sustain My covenant between Me and you and your descendants after you throughout their generations, an eternal covenant; I will be a God to you and your offspring after you.**

### ❋ *The Talmud Teaches*
*to you and your offspring* Whoever does not get married causes the Shechinah to leave Israel. For it says "I will be a God to you and your offspring." The implication is that as long as there is offspring, the Shechinah is present, but if there is no offspring, on whom should the Shechinah rest? On wood and stones (*Yevamot* 64a)?

*for Sarah is her name* Sarah is the same as Sarai. At first, she became a princess of her own people, but later she became a princess of the entire world (*Berachot* 13a).

NOTE: *Sarai* translates "my princess," whereas *Sarah* means just "princess," that is, she is universally accepted as princess.

**(17:19) God said, "Still, your wife Sarah will give birth to a son. You must name him Isaac. I will keep My covenant with him as an eternal treaty, for his descendants after him."**

### ❋ *The Jerusalem Talmud Teaches*
*You must name him Isaac* Why were the names of Abraham and Jacob changed and not that of Isaac? Abram's name was changed to Abraham; Jacob's name to Israel. The names Abram and Jacob were given them by their parents, but in the case of Isaac, it was God who gave him his name, for it says "God said, '. . . You must name him Isaac'" (Jerusalem Talmud, *Berachot* 1:6).

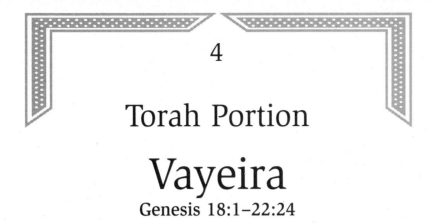

# 4

## Torah Portion

# Vayeira

### Genesis 18:1–22:24

### THE THREE VISITORS

**(18:2) Abraham lifted his eyes and he saw three strangers standing a short distance from him. When he saw them from the entrance of his tent, he ran to greet them, bowing down to the ground.**

### ✳ *The Talmud Teaches*
*He saw three strangers* Who were these three strangers? The angels Michael, Gabriel, and Raphael disguised as Arab way- farers. Michael came to announce to Sarah that she would give birth to a son; Raphael came to heal Abraham from his circum- cision; and Gabriel's mission was to overturn Sodom (*Bava Met- zia* 86b).

**(18:3) He said, "My Lord, if you would, please do not go away from Your servant."**

### ✳ *The Talmud Teaches*
*Please do not go away* Rav Yehudah said: Offering hospitality to guests is greater than having a revelation of the Divine Pres- ence. For it says [that] when Abraham wanted to welcome the three wayfarers, he interrupted the vision of God he was hav- ing and asked God to wait. Abraham said to God, "My Lord, if you would, please do not go away from Your servant."

R. Elazar said: Notice how the nature of God differs from that of mortal man. The nature of man is such that an unimportant person cannot tell a great man: Wait for me until I come to you. But when speaking to God, Abraham said: Please do not go away. Wait for me, and I will come back to You (*Shabbat* 127a).

NOTE: Although God is exalted above all, His hallmark is humility.

**(18:4) Abraham said: Let some water be brought, and wash your feet. Rest under the tree. (18:8) Abraham took cream and milk, and the calf that he prepared, and he placed it before his guests. He stood over them under the tree, and they ate.**

### ※ The Talmud Teaches
*Let some water be brought*  As a reward for three things that Abraham did, his descendants merited three things. As a reward for the cream and milk he served the three strangers (18:8), his descendants received the manna. As a reward for "and he stood over them" (18:8), they received the pillar of cloud that showed them the way through the wilderness (Exodus 17:6). As a reward for "Let some water be brought," they merited the Well of Miriam that accompanied them on their wanderings through the desert and supplied them with water (*Bava Metzia* 86b).

*and they ate*  R. Tanchum b. Chanila'i said: A person should never deviate from the custom of the place where he is staying as a guest. For when Moses went up to heaven, he did not eat bread because angels do not eat or drink; and when the angels came down to earth they did eat bread, for it says "and they ate," each following the custom of the place they were visiting (*Bava Metzia* 86b).

**(18:13) God said to Abraham, "Why did Sarah laugh and say, 'Can I really have children when I am so old?'"**

### ※ The Talmud Teaches
*When I am so old*  In the yeshiva of R. Yishmael, they taught: You see how precious peace is, for even God altered Sarah's words for the sake of peace. For she said, "How can I have chil-

dren; my husband is so old." Had Abraham heard that, he would have resented it. But to save domestic peace, God told Abraham that Sarah said, "How can I have children since *I* am so old" (*Bava Metzia* 87a).

## SODOM AND AMORAH

**(18:19) God said: For I have loved Abraham, because he commands his children and his household after him that they keep the way of God, doing charity and justice, in order that God might then bring upon Abraham that which He had spoken of him.**

### ✳ *The Talmud Teaches*
***Doing charity and justice*** The nation of Israel is known by three characteristics: They are compassionate, humble, and benevolent. We know that they are benevolent, for it says "That they keep the way of God, doing charity and justice" (*Yevamot* 79a).

**(18:20) God said, "The outcry against Sodom and Amorah is so great, and their sin is so very grave."**

### ✳ *The Talmud Teaches*
***The outcry . . . is so great*** An example of the unspeakable crimes of the Sodomites: There was a certain kindhearted young woman who would bring bread in her pitcher to the poor. The matter was eventually discovered by the ruthless Sodomites, who prohibited any display of mercy and compassion. To punish her, they smeared her with honey and placed her on the top of the city wall. Attracted by the honey covering her, bees swooped down and devoured the young woman. This is the Sodomites' crime that is alluded to in the verse "The outcry against Sodom and Amorah is so great *[rabbah].*" Sodom was destroyed because of the affair of the young woman *[rivah]* who was killed for being kind and benevolent, *rivah* (*Sanhedrin* 109b).

NOTE: In Hebrew, *rabbah* and *rivah* have the same letters.

Rashi explains that whenever she had to draw water, she would hide bread in her pitcher and go out to the well. When no one was looking, she would give the bread to a poor man.

**(18:27) Abraham spoke up and said, "I have already said too much before my Lord! I am mere dust and ashes!"**

### ✳ *The Talmud Teaches*

*dust and ashes* Rava expounded: For the humility Abraham displayed by saying, "I am mere dust and ashes," he was rewarded that his descendants received two mitzvoth that have to do with dust and ashes, namely, the ashes of the red cow and the dust used in the ceremony of the *sotah*, the suspected adulteress.

The Gemara asks: But there is another mitzvah that involves dust, namely that of covering the blood of slaughtered fowl with dust (Leviticus 17:13). Why didn't the Gemara mention that mitzvah too? The Gemara answers: In the case of the mitzvah of covering the blood, there is no benefit to the one who performs it. However, the mitzvah of the dust of the *sotah* entails the benefit that if she is cleared, domestic peace will be restored. The ashes of the red cow have the benefit that a ritually unclean person becomes clean by being sprinkled with them (*Sotah* 17a).

NOTE: The chapters of the red cow and the *sotah* are in Numbers 19 and 5:11–31, respectively.

**(20:17) Abraham prayed to God, and God healed Avimelech, as well as his wife and his slavegirls, so that they were able to have children.**

### ✳ *The Talmud Teaches*

*Abraham prayed to God* Rava said: From where do we know that a person who prays for his neighbor while he himself needs the same thing, he will be answered first? For it says "Abraham prayed to God, and God healed Avimelech, as well as his wife"; and immediately after that, it says "God remembered Sarah as he had . . . said," that is, as Abraham had prayed and said concerning Avimelech. And the next verse says "And Sarah became pregnant" (*Bava Kamma* 92a).

NOTE: Abraham prayed for Avimelech and his wife, who had become barren; and Sarah, who was barren, was helped first.

## ISAAC AND ISHMAEL

**(21:7) Sarah said, "Who would have even suggested to Abraham that Sarah would be nursing children? But here I have given birth to a son in Abraham's old age!"**

※ *The Talmud Teaches*
**Sarah would be nursing children** The Gemara asks: It says *children* in the plural. How many children did Sarah nurse when Isaac was her only child? R. Levi said: On the day that Abraham weaned his son Isaac, he made a great banquet, and all the people were skeptical, saying, "Have you seen that old man and woman? They picked up an abandoned child off the street and say it is their son." What did our father Abraham do? He invited all the important people of his time, and our mother Sarah invited their wives. Each one brought her child along, but not the wet nurse. A great miracle occurred to our mother Sarah. Her breasts opened like two wells, and she nursed all the children. Thereupon, they all declared, "Abraham is Isaac's father" (25:19) (*Bava Metzia* 87a).

**(21:17) God heard the boy weeping. God's angel called Hagar from heaven and said to her, "What's the matter, Hagar? Don't be afraid. God has heard the boy's voice where he is."**

※ *The Talmud Teaches*
**Where he is** These words seem unnecessary. R. Yitzchak explained: A person is only judged based on his actions up to that point in time and not for evil deeds he will commit later in life, as it says "God has heard the boy's voice where he is," right now, although later he will commit many crimes. God saved Hagar's son Ishmael's life, because at that moment he was still an innocent child (*Rosh Hashanah* 16b).

**(21:33) Abraham planted a tamarisk tree in Beer-sheba, and there he proclaimed the name of God, Lord of the Universe.**

※ *The Talmud Teaches*
**There Abraham proclaimed [vayikra] the name of God** Resh Lakish said: Don't read *vayikra*, "he proclaimed." Read instead

*vayakri*, "he caused the name of God to be uttered" by every person that passed by his tent. How did he accomplish that? He invited passing wayfarers to come in for a meal. After the guests finished eating and drinking, they got up to bless and thank Abraham. But Abraham told them, "Why are you thanking me? Did you eat *my* food? The food you ate belongs to the God of the universe. You should thank, praise, and bless Him Who spoke and the world came into being" (*Sotah* 10b).

## THE BINDING OF ISAAC ON THE ALTAR

**(22:1) After these events, God tested Abraham.**

### ✳ *The Talmud Teaches*

**After these events** Literally, "After these words." After which words? R. Yochanan said: After the words of Satan, who criticized Abraham before God. For it says "The child grew and was weaned. Abraham made a great feast on the day that Isaac was weaned" (21:8). Satan said to God, "You granted this old man a son at the age of a hundred years. From the entire feast that he made to celebrate, couldn't he have offered at least one turtledove or one young dove to You?" Then God said to Satan, "Did he make the feast for any reason other than his son? Still, if I would tell him, 'Sacrifice your son before Me,' he would sacrifice him immediately." Thereupon, the verse says "God tested Abraham" (*Sanhedrin* 89b).

**After these events** Literally, "after these words." R. Levi said: After Ishmael's words to Isaac. Ishmael was the son of Abraham and Hagar, Sarah's maidservant.

Said Ishmael to Isaac, "I am greater than you in the observance of the commandments, for you were circumcised when you were merely eight days old, whereas I was circumcised when I was thirteen years old." Ishmael meant to say: At eight days, you could not protest; but at thirteen years of age, I could have protested, yet I did not object to being circumcised. Isaac answered, "Do you challenge me from merely one limb, the male organ? If God would tell me, 'Sacrifice yourself before Me,' I would sacrifice myself willingly." Thereupon, it says "God tested Abraham" (*Sanhedrin* 89b).

**(22:2) Take your son, the only one, whom you love—Isaac— and go to the land of Moriah; bring him up there as an offering upon one of the mountains which I shall tell you.**

### ✳ *The Talmud Teaches*
***Take your son*** God told Abraham, "Take your son." Abraham replied, "I have two sons, Isaac and Ishmael! Which should I take?" God continued, "Your only one!" Abraham responded, "But this one is the only one of his mother, and that one is the only son of his mother." God said, "Whom you love!" Abraham replied, "But I love both of them." Finally, God said, "Isaac."

The Gemara asks: And why was this long-winded request necessary? Why didn't God say from the start, "Take Isaac"? The Gemara answers: So that Abraham should not be shocked at the sudden demand to sacrifice his son (*Sanhedrin* 89b).

**(22:3) Abraham got up early in the morning and saddled his donkey. He took his two men with him, along with his son Isaac.**

### ✳ *The Talmud Teaches*
***Abraham got up early*** The whole day is appropriate for circumcision, but the zealous perform the mitzvah as early as possible, for it says "Abraham got up early in the morning" (*Pesachim* 4a).

***He saddled his donkey*** It was taught in the name of R. Shimon b. Elazar: The fact that Abraham saddled his donkey himself shows that love is blind (*Sanhedrin* 105b).

NOTE: Out of Abraham's great love of God and eagerness to carry out His command, he disregarded his prominent status and saddled his donkey himself rather than have a servant do this lowly chore.

**(22:13) Abraham looked up and saw a ram—afterward, caught in the thicket by its horns. He went and got the ram, and offered it up as an offering instead of his son.**

### ❖ *The Jerusalem Talmud Teaches*

*Abraham saw a ram—afterward* What is the meaning of the awkward insertion of the word *afterward?* R. Yuda b. Simon said: God said to Abraham, "After many generations, your children will be involved in sin and go through suffering, but 'afterward,' in the end, they will be saved by the horns of this ram, that is, in the merit of the binding of Isaac, for it says in the prophecy about the coming of Mashiach [Messiah], 'The Lord God will blow with a shofar [horn]'" (Zechariah 9:14) (Jerusalem Talmud, *Taanit* 2:4).

5

## Torah Portion

# Chayei Sarah

### Genesis 23:1–25:18

## SARAH'S DEATH

**(23:2) Sarah died in Kiryat Arba which is Hebron in the land of Canaan; and Abraham came to eulogize Sarah and to weep for her.**

⁂ *The Talmud Teaches*
*in Kiryat Arba* Literally, in the "City of Four." Why is Hebron called City of Four? R. Yitzchak said: Because of the four couples that are buried there: Adam and Eve; Abraham and Sarah; Isaac and Rebeccah; Jacob and Leah (*Eruvin* 53a).

NOTE: Rachel died on the way back from Haran and was buried in Bethlehem (Genesis 35:19).

**(24:1) Abraham was old, well advanced in years, and God had blessed Abraham with everything.**

⁂ *The Talmud Teaches*
*Abraham was old* Until Abraham, there were no signs of old age. In fact, Abraham and Isaac looked exactly alike. So Abraham prayed for marks of old age; and old age came into existence, as it says "Abraham was old, well advanced in years" (*Bava Metzia* 87a).

NOTE: The redundancy of this phrase tells us that Abraham was old and had the marks of old age.

***with everything*** What is meant by "with everything"? The Rabbis taught: God gave Abraham a foretaste of the world to come while he was still in this world in the following ways: in that he did not have to struggle with the evil impulse; also, the angel of death had no power over him, so that he was spared the agony associated with dying, but died peacefully, and maggots had no dominion over his body. For it says "God blessed Abraham with everything," meaning, none of the good things of the world to come were withheld from him (*Bava Batra* 17a).

***God blessed Abraham with everything [bakol]*** What is meant by *bakol*, "with everything"? R. Meir said: He was blessed in not having a daughter. R. Yehudah said: He was blessed in having a daughter. Others say that Abraham had a daughter whose name was Bakol, and Bakol was God's blessing. R. Elazar Hamoda'i said: Abraham was blessed in that he was an expert astrologer, and all the kings of the East and the West used to get up early in the morning to seek his advice. R. Shimon b. Yochai said: Abraham had a precious jewel hanging from his neck, and any sick person who looked at it was healed immediately.

Another explanation of God's blessing is that Esau did not rebel against God as long as Abraham was alive. Yet another explanation is that Ishmael repented while Abraham was still alive (*Bava Batra* 16b, 17a).

## FINDING A WIFE FOR ISAAC

**(24:14) Eliezer, Abraham's servant, said, "If I say to the girl, 'Tip over your jug, and let me have a drink,' and she replies, 'Drink, and I also will water your camels,' she will be the one whom You have designated for Your servant Isaac."**

### ❈ The Talmud Teaches
***If I say to the . . . girl*** Eliezer asked in an improper manner, for it says "If I say to the girl, 'Tip over your jug, and let me have a drink' . . . she will be the one whom You have designated for Your servant Isaac." How could he make such a stipulation? The girl who showed up at the well might have been lame or blind! Nevertheless, he was answered properly in that God made Rebeccah appear on the scene (*Taanit* 4a).

**(24:25) Eliezer said, "I am Abraham's servant."**

### ※ *The Talmud Teaches*
*I am Abraham's servant* Rava asked Rabbah b. Mari: From where do we derive the popular saying, "If there is a flaw in your background, you be the first to tell it"? He replied: From Eliezer, for he introduced himself as "Abraham's servant," immediately mentioning his inferior rank (*Bava Kamma* 92b).

**(24:42) Eliezer said, "Now today I came to the well, and I prayed, 'O God, Lord of my master Abraham, if You will, grant success to this mission that I am undertaking.'"**

### ※ *The Talmud Teaches*
*Now today I came to the well* The earth shrank for Eliezer's sake, for it says "Now today I came to the well," implying that he had set out on that day (*Sanhedrin* 95a).

NOTE: Because the journey from Hebron to Aram Naharayim is approximately 450 miles, it could not be done in a day. Therefore, the earth must have shrunk for him.

**(24:50) Laban and Bethuel both spoke up. "The matter stemmed from God," they said. "We cannot say anything to you, bad or good."**

### ※ *The Talmud Teaches*
*The matter stemmed from God* Rav said: We can prove from a verse in the Torah that it is decreed by God who should become your wife. For it says: When Eliezer came to get Rebeccah for Isaac, "Laban and Bethuel both spoke up. 'The matter stemmed from God,' they said" (*Mo'ed Katan* 18b).

**(24:61) Rebeccah set off with her girls, and they rode on the camels and proceeded after the man Eliezer. The servant thus took Rebeccah and left.**

### ※ *The Talmud Teaches*
*They proceeded after the man, Eliezer* It says "After the man" but not "in front of the man." This teaches you that a man should

not walk behind a woman because this may give rise to pro-vocative thoughts (*Berachot* 61a).

### (25:1) Abraham married another woman whose name was Keturah.

### ※ The Talmud Teaches
**Abraham married another woman** Rava asked Rabbah b. Mari: From where is derived the popular saying: Sixty-one pains reach the teeth of a person who hears the noise made by some-one eating while he himself does not eat? Meaning: It is painful to watch people eat while you are hungry. For it says "Isaac married Rebeccah . . . and he loved her." And in the next verse, it says "Abraham married another woman" (*Bava Kamma* 92b). Seeing his son Isaac happily married, Abraham decided to get married again too.

### (25:5) Abraham gave all that he owned to Isaac.

### ※ The Talmud Teaches
**Abraham gave all that he owned to Isaac** The Arabs, the de-scendants of Ishmael, Abraham's oldest son, and the descen-dants of Keturah, the wife Abraham took after Sarah's death, came to contend with the Jews before Alexander the Great. These enemies of the Jews said to Alexander: The land Canaan belongs to us *and* the Jews. For it says "And these are the descendants of Ishmael the son of Abraham" (25:12), and it also says "These are the descendants of Isaac the son of Abra-ham" (25:19). Both are descendants of Abraham, and God promised the land of Canaan to Abraham and his descendants, so we lay claim to the land. Whereupon Geviha ben Pesisa, the Jewish spokesman, said: But it says "Abraham gave all that he owned to Isaac. And to the concubine-children whom Abraham had, Abraham gave gifts, and he sent them away from Isaac, his son, while he was still alive, to the east country" (25:6). Now, if a father gave legacies to his sons in his lifetime and then sent one son away to prevent rivalry after his death, does one son have any claim on the other? Certainly not! Therefore, you have no claim on the Land of Israel; for Abraham gave your ances-

tors part of his possessions and then sent them out of the Land of Israel, thereby indicating that they were to have no part of the Land of Israel. The descendants of Ishmael could not come up with a convincing answer, so they fled (*Sanhedrin* 92b).

**(25:11) After Abraham died, God blessed Isaac, his son. Isaac lived in the vicinity of Beer Lachai Ro'i.**

### ※ *The Talmud Teaches*
*God blessed Isaac* Because it does not say what the blessing consisted of, we conclude that God came to comfort him with the comfort of mourners. This teaches us that one of the attributes of God is that He comforts the bereaved (*Sotah* 14a).

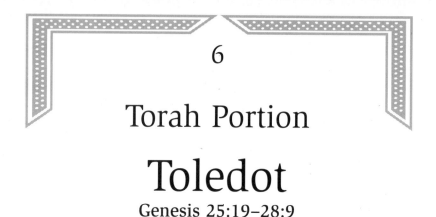

# 6

# Torah Portion

# Toledot

### Genesis 25:19–28:9

## JACOB AND ESAU

**(25:19) These are the offspring of Isaac son of Abraham. Abraham was Isaac's father.**

✳ *The Talmud Teaches*
*Abraham was Isaac's father* This phrase seems to be redundant, because [the verse] already says "Isaac son of Abraham." Why the repetition? When Sarah gave birth to Isaac, people made fun of Abraham, saying, "Could Abraham father a child at the age of one hundred?" Immediately, Isaac's facial features changed, and he came to look exactly like Abraham. Seeing this, they all cried out, "Abraham is Isaac's father!" (*Bava Metzia* 87a).

**(25:21) Isaac pleaded with God opposite his wife, because she was barren. God granted his plea, and Rebeccah became pregnant.**

✳ *The Talmud Teaches*
*opposite his wife* It does not say "concerning his wife" but "opposite his wife." From here we see that both Rebeccah and Isaac were infertile, and both Isaac and Rebeccah prayed to be healed from their condition. And why is it that our forefathers were incapable of having children? Said R. Yitzchak: God yearns to hear the prayers of the righteous; that's why He withholds

52

favors from them, so that they will pray to Him to be helped (*Yevamot* 64a).

**God granted his plea** Because both Isaac and Rebeccah were praying, it should say, "God granted their plea." The Gemara answers: Because the prayer of a righteous man (Isaac) who is the son of a righteous man—Abraham—is more powerful than the prayer of a righteous man who is the son of a wicked man. Rebeccah's father, Bethuel, was a wicked man (*Yevamot* 64b).

NOTE: The prayer of a *tzaddik* (righteous man) who is the son of a *tzaddik* is more effective because it is reinforced by the merits of his father. That's why Isaac's prayer was answered.

**(25:23) God said to her, "Two nations are in your womb. Two governments will separate from inside you. The upper hand will go from one government to the other. The elder will serve the younger."**

※ *The Talmud Teaches*
*The upper hand will go from one government to the other* R. Nachman b. Yitzchak said: Rome and Jerusalem will never flourish at the same time. If someone tells you that both Caesarea and Jerusalem are laid waste, don't believe it, or that both are settled, don't believe that either. But if someone says that Caesarea is laid waste and Jerusalem is settled, you may believe it, or that Jerusalem is laid waste and Caesarea is settled, you may believe it. For it says "The upper hand will go from one government to the other" (*Megillah* 6a).

NOTE: Caesarea is an ancient port in the Land of Israel that the Romans conquered. Rome is considered heir to the biblical nation of Edom, whose founder was Esau.

**(25:29) Jacob was simmering a stew, when Esau came exhausted from the field.**

※ *The Talmud Teaches*
*Jacob was simmering a stew* It was the day that Abraham died, and Jacob made a stew of lentils to comfort his father, Isaac. Why lentils? In Eretz Yisrael, they said in the name of

Rabbah b. Mari: Just as the lentil has no mouth, that is, no crack like other kinds of peas or beans, so the mourner has no mouth for speech (*Bava Batra* 16b).

***Esau came exhausted from the field*** It was the day that Abraham had died. R. Yochanan said: The wicked Esau committed five sins on that day: He raped a betrothed girl, committed murder, denied God, denied the revival of the dead, and rejected his birthright (*Bava Batra* 16b).

**(26:3) God said to Isaac, "Remain a stranger in this land. I will be with you and bless you, since it will be to you and your offspring that I will give these lands. I will thus keep the oath that I made to your father Abraham."**

### ※ The Talmud Teaches
***Remain a stranger in this land*** God said to Moses: I miss the patriarchs who are gone and no more to be found. I appeared to Abraham, Isaac, and Jacob many times, promising the Land of Israel to them, and they did not question My ways. I said to Isaac, "Remain a stranger in the land. I will be with you and bless you." Subsequently, his servants looked for water to drink and could not find any until they quarreled with the local inhabitants, as it says "The herdsmen of Gerar quarreled with Isaac's herdsmen, saying, 'The water is ours!'" (26:20). Still, although that was the very land that had been promised to him, he did not question My ways. Nor did any of the patriarchs ask Me, "What is Your name?" On the other hand, when I first spoke to you, Moses, you said to Me, "What is Your name?" (*Sanhedrin* 111a).

NOTE: Rashi explains: God is saying that He sorely misses the patriarchs. They were men of true faith who never questioned My ways, unlike you, Moses, who are quick to do so.

**(26:5) All this is because Abraham obeyed My voice, and kept My charge, My commandments, My decrees, and My laws.**

### ※ The Talmud Teaches
***My commandments, My decrees, and My laws*** Rav said: Abraham our Father kept the entire Torah long before it was given,

for it says "Abraham obeyed My voice, and kept My charge, My commandments, My decrees, and My laws." The Gemara asks: Perhaps the verse means that he observed the seven laws that were given to Noah that all humankind is obligated to observe? The Gemara answers: If this is so, why does the Torah say, "My decrees and My laws"? which implies much more than the seven Noahide laws. Thus, he obeyed all 613 mitzvoth (*Yoma* 28b).

NOTE: The seven Noahide laws are the command to administer justice and the six prohibitions against blasphemy, idolatry, murder, immorality, theft, and eating flesh torn from a living animal.

**(26:19) Isaac's servants then dug in the valley and found a well brimming over with fresh water.**

### ※ *The Talmud Teaches*
*fresh water* R. Natan said: If you see a well in your dream, you will find Torah, for it says "For one who finds me, the Torah, finds life [*chayim*]" (Proverbs 8:35). And it says here, "a well brimming over with fresh water, *mayim chayim*" (*Berachot* 56b).

NOTE: A well symbolizes water; water gives life; and the Torah represents life. Thus, a well epitomizes Torah.

## THE BLESSING

**(27:1) Isaac had grown old and his eyesight was fading. He summoned his elder son Esau. He said to him, "My son." He replied, "Here I am."**

### ※ *The Talmud Teaches*
*His eyesight was fading* R. Elazar said: If a person gazes at a wicked man, his eyesight becomes dimmed, for it says "Isaac had grown old and his eyesight was fading." Because he gazed at the wicked Esau, his eyesight was dimmed (*Yoma* 28b).

NOTE: This means gazing intently, not casually glancing.

**(27:22) Jacob came closer to his father Isaac, and [Isaac] touched him. He said, "The voice is Jacob's voice, but the hands are the hands of Esau."**

### ※ *The Talmud Teaches*
*. . . is Jacob's voice* signifies the wailing caused by Emperor Vespasian when he killed in the city of Betar four hundred thousand myriad, or, as some say, four thousand myriad.

NOTE: Betar was the city where the Jews made their last stand in the time of the Bar Kochba rebellion against the Romans (132 C.E.).

*The hands are the hands of Esau* alludes to the Roman Empire, which has destroyed our Temple and burned our sanctuary and driven us out of our land (*Gittin* 57b).

*The voice is Jacob's voice* Whenever a prayer is answered, there is a descendant of Jacob praying for that purpose. "The hands are the hands of Esau": If a war ends in victory, you can be sure that a descendant of Esau is involved in it (*Gittin* 57b).

**(27:29) Peoples will serve you, and regimes will bow down to you. You shall be like a lord over your brother; your mother's children will prostrate themselves to you. Those who curse you are cursed, and those who bless you are blessed.**

### ※ *The Jerusalem Talmud Teaches*
*Those who curse you are cursed* Once, a heathen happened to meet R. Yishmael and blessed him. Said R. Yishmael, "The blessing you just gave is nothing new." Another heathen then ran into R. Yishmael and cursed him. Said R. Yishmael, "Your curse is nothing new." Bewildered, the disciples asked him, "How is it that you said the same to both of them?" He replied, "Well, it says in the Torah, 'Those who curse you are cursed, and those who bless you are blessed'" (Jerusalem Talmud, *Berachot* 88:8).

**(27:45) Rebeccah said to Jacob, "When your brother has calmed from his rage against you, and has forgotten what you have done to him, I will send word and summon you home. But why should I lose both of you on the same day?"**

## ※ The Talmud Teaches
**On the same day** When Jacob's remains were brought to the Cave of Machpelah for burial, Esau held up the funeral. Chushim the son of Dan who was there took a club and clobbered Esau on the head so that he died and his eyes dropped out and fell to Jacob's feet. At that moment, the prophecy of Rebeccah came true, for she said, referring to Jacob and Esau, "Why should I lose both of you on the same day?" Although they did not both die on the same day, still both were buried on the same day (*Sotah* 13a).

**(28:9) Esau went to Ishmael and married Machalat, the daughter of Ishmael son of Abraham, a sister of Nebayot, in addition to his other wives.**

## ※ The Talmud Teaches
**Esau went to Ishmael** Rava asked Rabbah b. Mari: What is the source for the popular saying: A bad palm will usually make its way to a grove of barren trees? Or birds of a feather stick together? He replied: It says so in the Torah, "Esau went to Ishmael and married Machalat, the daughter of Ishmael son of Abraham." Esau and Ishmael were equally vicious and corrupt.

## ※ The Jerusalem Talmud Teaches
**Esau married Machalat** Was her name then Machalat? Surely, it was Basemat he married (36:3)! The name Machalat teaches us that all Esau's sins were forgiven. From this we can infer that on his wedding day a bridegroom's sins are forgiven (Jerusalem Talmud, *Bikkurim* 3:3).

NOTE: The name *Machalat* is taken as derived from *machal*, "to forgive." Esau's sins were forgiven because he married Machalat, the daughter of Ishmael, in order to please his father (28:8, 9).

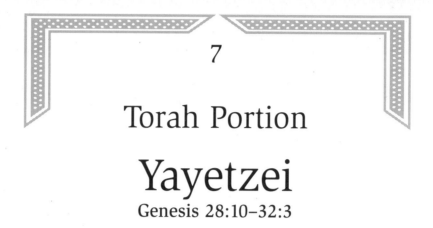

# 7

# Torah Portion

# Yayetzei
### Genesis 28:10–32:3

## JACOB'S VISION

**(28:11) Jacob came to a familiar place and spent the night there because the sun had already set. Taking some stones, he placed them at his head and lay down to sleep there.**

✳ *The Talmud Teaches*

*He came to a familiar place* The earth shrank for our father Jacob, for it says "Jacob left Beer-sheba and went to Haran, and he arrived there" (28:10). Then it says "He came to a familiar place—that is, Beth El—and slept there because the sun had already set."

NOTE: The two verses seem to contradict each other. First, he arrived in Haran, which is far beyond the borders of Eretz Yisrael; and then, he spent the night in Beth El, which is inside Eretz Yisrael, implying that he did not go as far as Haran!

The Gemara explains: This is what happened: Jacob did get as far as Haran, but once he reached Haran, he said to himself: Is it possible that I passed the place where my fathers prayed, that is, Beth El, and I did not pray there myself? I must go back to Beth El and correct my oversight. And as soon as he thought of going back, the earth between Haran and Beth El shrank for him, so that he instantly found himself back in Beth El. That is why immediately after Jacob reached Haran it says

"He came to the place," that is, Beth El, which proves that the earth shrank for him (*Sanhedrin* 95b).

***because the sun had already set*** After Jacob prayed in Beth El, he wanted to return to Haran. But God declared, "This righteous man has come to My lodging place—Beth El is the future site of the Temple—shall he leave without spending a night? Certainly not!" Thus, a miracle took place, and the sun set before its time, forcing Jacob to spend the night there (*Sanhedrin* 95b).

***taking some stones*** It says "Preparing to go to sleep, Jacob took some stones," *stones* in the plural. But further on, it says "Early in the morning he took the stone," *stone* in the singular (28:18). How can this variance be reconciled? R. Yitzchak said: This tells us that when Jacob lay down, all those stones gathered into one place; and each one said, "The *tzaddik* should rest his head on me!" Thereupon, all the stones were fused into one (*Chullin* 91b).

**(28:13) Suddenly he saw God standing over him. God said, "I am God, Lord of Abraham your father, and Lord of Isaac. I will give to you and your descendants the land upon which you are lying."**

***The Talmud Teaches***

***The land upon which you are lying*** What is so great about that? The land on which he was lying was no more than four cubits! Said R. Yitzchak: This teaches us that God rolled up the whole of Eretz Yisrael and put it under our father Jacob, as an omen that it would be as easy for his descendants to conquer as occupying the four cubits of the ground on which he was lying and so that no one could dispute Israel's right to the Land of Israel (*Chullin* 91b).

## RACHEL AND LEAH

**(29:12) Jacob told Rachel that he was her father's brother, and that he was Rebeccah's son; then she ran and told her father.**

※ *The Talmud Teaches*

*that he was her father's brother* Now, was Jacob really her father's brother? Wasn't he rather the son of Rebeccah, her father's sister? This is what happened: Jacob said to Rachel, "Will you marry me?" She answered, "Yes. But I must warn you that my father is a deceiver, and you will not be able to outwit him. He will try to trick you into marrying my sister." Jacob replied, "I am his brother in deceit" (*Megillah* 13b).

NOTE: Jacob implied, "I am just as shrewd as he is."

**(29:17) Leah's eyes were weak, while Rachel was shapely and beautiful.**

※ *The Talmud Teaches*

*Leah's eyes were weak* What is meant by *rakkot*, "weak"? Do you think that it means that her eyes were actually weak? Certainly not. So what is meant by *rakkot*?

Rav said: Her eyes were in fact weak, but that casts no aspersions on her; rather, it is an expression of high praise. She had poor eyesight because when she would hear people gossiping, "Rebeccah has two sons, and Laban has two daughters; the older daughter, Leah, should be married to the older son, Esau, and the younger one, Rachel, to the younger son, Jacob," Leah would inquire, "What kind of person is the older son?" They told her, "He is a bad man. He robs and pillages." She then asked, "What is the younger one like?" "He is a scholarly man who stays in tents," she was told. Hearing this, she cried until her eyelashes fell out. Thus, the fact that her eyes were weak attests to her virtue (*Bava Batra* 123a).

**(29:25) In the morning, Jacob discovered that it was Leah. He said to Laban, "How could you do this to me? Didn't I work with you for Rachel? Why did you cheat me?"**

※ *The Talmud Teaches*

*In the morning, Jacob discovered that it was Leah* Does this mean that until the morning it was not Leah? Of course not! To prevent Laban from substituting Leah for Rachel, Jacob had given Rachel a password through which he would be able to identify her as Rachel. When Rachel saw that her father was indeed planning to have Leah take her place, she gave the password to Leah to save her the embarrassment of being exposed. Because of the prearranged signs that Rachel divulged to Leah, Jacob did not know in the morning that it was Leah and not Rachel. When he heard the password, he thought that it was Rachel (*Megillah* 13b).

**(29:31) God saw that Leah was hated and He opened her womb. Rachel remained barren.**

*The Talmud Teaches*

***Leah was hated*** What could be the meaning of the phrase, "Leah was hated"? Surely Jacob did not really hate her! What it means is: God saw that Esau's behavior "was hated" in Leah's eyes. Therefore, "He opened her womb," and that is why Leah deserved to have the firstborn son, although originally Rachel was destined to give birth to the firstborn (*Bava Batra* 123a).

**(29:32) Leah became pregnant and gave birth to a son. So she named him Reuben. "God has seen my troubles," she said. "Now my husband will love me."**

*The Talmud Teaches*

***She named him Reuben*** Why was he called Reuben?

NOTE: The name *Reuben* is seen as a combination of *re'u,* "see," and *bein,* "between."

Leah said: *See* (*re'u*) the difference *between (bein)* my son Reuben and Esau, the son of my father-in-law. Esau, the son of my father-in-law, sold his birthright contemptuously to Jacob and then vowed to kill him! But my son Reuben lost his cherished birthright to Joseph, as it says "Reuben was the firstborn, but when he defiled his father's bed, his birthright was given to the sons of Joseph" (1 Chronicles 37:21). And not only did he not hate him, he tried to save his life, for it says "Reuben heard these words and tried to rescue Joseph from his brothers" (37:21) (*Berachot* 7b).

NOTE: Rashi on 35:22 explains that the phrase "He defiled his father's bed" refers to the following incident: After Rachel's death, Jacob moved his bed from Rachel's tent to the tent of Rachel's handmaid, Bilhah, rather than to the tent of Leah. Resenting his mother Leah's humiliation, Reuben placed Jacob's bed into Leah's tent. So Reuben did not do anything immoral.

**(30:1) Rachel realized that she was not bearing any children to Jacob. She was jealous of her sister and said to Jacob, "Give me children, otherwise I am dead!"**

### ※ *The Talmud Teaches*
*otherwise I am dead!* R. Yehoshua b. Levi said: A person who has no children is considered dead, for it says "Rachel who was childless said, 'Give me children, otherwise I am dead!'" (*Nedarim* 64b).

NOTE: Life is a continuous thread that connects parents with their children. Because a childless person's thread of life is broken, he is considered as dead.

**(30:21) Afterward Leah had a daughter, and she named her Dinah.**

### ※ *The Talmud Teaches*
*Afterward Leah had a daughter* After what? After Leah passed judgment, *din*, on herself, saying, "Jacob is destined to father twelve tribes. I have already borne six, and each of the handmaids has borne two, making a total of ten. If the child I am carrying is a male, then my sister Rachel will not even be equal to one of the handmaids, for she will have only one tribe, whereas the handmaids each have two." In order to spare Rachel such humiliation, Leah prayed for a miracle—that the fetus be changed to a female. Right away, the child was turned into a girl, as it says "She named her Dinah" (*Berachot* 60a).

NOTE: The name *Dinah* comes from *din*, "judgment."

**(30:22) God remembered Rachel. God heard her prayer and He opened her womb.**

### ✳ *The Talmud Teaches*
*He opened her womb*  R. Yochanan said: The key for childbirth is in the hand of God Himself. It is not assigned to an angel. For it says "God remembered Rachel. God heard her prayer, and He opened her womb" (*Taanit* 2a).

NOTE:  The inference is drawn from the words, "*He* opened her womb," and also from the fact that the Torah repeats God's name twice in this verse, rather than stating, "God remembered Rachel, heard her prayer, and opened her womb."

**(31:24) God appeared to Laban the Aramean that night in a dream and said, "Be very careful not to say anything, good or bad, to Jacob."**

### ✳ *The Talmud Teaches*
*Good or bad*  It is perfectly understandable that God warned Laban not to say anything "bad" but why not "good"? We can learn from this that all the good wishes of the wicked are harmful for the righteous. What harm could result from Laban saying something good? He might wish him good things in the name of his idol (*Yevamot* 103b).

NOTE:  It is forbidden to cause a heathen to mention the name of an idol, for it says "You must not cause the name of another deity to be heard" (Exodus 23:13).

8

# Torah Portion

# Vayishlach

### Genesis 32:4–36:43

## JACOB'S ENCOUNTER WITH ESAU

**(32:8) Jacob was very frightened and distressed. He divided the people accompanying him into two camps, along with the sheep, cattle, and camels.**

✳ *The Talmud Teaches*
*Jacob was very frightened* R. Yaakov b. Dimi pointed out a contradiction: It says "God said to Jacob, 'I am with you. I will protect you wherever you go'" (28:15). But here it says "Jacob was very frightened." Because God promised to protect him, what was he afraid of? He was afraid that some sin might cause God's promise not to be fulfilled (*Berachot* 4a).

NOTE: The Midrash explains that Jacob's perceived sin was his inability to honor his father during the fourteen years he stayed with Laban, while Esau honored his father all that time.

**(32:11) Jacob prayed, "I have been diminished because of all the kindnesses and faith You have shown me. When I left home I crossed the Jordan with only my staff, and now I have become two camps."**

✳ *The Talmud Teaches*
*I have been diminished* R. Yannai said: A person should never stand in a dangerous place expecting a miracle to be performed

for him, because the miracle may not happen. And if a miracle does happen, it will be deducted from the merits he has earned for his good deeds.

R. Chanin said: What verse tells us this? Jacob prayed, "I have been diminished—that is, my merits have decreased—because of all the kindness and faith that You have shown me" (*Shabbat* 32a).

**(32:25) After Jacob had taken his family and his possessions across the Jabbok River, Jacob remained alone. A man appeared and wrestled with him until just before daybreak.**

※ *The Talmud Teaches*
*Jacob remained alone* R. Elazar said: Having brought all his possessions across the river, Jacob returned, risking his life to pick up some small jugs he had forgotten to take. This shows us that the righteous place a higher value on their possessions than on their body. Why? Because they do not engage in robbery, and everything they own is dear to them because it was acquired through honest labor (*Chullin* 91a).

**(33:10) When meeting Esau, Jacob said, "No, I beg of you! If I have now found favor in your eyes, then accept my tribute from me, inasmuch as I have seen your face, which is like seeing the face of a divine being, and you have received me so favorably."**

※ *The Talmud Teaches*
*like seeing the face of a divine being* What did Jacob mean when he said this? R. Levi said: To what can we compare this conversation between Jacob and Esau? To a person who invited his neighbor to a meal, and the guest noticed that the host was trying to poison him. So the guest said, "This dish has the same aroma as the dish I was served at the royal palace." The host said to himself, "Obviously, he must know the king. I'd better not harm him." So he did not poison him. The same way, Jacob spoke of "seeing the face of the divine" in order to frighten Esau (*Sotah* 41b).

**(35:3) Jacob said to his household, "Then come, let us go up to Beth-el; I will make there an altar to God Who answered**

me in my time of distress and was with me on the road that I traveled."

### ※ *The Talmud Teaches*
*to God Who answered me*  R. Yochanan said: In all the passages that the *minim*—heretics, probably early Christians—have taken as grounds for their heresy, to prove that God is not one, they are refuted on the spot.

They used the passage, "For it was here that God had been revealed to him—*niglu*, plural" (35:7). They are refuted immediately in "the God Who answered me—*oneh*, singular" (35:3) (*Sanhedrin* 38b).

NOTE: R. Yochanan is referring to verses that speak of God in the plural, which the heretics use as proof that God is not the One and Only. Their claims are quashed in a nearby verse that speaks of God in the singular. When the Torah occasionally refers to God in the plural, it is done in the sense of the royal *we,* the way a king or queen uses *we* instead of *I* in official pronouncements.

**(35:11) God said to Jacob, "I am *El Shaddai,* God Almighty. Be fruitful and multiply. A nation and a community of nations will come into existence from you."**

### ※ *The Talmud Teaches*
*I am El Shaddai, God Almighty*  What is meant by "I am *El Shaddai,* God Almighty"? It means: I am He Who said the word *dai!* "Enough!" Stop right now! Had God not called out *dai!* "Enough!" to heaven and earth, they would go on evolving infinitely (*Chagigah* 12a).

**(35:22) While Jacob was living undisturbed in the area, Reuben went and lay with Bilhah, his father's concubine. Jacob heard about it. Jacob had twelve sons.**

### ※ *The Talmud Teaches*
*Reuben went and lay with Bilhah*  R. Shmuel b. Nachmani said: Whoever said that Reuben sinned is making a mistake. For it says in the same verse, "Jacob had twelve sons," implying that all of Jacob's sons were equally virtuous.

But what do you do with the verse, "Reuben lay with Bilhah, his father's concubine"? It teaches you that he moved his father's bed and placed it in Leah's tent, and Scripture considers that as if he had lived with her.

NOTE: The sisters Leah and Rachel were both married to Jacob. Leah was Reuben's mother; Rachel's maidservant was Bilhah. After Rachel's death, Jacob moved his bed from Rachel's tent into Bilhah's tent. Reuben, in defense of his mother's honor, placed Jacob's bed in Leah's tent.

R. Shimon b. Elazar explains: The righteous Reuben never committed that sin. If so, how do you explain the passage, "Reuben lay with Bilhah, his father's concubine"? The answer is: He stood up for his mother's humiliation. Reuben said: I can live with the fact that my mother's sister, Rachel, was a rival to my mother. But that Bilhah, the maidservant of my mother's sister, should be a rival to my mother now that Rachel has died, this is too much for me to swallow. Thereupon, Reuben took the initiative and changed his father's sleeping arrangements, moving Jacob's bed from Bilhah's into Leah's tent.

Others say: Reuben mixed up two beds, one of the Shechinah, the other of his father.

NOTE: Rashi explains that Jacob prepared a bed for the Shechinah in the tents of his four wives; in whichever tent he perceived the Shechinah, that is where he spent the night. And so before his death, Jacob reproached Reuben for rearranging the beds, saying, "Because you were impetuous as water, you will no longer be first. For when you moved your father's beds, you disgraced the Shechinah that went up on my bed" (Genesis 49:4) (*Shabbat* 55b).

## ESAU'S DESCENDANTS

**(36:12) And Timna became a concubine of Esau's son Eliphaz and she bore Eliphaz's son Amalek.**

### ✽ *The Talmud Teaches*
*Timna became a concubine of Esau's son Eliphaz* What is the significance of this? Timna was a royal princess, the sister of

Lotan, and it says "Chief Lotan" (Genesis 36:40). Because Lotan was a chieftain and Timna was his sister, it follows that she was a princess. Timna wanted to convert to the faith of Abraham, so she came to Abraham, Isaac, and Jacob for that purpose; but they did not accept her as a convert. Thereupon, she became a concubine of Eliphaz, the son of Esau, saying: I'd rather be a maidservant to this nation than a princess to any other nation. She therefore accepted the lowly rank of concubine to Eliphaz, because he was Isaac's grandson.

From her issued Amalek, Israel's perennial archenemy, who distressed Israel so greatly. Why was Amalek able to cause Israel so much anguish and pain? It was because Abraham, Isaac, and Jacob should not have rejected Timna (*Sanhedrin* 99b).

NOTE: The reason they did not accept Timna was because she wanted to convert in order to gain status by marrying into Abraham's family. This was not the sincere motivation that is needed for conversion.

**(36:20) These are the children of Seir the Chorite, who were settled in the land: Lotan, Shoval, Tziv'on, and Anah.**

※ *The Talmud Teaches*
*the Chorite who were settled in the land* Literally: "the Chorite, inhabitants of the earth." Does that mean that all other people are inhabitants of heaven? "Inhabitants of the earth" means that the Chorites were experts in the science of agriculture. They were able to say: This piece of land is best suited for planting olive trees; this piece of land is best suited for grapevines; and this is best suited for fig trees. The name *Chori*, "Chorites," implies that they smelled the earth, for by transposing the letters of Chori you obtain *rei'ach*, "smell." Thus, by the smell of the earth, they could tell what crop would thrive in a given piece of land (*Shabbat* 85a).

*Anah was the one who discovered how to breed mules* R. Shimon b. Gamliel said: The mule came into existence in the days of Anah. Those who expound the verse in a figurative sense used to say: Anah was illegitimate, born of an incestuous union;

therefore, he brought a mixed breed of animal into the world, because the mule is a crossbreed between a horse and a donkey (*Pesachim* 54a).

**(36:43) These are the tribes of Esau, each with its own settlement in its hereditary land—he is Esau, father of Edom.**

***The Talmud Teaches***

***He is Esau*** This seems to be redundant. The phrase teaches us that Esau remained in his wicked ways from beginning to end (*Megillah* 11a).

NOTE: Maharsha explains: He was wicked in his younger days, which he demonstrated by his selling his birthright at the age of fifteen. He was equally wicked when, in the last moments of his life, he objected to the burial of his brother Jacob in the Cave of Machpelah (*Megillah* 11a).

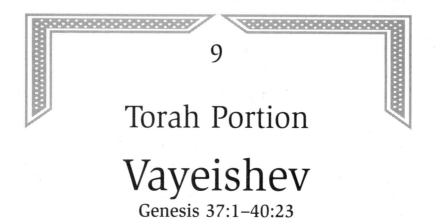

9

# Torah Portion

# Vayeishev
### Genesis 37:1–40:23

## JOSEPH'S TRAVAIL

**(37:1) After his long exile and his many trials, Jacob settled, in the land where his father had lived, in Hebron, in the land of Canaan.**

✳ *The Talmud Teaches*
***Jacob settled [vayeishev]*** R. Yochanan said: Wherever the word *vayeishev,* "he settled," is mentioned in Scripture, it introduces a painful episode. For example, "Jacob settled in the land where his father had lived" is followed by "and Joseph brought evil reports about his brothers to his father." And this brought on the tragic selling of Joseph by his brothers (*Sanhedrin* 106a).

NOTE: Rashi comments: Whenever a person wants to settle down and live at ease, he is reminded of his true purpose in life by events that jolt him out of his complacency.

**(37:2) These are the chronicles of Jacob: Joseph was seventeen years old. As a lad he would tend the sheep with his brothers, the sons of Bilhah and Zilpah, his father's wives. Joseph brought his father a bad report about them.**

✳ *The Talmud Teaches*
***These are the chronicles of Jacob*** The Rabbis taught: Joseph was worthy that twelve tribes should issue from him, just as his

father Jacob fathered twelve tribes, as it says "These are the chronicles of Jacob: Joseph." We would expect the verse to mention Reuben, the oldest son, rather than Joseph. But because the name Jacob is associated with Joseph, the Gemara equates them, expounding that Joseph too should have had twelve sons. However, Joseph did not have twelve sons because his power to beget was reduced when he let his seed go to waste when Potiphar's wife tried to seduce him, so that he had only two sons, Ephraim and Manasseh. The other ten were fathered by his brother Benjamin, and Benjamin named all his sons after events in the life of Joseph (*Sotah* 36b).

**Joseph was seventeen years old**  R. Levi said: A person should always expect a good dream to come true even if it takes as long as twenty-two years. How do we know this? From Joseph. For it says "Joseph was seventeen years old." Furthermore, it says "Joseph was thirty years old when he stood before Pharaoh" (41:46). How long is it from the age of seventeen to thirty? Thirteen. Add to this the seven years of plenty and two years of famine, for it was at that point in time that Joseph revealed himself to his brothers, and his dream came true. So you see that it can take as long as twenty-two years for a dream to come true (*Berachot* 55b).

### ▓ The Jerusalem Talmud Teaches
**Joseph brought his father a bad report about his brothers**  What did he say about his brothers? R. Meir said: He would report that they ate a limb cut off from a living animal, which is forbidden by one of the seven Noahide laws. R. Yehudah said: He would report that they disdained the sons of the handmaidens, Bilhah and Zilpah, treating them as slaves. R. Shimon said: He would report that they gazed at the local girls. And for all three counts, Joseph was punished: He reported that they ate a part cut off from a live animal, but it says that, after selling him, "They slaughtered a young goat" (37:37), proof that they always slaughtered an animal before eating from it. For reporting that they treated the sons of the handmaidens as slaves, Joseph was sold as a slave. He reported that they gazed at the local girls; for that, "His master's wife cast her eyes on Joseph" (39:7) (Jerusalem Talmud, *Pe'ah* 1:1).

**(37:3) Israel loved Joseph more than any of his other sons since he was a child of his old age. He made Joseph a colorful silk coat.**

### ✺ The Talmud Teaches
*A colorful silk coat* R. Chama b. Guriah said: A person should never favor one child over his other children, for because of two *sela*'s weight of silk—that is, the coat of many colors—that Jacob gave to Joseph over and above what he gave to his other children, his brothers became jealous of him, and ultimately this led to our forefathers' descent into Egypt (*Shabbat* 10b).

**(37:13) Jacob said to Joseph, "See how your brothers and the sheep are doing, and bring me back word." So he sent him from the depth of Hebron, and he arrived in Shechem.**

### ✺ The Talmud Teaches
*He sent him from the depth of Hebron* R. Chanina b. Papa said: But Hebron is situated on a mountain! Rather, the term *depth of Hebron* is to be understood figuratively: Jacob's decision to send Joseph to his brothers who sold him into slavery was in fulfillment of the "deep" design that had been confided to Abraham, who was buried in Hebron, as it says "God said to Abraham, 'Know for sure that your descendants will be foreigners in a land that is not theirs'" (14:13) (*Sotah* 11a).

NOTE: The expression "from the depth of Hebron" implies that Joseph's assignment was the first step toward the fulfillment of God's prophecy to Abraham of the descent of Israel into Egypt.

**(37:24) The brothers took Joseph and threw him into the well. The well was empty; there was no water in it.**

### ✺ The Talmud Teaches
*The well was empty; there was no water in it* R. Natan b. Minyumi expounded: What is the meaning of "The well was empty; there was no water in it"? When it says "The well was empty," isn't it obvious that there was no water in it? But what does the phrase "there was no water in it" come to teach us? There was

no water in it, but there were snakes and scorpions in it (*Shab-bat* 22a).

NOTE: Reuben did not know that the well contained snakes and scorpions. Thinking that the well was empty, he planned "to rescue Joseph and bring him back to his father" (37:22). It was a miracle that Joseph was not killed by the snakes and scorpions.

## JUDAH AND TAMAR

**(38:15) Judah saw Tamar, and because she had covered her face, he assumed that she was a prostitute.**

### ※ *The Talmud Teaches*

*Because she had covered her face* Is the fact that she had covered her face a reason for Judah to assume that she was a prostitute? R. Elazar said: She had covered her face while she lived in her father-in-law Judah's house. That's why Judah never saw her and did not recognize her when she was sitting by the crossroads. For R. Shmuel b. Nachmani said in the name of R. Yonatan: A daughter-in-law who is modest in her father-in-law's house deserves that kings and prophets descend from her (*Sotah* 10b).

NOTE: The prophet Isaiah and King David descended from Tamar.

**(38:25) When Tamar was being taken out to be burned, she sent the proofs to her father-in-law, Judah, with the message, "I am pregnant by the man who is the owner of these articles." And she said, "Please identify these objects. Who is the owner of this seal, this wrap, and this staff?"**

### ※ *The Talmud Teaches*

*The man who is the owner of these articles* Why did she speak in such a roundabout way? Why didn't she say bluntly: "Judah, you are the father of my child, and here are your articles to prove it"? R. Zutra b. Tuvyah said: It is better for a person to cast himself into a fiery furnace rather than put his fellow to shame in public. From where do we know this? From Tamar (*Sotah* 10b).

NOTE: Rashi explains: Tamar would rather die than publicly embarrass Judah by saying, "Judah, you are the father of my child, and here are the articles to prove it." She showed the articles to Judah. If he was going to admit that he was her unborn baby's father, fine. If not, she would rather be burned than expose and shame him.

**Tamar said, "Please identify these objects"**  Said R. Chama b. R. Chanina: Tamar used the phrase, "Please identify" in addressing Judah. The same phrase was used by Judah announcing to his father Jacob the bad tiding of Joseph's disappearance, saying, "Please identify it. Is it your son's coat or not?" (37:32) (*Sotah* 10b).

NOTE: The underlying idea is that both the selling of Joseph into slavery and the union of Judah and Tamar were shameful acts that had an auspicious outcome. The selling of Joseph brought in its wake the exile of the Jews in Egypt, which in turn reached a climax in the giving of the Torah; the union of Judah and Tamar produced the Davidic royal line that culminates in Mashiach.

## JOSEPH RESISTS TEMPTATION

**(39:9) Joseph said to his master's wife, "There is no one greater in this house than I, and he has denied me nothing but you, since you are his wife; how could I do such a great wrong? It would be a sin before God!"**

### ▒ *The Jerusalem Talmud Teaches*
*It would be a sin before God!*  This teaches us that for committing immorality one is punished in this world, but the sin remains intact in the world to come, because it says "How could I do such a great wrong? It would be a sin before God!" (Jerusalem Talmud, *Pe'ah* 1:1).

NOTE: Joseph implied: It is self-understood that by sleeping with you I am committing a sin against your husband, Potiphar, in this world, but in addition, I will be punished for it in the world to come.

**(39:10) She spoke to Joseph every day, but he would not pay attention to her. He would not even lie next to her, to be with her.**

### ※ The Talmud Teaches
**She spoke to Joseph every day** Every day, Potiphar's wife tried to seduce him with her talk. She said to him, "Surrender to me!" He replied, "No, I won't!" She said, "I'm going to have you locked up in prison." He said, "God sets prisoners free" (Psalms 146:7). She said, "I'm going to bend your proud stature; I'm going to disgrace you." He answered, "God makes those who are bent stand straight" (146:8). She said, "I'm going to blind your eyes." He replied, "God restores sight to the blind" (146:8). She offered him a thousand talents of silver to make him give in to her, "to lie next to her, to be with her," but "he would not pay attention to her" (*Yoma* 35b).

**to lie with her, to be with her** He would not lie with her in this world, for then he would have to be with her in the world to come. Said R. Eliezer: From here, we know that if a person commits the sin of sexual immorality, it stays tied to him like a dog and is never erased (*Avodah Zarah* 5a).

**(39:11) One day, Joseph came to the house to do his work. None of the household staff was inside.**

### ※ The Talmud Teaches
**none of the household staff** Is it possible that there was no one present in a huge mansion like that? In the yeshiva of R. Yishmael, they taught: That day was a pagan festival, and they all went to their temple; but she claimed that she was sick. She thought that this was a perfect opportunity for her to seduce Joseph (*Sotah* 36b).

NOTE: *Torah Temimah* explains that they made a celebration on the day the waters of the Nile began to rise.

## THE DREAMS OF THE TWO PRISONERS

**(40:11) Pharaoh's cup was in my hand. I took the grapes and squeezed them into Pharaoh's cup. Then I placed the cup in Pharaoh's hand.**

⚜ *The Talmud Teaches*
*Pharaoh's cup was in my hand* Why is the word *cup* repeated three times in this verse in connection with Pharaoh? What do the three cups signify? The three cups portend the three calamities that were to befall Egypt. One refers to the cup of ruin that Egypt drank in the days of Moses and the Exodus; another refers to the cup of ruin Egypt drank in the days of Pharaoh Necho when Egypt was defeated by the Babylonians under Nebuchadnezzar (Jeremiah 46:2, 13); and the third cup refers to the cup of disaster Egypt is destined to drink together with all the heathen nations in the time to come (*Chullin* 92a).

NOTE: The word *cup* is a symbol of calamity, as in "Jerusalem, you have drunk from the hand of God the cup of His fury" (Isaiah 51:17).

**(40:16) The chief baker saw that Joseph had interpreted well. He said to Joseph, "I also saw myself in my dream. There were three baskets of fine bread on my head."**

⚜ *The Talmud Teaches*
*The chief baker saw that Joseph had interpreted well* How did he know that? R. Elazar said: Both the butler and the baker had a dream, and each also dreamed the interpretation of the other one's dream (*Berachot* 55b).

NOTE: The Gemara infers this from the wording "the baker *saw*," that is, he understood, rather than "the baker heard."

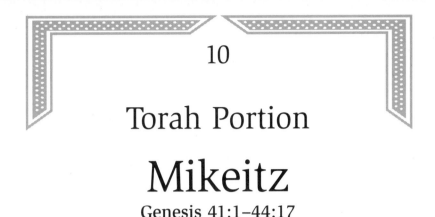

# 10

## Torah Portion

# Mikeitz

### Genesis 41:1–44:17

## JOSEPH APPOINTED VICEROY OF EGYPT

**(41:13) The butler said: And things worked out just as Joseph said they would. I was given back my position, while the baker was hanged.**

✳ *The Talmud Teaches*
*And things worked out just as Joseph said they would*  R. Elazar said: How do we know that all dreams follow the suggestion of the interpreter? Because it says "The butler said to Pharaoh, 'Things worked out just as Joseph said they would.'"

Rava added: Don't think that whenever an interpreter says something it invariably comes true. It only does if the interpretation fits the dream, for it says "He interpreted each dream according to its content" (41:12) (*Berachot* 55b).

NOTE: Because all dreams follow the suggestion of the interpreter, if you have a dream that can be interpreted either in a beneficial or a harmful sense, you should give it the beneficial interpretation.

**(41:32) Joseph said to Pharaoh, "The reason that Pharaoh had the same dream twice is because the process has already been set in motion by God, and God is rushing to do it."**

## ※ *The Talmud Teaches*

**The reason that Pharaoh had the same dream twice**  A dream
that is repeated comes true. For it says Joseph saw significance
in the fact "that Pharaoh had the same dream twice" (*Berachot*
55b).

**(41:43) Pharaoh also had Joseph ride in the second royal
chariot, and those going ahead of him announced, *"Avrech!"*
Thus he appointed him over all the land of Egypt.**

## ※ *The Talmud Teaches*

**Those going ahead of him announced, *"Avrech!"***  What does
*avrech* mean? It is a composite of the words: *av*, "father," and
*rech*, "king," from the Latin *rex*. Thus, it means "father of the
king." Indeed, Joseph sent a message to his father, "God has
made me father to Pharaoh" (45:8) (*Bava Batra* 4a).

**(41:44) Pharaoh said to Joseph, "I am Pharaoh. Without your
say, no man will lift a hand or foot in all Egypt."**

## ※ *The Talmud Teaches*

**Without your say**  Pharaoh's astrologers complained, "What!
A slave who was bought for twenty pieces of silver you put in
charge of us!" "I see in him characteristics of a king," Pharaoh
replied. "If that is the case," the astrologers retorted, "he should
at least know the seventy languages of the world." The angel
Gabriel came and taught Joseph all seventy languages, but he
could not grasp them. So one letter of the name of God, Y-H-V-H,
namely, the letter *hei*, was added to his name, and that gave him
the ability to learn the seventy languages he needed to know to
become viceroy. For it says "He appointed it as a testimony for
Joseph—written: *Yehosef*, with an extra letter *hei*—when he
went out over the land of Egypt, where I—Joseph—heard a language unknown to me" (Psalms 81:6) (*Sotah* 36b).

NOTE: An allusion to the seventy languages of the world may
be found in the fact that this verse begins and ends with the letter *ayin*, whose numeric value is seventy. It begins with the
word *eidut*, whose first letter is an *ayin*, and it ends with the word

*eshma,* whose last letter is also an *ayin.* In the Hebrew alphabet, each letter has a numeric value. For example, the letter aleph equals 1, bet equals 2, yud equals 10, lamed equals 30, ayin equals 70, and so on.

**(41:50) Joseph had two sons before the famine years came, born to him by Asenath, daughter of Potiphera, priest of On.**

※ *The Talmud Teaches*
*Joseph had two sons before the famine years came* Resh Lakish said: A person should not have marital relations during famine years, for it says "Joseph had two sons *before* the famine years came." Although Joseph, being the viceroy in charge of food allocation, did not himself suffer from hunger, he nevertheless abstained from marital relations out of sympathy and fellowship with the people (*Taanit* 11a).

## JOSEPH CONFRONTS HIS BROTHERS

**(42:1) Jacob learned that there were provisions in Egypt, so Jacob said to his sons, "Why do you make yourselves conspicuous?"**

※ *The Talmud Teaches*
*Why do you make yourselves conspicuous?* Jacob was telling his sons: "Even though you have enough food, do not make it obvious to your neighbors, the children of Esau and the children of Ishmael, that you are satiated, so that they should not become jealous of you" (*Taanit* 10b).

NOTE: Jacob implied: Even though you still have grain in your storehouse, go to Egypt to buy food, so as not to arouse your neighbors' envy. From this, we derive that a person who has a valid reason not to fast on a public fast day should not show that he is content, so as not to cause anguish to the people who are fasting (*Sanhedrin* 29b).

**(42:8) Joseph recognized his brothers, but they did not recognize him.**

## ❋ The Talmud Teaches
**but they did not recognize him**  R. Chisda said: This teaches us that when Joseph left them he did not even have a trace of a beard, and now he appeared with a full beard (*Yevamot* 88a).

NOTE:  When Joseph left, his brothers all had full beards, so their appearance did not change drastically. That is why he was able to recognize them.

**(42:36) Their father Jacob said to them, "You're making me lose my children! Joseph is gone! Simeon is gone! And now you want to take Benjamin! Everything is happening to me!"**

## ❋ The Talmud Teaches
**Joseph is . . . gone!**  R. Shimon b. Elazar said: If a person's first undertaking after a happy event such as acquiring a house, the birth of a child, or his marriage turns out to be successful, he may regard it as an auspicious sign and a portent of success in future undertakings of a similar nature. On the other hand, if a person's first undertaking proves unsuccessful, he should in the future be wary of similar undertakings.

　　R. Elazar commented: Provided the same thing happppened three times, that is, he had three successes or three reverses in a row. As it says "Joseph is gone!—one—Simon is gone!—two—, and now you want to take Benjamin—three—, then everything is happening to me!" (*Chullin* 95b).

NOTE:  Rashi explains: Although the Torah forbids believing in lucky times or acting on the basis of good or bad omens (Leviticus 19:26), it is permitted to regard this as an indication of the future.

**(42:37) Reuben said to his father, "If I do not bring Benjamin back to you," he said, "you can put my two sons to death. Let him be my responsibility, and I will bring him back to you."**

## ❋ The Talmud Teaches
**You can put my two sons to death**  Reuben spoke in an improper way, saying, "You can put my two sons to death," as opposed to Judah, who did speak in a proper way when he said,

"I myself will be responsible for him" (43:9) (*Avot d' Rabbi Natan,* Chapter 37).

NOTE: Rashi comments: Jacob said: Reuben is a fool. He suggests that I should kill his two sons. Aren't his sons also my sons?

**(42:38) Jacob said, "My son shall not go down with you, for his brother is dead, and he is all I have left. Something may happen to him along the way, and you will bring my white head to the grave in misery."**

### ▩ *The Jerusalem Talmud Teaches*
***Something may happen to him along the way*** Disaster strikes when a person is on the road, not when he is at home. Jacob was afraid that something might happen on the road because Rachel died on the road and Joseph and Simon met with misfortune while away from home. He was concerned because disaster had struck on the road three times, as R. Elazar said earlier (Jerusalem Talmud, *Shabbat* 2:6).

**(43:16) When Joseph saw Benjamin with them he said to the overseer of his household, "Bring these men to the palace. Have meat slaughtered and prepare it. These men will be eating lunch with me."**

### ▨ *The Talmud Teaches*
***Have meat slaughtered and prepare it*** R. Yose b. R. Chanina said: What is the meaning of the passage, "Have meat slaughtered and prepare it"? Joseph said, "Have meat slaughtered," implying, uncover for them the place where the animal has been slaughtered to show them that the animal was slaughtered by *shechitah* [ritual slaughter].

"And prepare it," implying, remove the sciatic nerve in front of them, for Jews may not eat the sciatic nerve (Genesis 32:33) (*Chullin* 91a).

NOTE: Rashi comments: Jacob's sons observed the Torah although it had not yet been given.

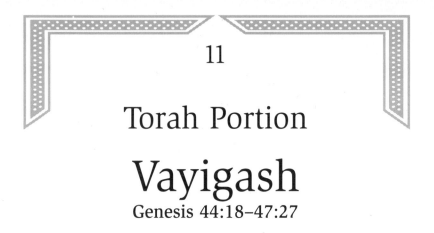

# 11

# Torah Portion

# Vayigash

Genesis 44:18–47:27

## JOSEPH REVEALS HIMSELF

**(45:3) Joseph said to his brothers, "I am Joseph! Is my father still alive?" His brothers were so startled, they could not respond.**

�֍ *The Talmud Teaches*
*His brothers were so startled, they could not respond* When R. Elazar came to this verse, he wept. He said: If the rebuke of flesh and blood—that is, Joseph—is so powerful as to stun the brothers, imagine how overwhelming the reproach of God will be when He takes me to task in the hereafter (*Chagigah* 4b).

NOTE: Joseph's reproach is contained in the words "Is my father still alive?" He implied: Is it possible that my father could survive the anguish you inflicted on him?

**(45:12) You and my brother Benjamin can see with your own eyes that it is my mouth that is speaking to you.**

✖ *The Talmud Teaches*
*You and my brother Benjamin can see with your own eyes* What is the meaning of "You and my brother Benjamin can see"? R. Elazar said: Joseph told his brothers: Just as I feel no resentment against Benjamin who was not yet born at the time of my sale, so I have no resentment against you (*Megillah* 16b).

*That it is my mouth that is speaking to you* R. Elazar said: Joseph told his brothers: As my mouth speaks, so does my heart feel (*Megillah* 16b).

**(45:14) Then he fell upon his brother Benjamin's neck and wept; and Benjamin wept upon his neck.**

※ *The Talmud Teaches*
*his brother Benjamin's neck* The word *tzaverei*, "neck," is written in the plural, as *necks*. Therefore, the Gemara asks: How many necks did Benjamin have? The Gemara answers: R. Elazar said: Scripture uses the plural to teach that Joseph wept over the two Temples that were destined to be in Benjamin's territory and were destined to be destroyed (*Megillah* 16b).

NOTE: Maharsha explains: The Temple is compared to a neck, which rests atop the body, because the Temple is the spiritual high point of Eretz Yisrael.

**(45:22) He gave each of his brothers an outfit of clothes. To Benjamin, however, he gave three hundred pieces of silver and five outfits.**

※ *The Talmud Teaches*
*Five outfits* The Gemara asks: Is it possible that the very thing that caused the righteous Joseph to suffer, namely, Jacob favoring Joseph over his brothers, Joseph himself should stumble over? How could Joseph make the same mistake! R. Binyamin b. Yefet said: By giving Benjamin these five outfits of clothing, Joseph hinted to him that in the future a descendant of Benjamin—Mordechai—would go forth from the king's palace dressed in five royal garments. As it says "And Mordechai left the king . . . in royal apparel of blue and white, with a large gold crown and a robe of fine linen and purple" (Esther 8:15) (*Megillah* 16b).

**(45:24) Joseph sent his brothers on their way. As they were leaving he said to them, "Do not become agitated on the way."**

### ❋ The Talmud Teaches

*Do not become agitated on the way*  R. Elazar said: Joseph told them, "Don't get involved in any discussions, not even debates about religious law, for you may be distracted and lose your way." In a Mishnah, it was taught: He told them, "Do not take big strides, and make sure you enter the city when the sun is still shining."

The Gemara elaborates: Taking big strides is harmful to one's eyesight, and a person should always travel in the daytime to be protected from wild animals, robbers, and from falling into a pit (*Taanit* 10b).

**(45:26) They broke the news to him, "Joseph is still alive. He is the ruler of all Egypt." [Jacob's] heart became numb, for he could not believe them.**

### ❋ The Talmud Teaches

*for he could not believe them*  R. Shimon said: Such is the punishment of a liar, that even when he speaks the truth, no one believes him. For that is what happened to the sons of Jacob. They deceived their father when they said, "We found this. Try to identify it. Is it your son's coat or not?" And he immediately recognized it and said, "It is my son's coat!" (37:31, 33). But in the end, although they spoke the truth, he did not believe them, for it says "Jacob's heart became numb, for he could not believe them." He only believed them after they showed him the wagons Joseph had sent and told him Joseph's password, which was the title of the last topic his father had taught him before his abduction (*Avot d'Rabbi Natan*, Chapter 30).

**(45:27) Then they related all the words that Joseph had spoken to them, and he saw the wagons that Joseph had sent to transport him. The spirit of their father Jacob was then revived.**

### ❋ The Talmud Teaches

*The spirit of their father Jacob was then revived*  Some say that the prophetic inspiration that had left Jacob came back to him at that moment, for it says "The spirit of their father Jacob was then revived." (*Avot d'Rabbi Natan*, Chapter 30).

NOTE: Grief and anxiety preclude prophecy. During the time Jacob mourned for Joseph, the divine inspiration withdrew from him until he received the news that Joseph was alive (Maimonides, *Eight Chapters*, Chapter 7).

**(47:14) Joseph collected all the money that was to be found in Egypt and Canaan in payment for the food the people were buying. Joseph brought all the money to Pharaoh's treasury.**

## ※ *The Talmud Teaches*

*Joseph collected all the money* Rav Yehudah said: Joseph collected the money of the whole world and brought it to Egypt— not just the money of Egypt and Canaan, because it says "The people from all over the earth came to Egypt" (41:57). And furthermore, it says "Joseph collected all the money." And when the Israelites left Egypt, they took this vast treasure along with them, as it says "The children of Israel drained Egypt of its wealth" (Exodus 12:35) (*Pesachim* 119a).

**(47:21) Joseph moved the population from one city to the other, from one end of Egypt to the other.**

## ※ *The Talmud Teaches*

*He moved the population* What does this have to do with us? He moved them around in order that his brothers should not be called immigrants. For now, all Egyptians were homeless strangers in the cities where Joseph resettled them, and they would not slur the children of Israel by calling them aliens (*Chullin* 60b).

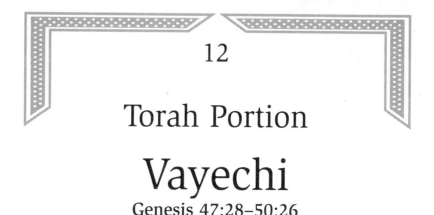

## 12

# Torah Portion

# Vayechi

### Genesis 47:28–50:26

## JACOB ON HIS DEATHBED

**(47:31) "Swear to me," said Jacob. Joseph made an oath to him, then Israel bowed toward the head of the bed.**

❋ *The Talmud Teaches*
*Israel bowed*  R. Binyamin b. Yefet said: This is what people mean with the adage: When the fox has his hour, bow to him (*Megillah* 16b).

NOTE: When Joseph—who is just a fox compared to Jacob—is the ruler, even the mighty lion—Jacob—pays homage to him.

**(48:1) A short time after this, Joseph was told that his father was sick. So Joseph went to his father, taking his two sons, Manasseh and Ephraim, along with him.**

❋ *The Talmud Teaches*
*His father was sick*  It was taught: Until Jacob's days, nobody became sick before he died; people died suddenly, without warning. Then Jacob prayed that a person should become sick before he died, so that he could convey his last wishes to his children, and sickness came into being (*Bava Metzia* 87a).

**(48:7) Jacob said to Joseph, "When I was coming from Padan, your mother Rachel died on me. It was in Canaan, a**

**short distance before we came to Ephrath. I buried her there along the road to Ephrath, which is Bethlehem."**

***The Talmud Teaches***

***Rachel died on me*** A Tanna [teacher of the Mishnah] taught: The death of a woman is felt by no one but her husband. For it says "When I was coming from Padan, Rachel died on *me,*" and the death of a man is felt by no one but his wife (*Sanhedrin* 22b).

**(48:19) His father refused and said, "I know my son. I know. The older one will also become a nation. He too will attain greatness. But his younger brother Ephraim will become even greater, and his descendants will be famous among nations."**

***The Talmud Teaches***

***His descendants will be famous among nations*** When did Ephraim's descendants become famous among nations? When the sun stood still for Joshua, who was an offspring of Ephraim. All the nations were afraid of Joshua when they heard about the great miracle God performed for him, when Joshua said, "Sun, stand still at Gibeon, and moon, in the Valley of Ayalon" (Joshua 10:12) (*Avodah Zarah* 25a).

**(48:22) And as for me, I have given you Shechem—one portion more than your brothers, which I took from the hand of the Emorite with my sword and my bow.**

***The Talmud Teaches***

***with my sword and my bow*** Did Jacob take Shechem with his sword and with his bow? Surely, it says "For I do not trust in my bow, nor does my sword save me" (Psalms 44:7). But *my sword* means "prayer" and *my bow* means "supplication" (*Bava Batra* 123a).

NOTE: The Kotzker Rebbe asks: How can prayer be compared to a bow? He explains: The closer you pull the string toward your heart, the farther the arrow will fly. So it is with prayer. The more fervently you pray, the more power your prayer has to penetrate the gates of heaven.

## JACOB BLESSES HIS SONS

**(49:22) Joseph is a charming son, a charming son to the eye; each of the girls climbed heights to gaze.**

### *The Talmud Explains*

***a charming son to the eye [alei ayin]*** R. Abbahu said: Don't read *alei ayin,* but *olei ayin,* "rising above the power of the evil eye." From here, we know that the evil eye has no power over the offspring of Joseph (*Berachot* 20a).

**(49:24) But his bow was firmly emplaced and his arms were gilded, from the hands of the mighty power of Jacob—from there he shepherded the stone of Israel.**

### *The Talmud Teaches*

***But his bow was firmly emplaced*** R. Yochanan said: At the moment when Potiphar's wife tried to seduce Joseph, grabbing him by his garment, his father's image appeared to him through the window and said, "Joseph, your brothers will have their names inscribed on the stones of the shoulder pieces of the *ephod*—one of the priestly garments—and yours among them. Do you want your name removed from it?" Immediately, "His bow was firmly emplaced," meaning that his passion subsided; "and his arms were gilded," meaning that he pressed his hands into the ground to cause himself pain, so that his desire should recede (*Sotah* 36b).

***From the hands of the mighty power of Jacob*** Who caused Joseph's name to be engraved on the stones of the *ephod,* if not the mighty power of Jacob? "From there he shepherded the stone of Israel": From there, Joseph was worthy to be made a shepherd, as it says "Give ear, O Shepherd of Israel who leads Joseph's sheep" (Psalms 80:2) (*Sotah* 36b).

NOTE: Rashi explains: The entire Jewish nation is called Joseph's sheep because he sustained them in Egypt during the famine (Psalms 80:2).

# JACOB'S BURIAL

**(49:33) Jacob thus concluded his instructions to his sons. He drew his feet back onto the bed, he breathed his last and passed away.**

### ※ *The Talmud Teaches*
*he breathed his last and passed away* R. Yochanan said: Jacob our father never died. R. Nachman asked R. Yitzchak: Was it for nothing that they eulogized, embalmed, and buried him? He replied: I derive it from scriptural verse, for it says "But as for you, have no fear, My servant Jacob. . . . for I will deliver you from far away, your children from the land of captivity" (Jeremiah 30:10). The verse compares Jacob to his children, the Jewish people. Just as the children of Jacob will be alive at the time of the redemption, so Jacob too will then be alive (*Taanit* 5b).

*He breathed his last, and passed away* R. Tarfon said: A person dies only through inactivity, for it says "He breathed his last and passed away." Jacob's death occurred *after* he finished giving his instructions to his sons—because so long as he was engaged in a task, death had no power over him (*Avot d'Rabbi Natan,* Chapter 11).

**(50:5) Joseph asked Pharaoh for permission to take Jacob's remains to Eretz Yisrael, saying, "My father bound me by oath and he declared, 'I am dying. You must bury me in the grave that I prepared for myself in the land of Canaan.' Now, if you allow me, I will go up and bury my father; then I will return."**

### ※ *The Talmud Teaches*
*My father bound me by oath* The Gemara in *Sotah* 36b relates that an Egyptian monarch had to know all the languages of the world. When Joseph was appointed viceroy of Egypt, he had mastered all the languages. But when he addressed Pharaoh in the Hebrew tongue, Pharaoh did not understand it. He then made Joseph swear not to reveal this to anyone, as this would

disqualify him from being the Egyptian ruler. Later on, when Joseph asked Pharaoh for permission to take his father's remains to the Land of Israel, saying, "My father bound me by oath that I should move his remains to the Land of Israel," Pharaoh replied, "Go and ask your father to release you from your oath," for he did not want Joseph to leave Egypt. Joseph answered, "In that case, at the same time, I will ask to be released from the oath I gave you not to reveal your ignorance of Hebrew." Hearing this, Pharaoh reluctantly told him, "Go and bury your father just as he had you swear" (50:6) (*Sotah* 36b).

**(50:16) The brothers instructed messengers to tell Joseph, "Before he died, your father gave us final instructions. He said, 'This is what you must say to Joseph: O please, kindly forgive the spiteful deed and the sin your brothers committed when they did evil to you.' Now please forgive the spiteful deed that [we], the servants of your father's God, have done."**

### ✕ *The Talmud Teaches*
***Your father gave us final instructions*** R. Ila'i said: You are allowed to stretch the truth for the sake of peace. For it says "[The brothers instructed messengers to tell Joseph,] 'Before he died, your father gave us final . . . instructions. . . . Forgive the spiteful deed and sin your brothers committed'" (*Yevamot* 65b).

NOTE: Jacob never gave such instructions. The brothers invented the statement for the sake of preserving the peace between themselves and Joseph (*Yevamot* 65b).

**(50:21) Joseph said to his brothers, "Now don't worry. I will fully provide for you and your children." He thus comforted them and spoke to their hearts.**

***He spoke to their hearts*** R. Binyamin b. Yefet said: This teaches that he reassured them. He said: If ten lights could not extinguish one light, that is, the actions of the ten of you could not harm me, on the contrary, they were the cause of my rise to greatness, how can one light extinguish ten lights? If ten brothers could not harm one, one certainly cannot harm ten (*Megillah* 16b).

# Exodus

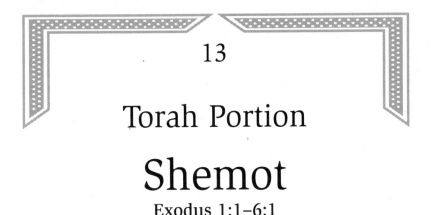

# 13

## Torah Portion

# Shemot
### Exodus 1:1–6:1

## THE BIRTH OF MOSES

**(1:6) Joseph, his brothers, and everyone else in that generation died.**

※ *The Talmud Teaches*
***Joseph, his brothers . . . died*** R. Chama b. R. Chanina said: Joseph lived 110 years, whereas his brothers lived 120 years. Why did Joseph die before his brothers? Because he behaved in a high-handed manner (*Berachot* 58a).

NOTE: *Pirkei d' R. Eliezer* explains that Joseph's life was shortened by ten years because he heard ten times his brothers referring to Jacob as "your servant, our father" without stopping them. Now in the Torah, this phrase is mentioned only five times, but Joseph heard it five times from his brothers and again five times from the interpreter, so that he heard it ten times. The five times are at Genesis 43:28; 45:25, 27, 30, 32.

**(1:8) A new king came into power in Egypt who did not know of Joseph.**

※ *The Talmud Teaches*
***A new king came into power*** Rav and Shmuel have different opinions about this passage. One says that it really was a new king; the other holds that it was the same old king but that he

issued new decrees. The one who holds that it was a new king does so because it says "a *new* king," and the one who maintains that it was the same king but that he issued new decrees argues that it does not say anywhere that he died and was succeeded by a new king (*Sotah* 11a).

**who did not know Joseph**   If it is the same old king, he certainly did know Joseph! He pretended that he had never heard of him (*Sotah* 11a).

**(1:10) Come, let us outsmart him, otherwise they may increase so much, that if there is a war, they will join our enemies and fight against us, driving us from the land.**

### ※ *The Talmud Teaches*

**Come, let us outsmart him**   It should say, "Let us outsmart *them*"! R. Chama b. R. Chanina said: Pharaoh was really trying to catch one person in his net. He meant to say: Let us outsmart God, the Redeemer of Israel. We know that God retaliates measure for measure. So with what shall we punish Israel? Shall we punish them with fire? If we did that, we know God will retaliate tit for tat, for it says "For behold, God will arrive in fire" (Isaiah 66:15). Shall we punish them by the sword? That would not do either, for the verse continues, "With his sword against all mankind," and God would bring down the sword on us. Said Pharaoh: Let's punish them with water by casting every newborn boy into the Nile. This way, God will not be able to retaliate against us, for He has already sworn that He would never again bring a flood on the world. But Pharaoh did not realize that God would not bring a flood on the entire earth, but on one nation He could bring a flood. Another miscalculation: God would not flood the Egyptians, but they would fall into the water. And that is exactly what the verse says: "The Egyptians were fleeing toward the water in confusion, but God swamped the Egyptians in the middle of the sea" (14:27) (*Sotah* 11a).

**(1:12) But as much as the Egyptians oppressed the Israelites, the more they will increase and the more they will spread. The Egyptians became disgusted because of the Israelites.**

✳ *The Talmud Teaches*
**The more they will increase and the more they will spread** It should say, "The more *they increased* and the more *they spread.*" Resh Lakish said: The Holy Spirit announced to the Egyptians what was going to happen: All your strategies to prevent them from increasing won't do you any good. The more you oppress them, "the more they will increase, and the more they will spread" (*Sotah* 16a).

**(1:17) The midwives feared God, and did not do as the Egyptian king had ordered them. They allowed the infant boys to live.**

✳ *The Talmud Teaches*
**They allowed the infant boys to live** We learned: Not only did they not drown them, but they supplied them with water and food. The verse does not say "they did not kill them." Therefore, the implication is that they nourished them (*Sotah* 11b).

**(1:22) Pharaoh gave orders to all his people: "Every boy who is born must be cast into the Nile, but every girl shall be allowed to live."**

✳ *The Talmud Teaches*
**Every boy must be cast into the Nile** Pharaoh's astrologers saw that Israel's savior would be punished through water, so they got up and decreed, "Every boy must be cast into the Nile." But they were misled, because after Moses' mother placed him into the Nile, they said: "We do not see that sign any longer," for once he was in the river, the prophecy had come true to a certain extent, so they told Pharaoh to cancel the decree. But they did not know that Moses was to be punished through the water of *Merivah,* the Waters of Dispute (Numbers 20:13), and this was what they actually saw in regard to water (*Sotah* 12b).

**(2:1) A man, Amram, of the house of Levi went and married Levi's daughter.**

✳ *The Talmud Teaches*
**A man, Amram . . . went** Where did he go? R. Yehudah b. Zevina said: He went and acted on the advice of his daughter.

We learned: Amram was the leader of his generation; when he saw that Pharaoh decreed that every boy who is born must be cast into the Nile, he said to himself: What is the point of having children? Thereupon, he divorced his wife. All the men of Israel followed suit and divorced their wives too. His daughter, Miriam, then said to him: Father, your decree is harsher than the wicked Pharaoh's decree because Pharaoh decreed only against the males, whereas you decreed against males and females; when all the men divorce their wives, neither boys nor girls will be born. Pharaoh decreed only regarding this world, because the children that are killed live on in the world to come, whereas you decreed regarding this world and the world to come, because unborn children cannot come to the world to come. Furthermore, if the wicked Pharaoh makes a decree, it is doubtful if it will be carried out, but you are a righteous man, and your decree will surely come to fruition. At that moment, Amram remarried his wife, and all the others followed suit and remarried their wives (*Sotah* 12b).

**(2:3) When she could no longer hide him, she took for him a box of bulrushes, coating it with clay and with tar; she placed the child into it and placed it among the reeds at the bank of the Nile.**

### ✳ *The Talmud Teaches*
**When she could no longer hide him** Why? She should have gone on hiding him! But whenever the Egyptians found out that a woman had given birth, they would bring one of their babies there so that it should hear them cry and cry together with them, for a baby will start crying when it hears other babies cry. As it says "Seize for us foxes, even small foxes that destroy the tiny grapes" (Song of Songs 2:15), which is a reference to the tiny Egyptian babies that caused the Jewish babies to reveal their hiding places (*Sotah* 12a).

**She took for him a box of bulrushes** Why inexpensive bulrushes? R. Elazar said: From the fact that she used bulrushes, which are less expensive than sturdy wood, you can infer that the righteous love money more than their own body. Why so?

Because the righteous never reach for things that do not belong to them, so whatever they have they earned by honest labor and is precious to them.

R. Shmuel b. Nachmani said: She used bulrushes because they are pliable and can withstand a collision with both hard and soft materials (*Sotah* 12a).

**Coating it with clay and with tar** We learned: The clay was on the inside of the box and the tar on the outside, so that the righteous child should not smell the bad odor of the tar (*Sotah* 12a).

**(2:5) Pharaoh's daughter went to bathe in the Nile, while her maids walked along the Nile's edge. She saw the box in the rushes, and sent her slave-girl to fetch it.**

### ※ The Talmud Teaches
**while her maids walked [holechot]** R. Yochanan said: The term *holechot*, "walked," is associated with death, and so it says "look I am going *[holech]* to die" (Genesis 25:12). Why did the maids of Pharaoh's daughter die? When the maids saw that she wanted to rescue Moses, they said to her: Princess, it is the custom that when a king makes a decree, although no one heeds it, at least his children and the members of his household obey it. But you are violating your father's decree! At that moment, Gabriel came and beat them to the ground; and they died, hence the term *holechot*, "they went to die" (*Sotah* 12b).

**She sent her slave-girl [amatah] to fetch it** R. Yehudah and R. Nechemiah differ in their interpretation of the word *amatah*. One says that the word means that she sent her "slave-girl," and the other says it means that she stretched out "her arm." The one who says that it means "her arm" bases his opinion on the fact that *amatah* can also mean "arm." The one who says that it means "her slave-girl" does so because the text does not say *yadah*, "her arm." The Gemara asks: But according to the one who says that it means "her slave-girl," you just said that Gabriel came and struck them all dead to the ground? So how could she have sent a slave-girl? The Gemara answers: Gabriel left her one; it is not proper for a princess to be unattended. But

according to the one who says that *amatah* means "her arm,"
it should have said *yadah* rather than *amatah!* It teaches that
miraculously her arm lengthened (*Sotah* 12b).

NOTE: Rashi says that she extended her arm, and miraculously
it became long enough to reach the basket. R. Mendel of Kotzk
asks: Why did she reach for the basket, when obviously it was
far beyond her grasp? This teaches that you should never
assume that a task is impossible. The basket was far away, yet
she reached for it, and God enabled her to attain her goal.

**(2:7) The infant's sister said to Pharaoh's daughter, "Shall I
go and call a Hebrew woman to nurse the child for you?"**

### ※ *The Talmud Teaches*
*a Hebrew woman to nurse the child*  Why did she emphasize
"a Hebrew woman"? It teaches us that they carried Moses
around to all the Egyptian women, but he would not nurse from
them. God said: Should the mouth that is destined to speak
with Me sip an unclean thing? (*Sotah* 12b).

NOTE: Egyptian women eat unclean food, traces of which show
up in the milk.

## THE BURNING BUSH

**(2:20) "And where is he now?" Jethro asked his daughters,
"Why did you abandon the stranger? Call him and let him
have something to eat."**

### ※ *The Talmud Teaches*
*And let him have something to eat*  R. Yochanan said: Giving
food to wayfarers is of great importance, for it draws near those
who are distant. You can see this from what happened to
Jethro. As a reward for Jethro's invitation to Moses, saying,
"Call him and let him have something to eat," his descendants
merited to sit in the chamber of hewn stone, that is, the seat of
the Great Sanhedrin (*Sanhedrin* 104a).

**(3:8) I have come down to rescue them from Egypt's power. I will bring them out of that land, to a good, spacious land, to a land flowing with milk and honey, the territory of the Canaanites, Hittites, Amorites, Perizzites, Hivites, and Jebusites.**

※ *The Talmud Teaches*
*a land flowing with milk and honey* R. Chisda said: What is meant by the verse, "I give you a cherished land, the heritage of the deer" (Jeremiah 3:10)? Why is the Land of Israel compared to a deer? To tell you that just as the skin of a deer, after it has been removed, cannot hold its body, because it shrinks, so too all the storehouses of the Land of Israel cannot hold its produce. Another explanation: Just as the deer is the swiftest of all animals, so does the produce of the Land of Israel ripen sooner than that of all other countries. Now, you may think that just as the deer is swift but its flesh is not fat, so is the fruit of the Land of Israel swift to ripen but it is not plump. Therefore, it says explicitly, "a land flowing with milk and honey" (Exodus 3:8), to tell you that its fruit is richer than milk and sweeter than honey (*Ketubot* 112a).

**(5:2) Pharaoh replied, "Who is God that I should obey Him and let Israel go? I do not recognize God. Nor will I let Israel leave."**

※ *The Talmud Teaches*
**Who is God?** God said to Israel: I love you because even when I bestow greatness on you, you humble yourselves before Me. I bestowed greatness on Abraham, yet he said to Me, "I am mere dust and ashes" (Genesis 18:27). I did the same to Moses and Aaron, but they said, "We are nothing" (Exodus 16:8). But the heathens react differently. I bestowed greatness on Pharaoh, and he said, "Who is God that I should obey Him?" (*Chullin* 89a).

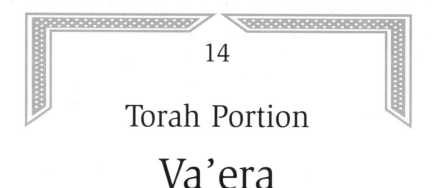

# 14

# Torah Portion

# Va'era

Exodus 6:2–9:35

## THE PLAGUES

**(6:4) I also made My covenant with them—the patriarchs—promising to give them the land of Canaan, the land of their sojourning, where they lived as foreigners.**

✳ *The Talmud Teaches*

*promising to give them* R. Simai says: Where do we find an allusion to the resurrection of the dead in the Written Torah? For it says "I also made My covenant with them—the patriarchs—promising to give them the land of Canaan." In this verse, God speaks to Moses, describing to him the covenant He made with the patriarchs Abraham, Isaac, and Jacob to give them the land of Canaan. Note that it does not say "to give *you*—the children of Israel" but rather "to give *them*—the patriarchs." The implication is that the patriarchs themselves are to inherit the land of Canaan. Because they had already died, the promise can only be fulfilled in the future when the patriarchs will be resurrected. Here, we have an allusion in the Torah to the resurrection of the dead (*Sanhedrin* 90b).

**(6:6, 7) Therefore say to the Israelites in My name, "I am God. I will take you away from your forced labor in Egypt and free you from their slavery. I will liberate you with a demonstration of My power, and with great acts of judgment. I will take you to Myself as a . . . nation."**

### ❊ The Jerusalem Talmud Teaches
*I will take you away* From where do we know that we have to drink four cups of wine on the night of Passover? R. Yochanan said: Analogous with the four expressions of redemption in this verse: "I will take you away"; "I will free you"; "I will liberate you"; and "I will take you" (Jerusalem Talmud, *Pesachim* 10:1).

**(6:23) Aaron married Nachshon's sister, Elisheva, daughter of Aminadav. She bore him Nadav, Avihu, Eleazar, and Ithamar.**

### ❊ The Talmud Teaches
*Aaron married Nachshon's sister, Elisheva, daughter of Aminadav* R. Elazar said: You should always marry into a good family. Moses who married the daughter of Jethro, the Midianite idolatrous priest, had a grandson Jonathan who served as priest in an idolatrous shrine (Judges 18:30), whereas Aaron who married Elisheva the daughter of the righteous Aminadav had a grandson Pinchas who zealously defended God's honor (Numbers 25:1 and following) (*Bava Batra* 109b).

*Nachshon's sister* Because it says "the daughter of Aminadav," is it not obvious that she is the sister of Nachshon? Then why does it say expressly, "Nachshon's sister"? From there, you can infer that when you take a wife, you should inquire about the character of her brothers. It was taught: Most children resemble the brothers of the mother. It says "Nachshon's sister" to tell us that Aaron married Elisheva because she was the sister of Nachshon, the righteous leader of the tribe of Judah (*Bava Batra* 110a).

**(6:26) These are Aaron and Moses, to whom God said, "Bring the Israelites out of Egypt according to their legions."**

### ❊ The Talmud Teaches
*These are Aaron and Moses* Throughout the Torah, Moses is always mentioned before Aaron, except in this verse, where Aaron precedes Moses. This teaches us that both were equal (*Tosefta,* end of *Keritot*).

**(7:15) God said to Moses, "Pay a call on Pharaoh in the morning, when he goes out to the water. Place yourself to meet**

him on the bank of the Nile. Take in your hand the staff that
was turned into a snake."

※ *The Talmud Teaches*
*Place yourself to meet him* R. Yochanan commented: God said
to Moses: Pharaoh is a king, and you must show him respect;
while Resh Lakish held that God said to Moses: He is a wicked
man, therefore you should be impudent toward him (*Zevachim*
102a).

(7:28) The Nile will swarm with frogs, and when they
emerge, they will be in your palace, in your bedroom, and
even in your bed. They will also be in the homes of your officials and people, even in your ovens and kneading bowls.

※ *The Talmud Teaches*
*in your ovens and kneading bowls* The text places ovens next
to kneading bowls. When is the kneading bowl found near the
oven? When the oven is hot. So when the frogs jumped into
the ovens, they would be burned; yet they did not hesitate to
do it. This is all the more surprising, because frogs are usually
in the water where it is cool. By jumping into the hot ovens,
they went against their nature (*Pesachim* 53a).

(8:2) Aaron stretched out his hand over the waters of Egypt,
and the frogs emerged, covering Egypt.

※ *The Talmud Teaches*
*and the frogs emerged* Literally, *the frog.* R. Akiva said: Why
doesn't it say "the frogs"? There was one frog that filled all of
Egypt by multiplying profusely. R. Elazar b. Azariah disagreed.
He said: What happened was that one frog croaked, and all others came running (*Sanhedrin* 67b).

(9:20) He that feared the word of God among the servants of
Pharaoh chased his servants and his livestock to the houses
before the hail would strike.

※ *The Jerusalem Talmud Teaches*
*He that feared the word of God* R. Yishmael taught: This was
Job, for Job was one of Pharaoh's servants; in fact, he was one

of his closest confidants. The fact that the verse refers to Job
can be seen in the fact that Scripture describes Job as a God-
fearing man, "Job was wholesome and upright, *he feared God
and shunned evil*" (Job 1:1); and the present verse uses the
same expression, "He that feared the word of God" (Job 1:1)
(Jerusalem Talmud, *Sotah* 5:6).

**(9:29) Moses said to Pharaoh, "When I go out of the city, I
will spread my hands in prayer to God. The thunder will
then stop, and there will not be any more hail. You will then
know that the whole world belongs to God."**

✳ *The Midrash Teaches*
**When I go out of the city**  But Moses did not want to pray inside the city. Why? Because the city was full of idols. He left the
city so that it could not be taken that he was appealing to one
of the Egyptian gods *(Mechilta)*.

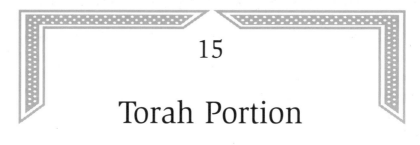

15

# Torah Portion

# Bo

## Exodus 10:1–13:16

### PRELUDE TO THE EXODUS

**(10:14) The locusts invaded Egypt, settling on all Egyptian territory. It was a very severe plague. Never before had there been such a locust plague, and never again would the like be seen.**

✳ *The Talmud Teaches*
*The locusts invaded Egypt* Why did God bring the plague of locusts on them? Because the Egyptians forced the Jews to plant wheat, barley, and various kinds of beans for them. They made the Jews do farm work so that they should be away from home and thus have fewer children. So God brought the locust on the Egyptians, and these creatures swallowed up all that the Jews had planted (*Tanna debei Eliyahu*, Chapter 7).

**(10:17) Pharaoh said to Moses, "Now forgive my offense just this one more time. Pray to God your Lord that He take away from me only this death, [that is], the locusts!"**

✳ *The Talmud Teaches*
*that He take away from me only this death* Why did Pharaoh say "*only* this death"? What did he want to exclude by saying "only"? In the days of R. Shmuel b. Nachmani, there was both a famine and an epidemic. People asked him: What shall we do? Shall we pray that God should take away both scourges?

That is not possible. So let us pray that God should eliminate the epidemic, and we will have to endure the famine. But R. Shmuel b. Nachmani told them: Let us pray that God eliminate the famine, because when the Merciful One grants abundance, He grants it to the living. For it says "You open Your hand, and satisfy the desire of every *living* thing" (Psalms 145:16), so He will remove the epidemic and keep us alive and well (*Taanit* 8b).

NOTE: *Torah Temimah* comments: The Midrash says that each of the ten plagues was accompanied by a serious epidemic; thus, along with the plague of locusts that caused a famine, there was also an epidemic. Faced with the twin scourges of famine and epidemic, and knowing that you cannot ask God for two calamities to be removed, Pharaoh said, "Pray that He take away from me *only* this death," meaning the famine. Then automatically, the epidemic would be removed too, for when God gives abundance, He gives it to the living.

**(11:2) God said to Moses, "Please speak in the ears of the people, and let each man request from his neighbor and each woman from hers, gold and silver articles."**

### ▒ *The Talmud Teaches*
**Please speak**  R. Yannai said: By saying "please," God was asking Moses to make a special effort to prevail upon the Jews to request valuables from their Egyptian neighbors. God requested this so that the righteous Abraham should not have a grievance against Him, saying, "You fulfilled the promise that the Jews 'will serve the Egyptians and be oppressed,' but You did not fulfill the other part of that promise, 'they will then leave with great wealth'" (Genesis 15:14, 15) (*Berachot* 9b).

**(11:7) But against any of the children of Israel, against neither man nor beast shall a dog snarl. You will then realize that God is making a miraculous distinction between Egypt and Israel.**

### ✳ *The Midrash Teaches*
**against neither man nor beast shall a dog snarl**  That is why the Torah says that the flesh of an animal attacked by a predator

in the field should be "cast to the dogs" (Exodus 22:30). For God does not withhold the reward from any creature. The dogs are rewarded for not snarling *(Mechilta, Mishpatim)*.

**(11:8) Moses said to Pharaoh, announcing the imminent death of the firstborn, "All your officials here will come and bow down to me."**

### ✵ *The Talmud Teaches*

***All your officials will come and bow down to me*** R. Yannai said: You should always be respectful toward the ruling monarch, for it says "Moses said to Pharaoh, 'All your officials will come and bow down to me,'" but he did not say this of Pharaoh himself. Out of respect for the monarchy, Moses did not say to Pharaoh, "*You* will come and bow down to me" (*Zevachim* 102a).

## THE PASSOVER

**(12:22) This month shall be for you the beginning of the months, it shall be for you the first of the months of the year.**

### ✵ *The Talmud Teaches*

***This month*** Rabbah b. Shmuel has taught: I might think that just as the year is prolonged in case of an emergency, so too the month may be prolonged to meet an emergency; to teach you otherwise, it says "This month shall be for you the beginning of the month," which implies: When you see the moon like this, then sanctify it, and declare *Rosh Chodesh,* the new month (*Rosh Hashanah* 20a).

NOTE: The Jewish year is based on twelve lunar revolutions. The twelve lunar months give us a year of twelve times 29.5 days, or about 354 days. The solar year—the period of time in which the earth completes one orbit around the sun—has 365 days. Consequently, the lunar year is about eleven days shorter than the solar year. This means that if in a given year Passover falls in April, then the next year it falls eleven days earlier and so on. If nothing were done to correct the situation, Passover and all the other holidays would be moving through the four seasons of the year. The Torah commands that Passover should be in the spring. "Safeguard the month of the standing grain so that you will be able to keep the Passover to God your Lord" (Deuteronomy 16:1). Therefore, the lunar calendar is adjusted to the solar year so that the month of Nisan remains in the spring. The correction is achieved by periodically inserting a thirteenth month, Adar II. The new moon appears on the thirtieth or thirty-first day of the previous month. To prevent inconvenience to the public, it is necessary sometimes to declare the new month on the thirtieth day, even though the new moon has not yet appeared. The Gemara interprets the statement "See the moon like this and then sanctify" to mean: In the first instance, you should sanctify the new month when you see the new moon; but if you sanctify the new month before you see the new moon, "Sanctify the moon, and then see it."

**(12:34) The people took their dough before it could rise. Their leftover dough was wrapped in their robes and placed on their shoulders.**

✳ *The Midrash Teaches*
**on their shoulders** Didn't they have animals to carry the dough? After all, it says "A mixture of nationalities left with them. There were also sheep and cattle, a huge amount of livestock" (12:33)! They carried the troughs with the dough on their shoulders because they loved the mitzvoth *(Mechilta)*.

**(12:40) The length of time that the children of Israel stayed in Egypt was 430 years.**

✳ *The Talmud Teaches*
*The length of time that the children of Israel stayed in Egypt*
When Alexander the Great conquered the Land of Israel, the Egyptians came before him to bring suit against the Jews. They said, "Give us back the silver and gold you took from us!" Geviha b. Pesisa, the spokesman of the Jews, said to the Egyptians, "It says 'The length of time that the children of Israel stayed in Egypt was 430 years.' So pay us the wages for the labor of the six hundred thousand men you enslaved for 430 years. This sum surely exceeds by far anything we owe you."

They searched but could not come up with an answer, so they ran away (*Sanhedrin* 91a).

**(13:9) And the tefillin shall be for you a sign on your arm and a reminder between your eyes. God's Torah will then be on your tongue—for with a strong hand God removed you from Egypt.**

�֍ *The Talmud Teaches*
*God's Torah will then be on your tongue*  Women are exempt from all commandments that must be done at a specific time, for it says that by wearing tefillin, "God's Torah will then be on your tongue." Hence, the whole Torah is compared to tefillin; just as tefillin are a commandment that is limited to time, and women are exempt, so are they exempt from all commandments that are limited to time (*Kiddushin* 35a).

NOTE: The law of tefillin (phylacteries) is the biblical commandment, "Bind these words as a sign on your hand, and let them be an emblem in the center of your head" (Deuteronomy 6:8). The tefillin consist of two leather boxes containing four selections from the Bible, inscribed on parchment, which proclaim the existence and unity of God and serve as a reminder of the liberation from Egypt. Every Jewish male having reached the age of bar mitzvah is required to wear them during the weekday morning prayers.

# 16

# Torah Portion

# Beshalach
### Exodus 13:17–17:16

## CROSSING THE RED SEA

**(13:19) Moses took Joseph's remains with him. Joseph had bound the Israelites by an oath: "God will grant you special providence, and you must then bring my remains out of here with you."**

※ *The Talmud Teaches*
***Moses took Joseph's remains*** In the manner that a person deals with others, God will deal with him. Moses earned merit by looking after the remains of Joseph, for it says "Moses took Joseph's remains with him." And no one in Israel was greater than Moses. So measure for measure, no one other than God Himself took care of his burial. For it says "And He buried Moses in the valley" (*Sotah* 9b).

***Moses took*** It says here, "Moses took Joseph's remains with him"; and in Joshua 24:32, it says "The remains of Joseph that the children of Israel brought up out of Egypt they buried in Shechem." The two verses contradict each other! R. Chama b. R. Chanina resolved the inconsistency, saying: If you perform a task without finishing it, and someone else completes it, Scripture credits the one who completed it as though he had done the whole task (*Sotah* 13b).

NOTE: The task was completed when Joseph was buried, and this Moses could not do because he died before entering the Land of Israel.

**(13:21) God went before them by day with a pillar of cloud, to guide them along the way, and by night in a pillar of fire to give them light. They could thus travel by day and night.**

### ✴ *The Talmud Teaches*

**God went before them** Rava asked Rabbah b. Mari: What is the Scriptural basis for the popular saying, "When we were young, we were treated like men; now that we have grown old, we are looked upon as children"? He replied: In the beginning, "God Himself went before the young nation . . . in a pillar of fire to give them light," but later it says "I will send an angel before you to safeguard you on the way" (23:20) (*Bava Kamma* 92b).

NOTE: Maharsha explains: When they were "young," immediately after the Exodus, God treated them like adults and marched ahead of them, but later He handled them like children, sending an angel to protect them every step of the way.

**God went before them** When Onkelos, son of Kalonymos, a nephew of Titus, became a convert to Judaism, the Roman emperor sent a unit of soldiers from Rome to arrest him. As they were about to take him away, he said to them, "Let me tell you just a simple thing: In a procession, a low-ranking official carries the torch in front of a high-ranking dignitary, a high-ranking dignitary in front of the senator, the senator in front of the duke, the duke in front of the governor, but does the governor carry a torch in front of the people that follow him?" "No" they replied. "But God does carry the light in front of Israel," he countered. For it says "God went before them . . . in a pillar of fire to give them light." Thereupon, they converted to Judaism (*Avodah Zarah* 11a).

NOTE: Usually, a low-ranking official marches in front of one of higher rank. But God went before Israel, holding a torch to give them light.

**(14:13, 14) "Don't be afraid!" said Moses to the people. "Stand firm and you will see what God will do to rescue you today. For as you have seen Egypt today, you shall not see them ever again! God will fight for you, but you must remain silent."**

### ✇ *The Jerusalem Talmud Teaches*

*Stand firm and you will see* Standing at the sea, the people split into four groups: One group said: Let's throw ourselves into the sea. Another said: Let's go back to Egypt. The third said: Let's fight against the Egyptians. The fourth said: Let's cry out to God that He may help us. To those who said: Let's throw ourselves into the sea, Moses said, "Stand firm and you will see what God will do to rescue you today!" To those who said: Let's go back to Egypt, Moses said, "For as you have seen Egypt today, you shall not see them ever again!" To those who said: Let's fight against them, Moses said, "God will fight for you!" And to those who said: Let's cry out to God, Moses said, "You must remain silent" (Jerusalem Talmud, *Taanit* 2:5).

**(14:20) The cloud came between the Egyptian and the Israelite camp. There was cloud and darkness that night for the Egyptians, and the pillar of light illuminated the night for the Israelites. And one did not draw near the other all night.**

### ✸ *The Talmud Teaches*

*And one did not draw near the other all night* This is expounded as referring to the ministering angels. R. Yochanan said: What is the meaning of "One did not come near the other all night"? When the Egyptians were drowning in the Red Sea, the ministering angels wanted to recite a song of praise. However, God reprimanded them, saying: My handiwork—the Egyptians who are also God's creatures—are drowning in the sea, and you utter a song of praise (*Megillah* 10b)?

NOTE: For this reason, we recite the entire Hallel only on the first two days of Passover, whereas on the last six days of Passover a shortened version is recited, to tone down our expression of joy.

**(15:2) My strength and song is God, and this is my deliverance; this is my God, and I will glorify Him; the God of my father, and I will exalt Him.**

### ※ *The Talmud Teaches*

*This is my God* R. Avira expounded: As a reward for the righteous women who lived in that generation, the Jews were delivered from Egypt. When they went to draw water, God arranged that small fishes should enter their pitchers, so that they drew up half water and half fishes. This they would feed to their husbands, who would thereby be encouraged to have intercourse with them. When the time came for them to give birth, they would go and give birth in the field. God sent down someone from on high who washed and straightened the limbs of the babies as a midwife straightens the limbs of an infant. And when God revealed Himself by the Red Sea, those infants were the first to recognize Him and cried out, "*This* is my God; I already know Him" (*Sotah* 11b).

*and I will glorify Him* This means: Beautify yourself before Him with mitzvoth: with a beautiful *sukkah*, a beautiful *lulav*, beautiful zizith, a beautiful Torah scroll written with the proper intention, with beautiful ink, with a beautiful quill, by an expert scribe, and wrap it with beautiful wrappings (*Shabbat* 133b).

NOTE: A *sukkah* is the thatched hut in which we dwell on the festival of Sukkot, the Feast of Booths, based on the verse, "I had the children of Israel live in huts when I brought them out of Egypt" (Leviticus 23:43). The *sukkah* with its see-through roof of plant material reminds us of the divine protection the Jews enjoyed during their wanderings in the wilderness after the Exodus from Egypt. The *lulav* is the palm frond to which are attached sprigs of willow and myrtle, and together with the *etrog*, "citron," it forms the "four species" over which a blessing is recited and which are waved daily during the Sukkot festival (Leviticus 23:34–43). Zizith are the tassels on the four corners of the tallith, which remind us to keep God's commandments (Numbers 15:38–41).

**(15:26) Moses said, "If you obey God your Lord and do what is upright in His eyes, carefully heeding all His command-**

ments and keeping all His decrees, then I will not strike you with any of the sicknesses that I brought on Egypt. I am God who heals you."

✳ *The Midrash Teaches*
*and you do what is upright in His eyes* This refers to honesty in business dealings. It teaches us that all who are honest in their business dealings are well liked by their fellowmen and are considered as if they had fulfilled the entire Torah because they have overcome many temptations *(Mechilta).*

※ *The Talmud Teaches*
*keeping all His decrees. Then I will not strike you with any of the sicknesses that I brought on Egypt.* From here, we know that if you occupy yourself with Torah study, you will be safe from afflictions *(Berachot 5a).*

## THE MANNA

(16:4) God said to Moses, "I will make bread rain down to you from the sky. The people will go out and gather enough for each day. I will test them to see whether or not they will keep My law."

※ *The Talmud Teaches*
*I will make bread rain down to you* Here, it says "bread," and in Numbers 11:8 the manna is described as "oil"; and then again in Exodus 16:31, it says that it tasted like "honey"! How can these disparities be reconciled? R. Yose b. R. Chanina said: For young men, it tasted like bread; for old men, it tasted like oil; and for children, like honey *(Yoma 75a).*

(16:17) Moses and Aaron said: In the morning you will see God's glory. He has heard your complaints, which are against God. After all, what are we that you should complain against us?

※ *The Talmud Teaches*
*what are we* Rava said: The statement Moses and Aaron made shows that they were more humble than Abraham. For Abraham

said, "I am mere dust and ashes" (Genesis 18:27), whereas Moses and Aaron said, "We are nothing," which is even less than dust and ashes (*Chullin* 89a).

## THE BATTLE AGAINST AMALEK

**(17:9) Moses said to Joshua, "Choose men for us, and prepare for battle against Amalek. Tomorrow, I will stand on top of the hill with the staff of God in my hand."**

✳ *The Midrash Teaches*
**Choose men for us** Moses did not say, "Choose men for *me*" but "Choose men for *us*," which implies that Moses placed Joshua on a par with himself. From here, we derive that a teacher should love his student as he loves himself *(Mechilta)*.

**(17:11) As long as Moses held his hands up Israel would be winning, but as soon as he let his hands down, the battle would go in Amalek's favor.**

✴ *The Talmud Teaches*
**As long as Moses held his hands up** Was it then Moses' hands that won the battle or lost the battle? Surely not. Rather, the Torah teaches you: As long as Israel looked toward heaven and subjected their hearts to their Father in heaven, they would win. But when they did not, they were defeated (*Rosh Hashanah* 29a).

**(17:12) When Moses' hands became weary, they took a stone and placed it under him, so that he would be able to sit on it. Aaron and Chur then held his hands, one on each side, and his hands remained steady until sunset.**

✴ *The Talmud Teaches*
**They took a stone** Did Moses have to sit on a bare stone? Didn't he have a cushion or a pillow to sit on? Moses said, "I insist on sitting on a stone. Since the children of Israel are in anguish, being attacked by Amalek, I will share their anguish with them." From here, it is derived that a person who is per-

fectly righteous must share in the lot of the many, even though
he had no part in the failings that brought on the calamity
(*Taanit* 11a).

**(17:16) Moses said, "The Hand is on God's Throne. God shall
be at war with Amalek for all generations."**

✳ *The Midrash Teaches*
*For all generations* R. Eliezer says: God has sworn by His
Throne of Glory that any non-Jew who comes to be converted
must be accepted. But if he is a descendant of Amalek and his
offspring, he should not be accepted. For it says "God shall be
at war with Amalek for all generations" *(Mechilta)*.

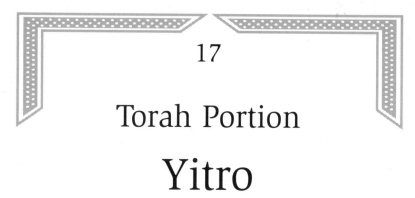

# 17

# Torah Portion

# Yitro

## Exodus 18:1–20:23

## JETHRO ADVISES MOSES

**(18:1) Jethro, the minister of Midian, the father-in-law of Moses, heard everything that God did to Moses and to Israel, His people—that God had taken Israel out of Egypt.**

✳ *The Talmud Teaches*
*Jethro heard* What news did he hear that prompted him to come and convert? R. Yehoshua says: He heard of the war with Amalek, because the present verse is preceded by "Joshua weakened Amalek and his people with the sword's blade" (17:13). R. Elazar Hamoda'i says: He came because he heard of the giving of the Torah, and this inspired him to convert. For when God gave the Torah to the people of Israel, the sound carried from one end of the world to the other.

R. Eliezer said: He heard of the parting of the sea, and that prompted him to come. For it says "It happened that when all the kings of the Amorites heard . . . that God had dried up the Jordan's waters . . ." (Joshua 5:1). Because the term *heard* in this verse refers to the drying up of the Jordan's water, it has a similar connotation when it is used in the present verse in connection with Jethro; he heard of the parting of the sea (*Zevachim* 116a).

**(18:4) The name of the other son was Eliezer, for Moses said, "My father's God—Eli—was my helper [ezer], and He saved me from the sword of Pharaoh."**

### ❖ The Jerusalem Talmud Teaches
**He saved me from the sword of Pharaoh** R. Eliezer said: When Pharaoh arrested Moses for killing the Egyptian who had struck a Jew, he condemned him to be beheaded; but the sword sprang from his neck to the executioner's neck and killed him. This is what Moses had in mind when he said, "He saved me from the sword of Pharaoh." He implied: He saved *me* and killed the executioner (Jerusalem Talmud, *Berachot* 9:1).

**He saved me from the sword of Pharaoh** It does not say "He saved me from Pharaoh" but "from the *sword* of Pharaoh" to teach you that even when a sharp sword is on a person's neck, he should not give up hope of being saved by God (Jerusalem Talmud, *Avodah Zarah* 1:3).

**(18:11) Jethro said: Now I know that God is the greatest of all deities, for the very thing they plotted came on them.**

### ❖ The Talmud Teaches
**The very thing they plotted came on them** What is meant by "the very thing they plotted came on them"? As the saying has it: In the pot that they cooked, they were cooked themselves. Which means: The Egyptians plotted to destroy the Jews by throwing their infant boys into the water, and it was by drowning in water that they themselves were destroyed. "He who digs a pit will fall into it" (Ecclesiastes 10:8) (*Sotah* 11a).

## THE TEN COMMANDMENTS

**(19:3) Moses went up to God. God called to him from the mountain and said, "This is what you must say to the house of Jacob and tell the children of Israel."**

### ❖ The Midrash Teaches
**This is what you must say [tomar] to the house of Jacob** "The house of Jacob" refers to the women, for they are the builders of the Jewish home. Speak gently, *tomar*, to them; give them a general outline of the laws. "Tell [*tageid*] the children of Israel" refers to the men. Present the laws to them in detail.

NOTE: The word *tomar* implies a mild form of speech, suited to a woman's compassionate and gentle nature. The word *tageid* suggests firmness. Thus, Moses was told to teach the commandments to the men in a firm and clear-cut manner (*Mechilta*).

**(19:17) Moses led the people out of the camp toward God. They stood at the bottom of the mountain.**

✳ *The Talmud Teaches*
**They stood at the bottom of the mountain** Literally, "beneath the mountain": This teaches us that God held the mountain over their heads like an overturned wine barrel and said, "If you accept the Torah, fine; if not, here will be your burying place!" (*Shabbat* 88a).

**(20:2) I am God your Lord, who brought you out of Egypt, from the place of slavery.**

✳ *The Talmud Teaches*
**I am God your Lord** Ullah Rabbah expounded: It says "All the kings of the earth will acknowledge You, God, because they heard Your statements" (Psalms 138:4). It does not say "Your statement" but "Your statements"—in the plural. Why so? When God said, "I am God your Lord" and "Do not have any other gods before Me," the idol worshippers said: He is looking only for His own glory. But when He said, "Honor your father and your mother" (20:12), they took it back, recognizing the correctness of the first commandments. Therefore, the kings acknowledged God when they heard *all* these statements (*Kiddushin* 31a).

**Who brought you out of the land of Egypt** R. Yehoshua b. Levi said: When Moses ascended on high to receive the Torah, the ministering angels said to God, "Master of the universe, this hidden treasure—the Torah that is Yours—do You really want to give to flesh and blood!" God then said to Moses, "*You* answer them!" Moses said to them, "What is written in this Torah? 'I am the Lord your God who brought you out of the land of Egypt.' Did you ever go down to Egypt? What else is written in it? 'Do not have any other gods before Me' (20:3). Do you live among the nations that worship idols? What else is written in it? 'Remember the Sabbath to keep it holy' (20:8). Do you do any work that you need to rest? What else? 'Do not take the name of God your Lord in vain' (20:7). Are there any business dealings among you that you need to swear? What else? 'Honor your father and mother' (20:12). Do you have parents? What else? 'Do not commit murder'; 'do not commit adultery'; 'do not steal' (20:13). Is there any envy among you? Do you have an evil impulse?" At this, they immediately agreed with God that the Torah should be given to the children of Israel (*Shabbat* 88b).

**(20:12) Honor your father and mother. You will then live long on the land that God your Lord is giving you.**

### ✖ *The Talmud Teaches*
*Honor your father and mother* Rebbi said: God knows full well that by nature a son honors his mother more than his father, for she persuades him with gentle words. That's why He placed the honor of one's father ahead of that of one's mother (*Kiddushin* 31a).

**(20:13) Do not commit murder. Do not commit adultery. Do not steal. Do not testify as a false witness against your neighbor.**

### ✖ *The Talmud Teaches*
*Do not steal* This verse speaks of one who kidnaps; but as far as stealing money is concerned, this is indicated in the verse, "Do not steal" (in Leviticus 19:11) (*Sanhedrin* 86a).

**(20:15) All the people saw the sounds, the flames, the blast of the ram's horn, and the mountain smoking. The people trembled when they saw it, keeping their distance.**

### ✳ *The Midrash Teaches*
*All the people saw* We derive from this that there were no blind people among them. And from where do we know that there were no mute people among them? From "And the people

answered" (24:7). And how do we know that there were no deaf ones among them? From "We shall do and we shall hear" (24:7). And that there were no lame ones? From "And they stood at the foot of the mountain" (19:17). And that there were no ignorant people among them? From "You have been shown so that you will know" (Deuteronomy 4:35).

NOTE: This is not to say that there were no disabled people before the giving of the Torah. Rather, at the giving of the Torah, they were cured from their infirmities. And when they sinned with the golden calf, their handicaps came back *(Mechilta)*.

**(20:17) Moses said to the people, "Do not be afraid. God only came to raise you up. His awe will then be upon your faces, and you will not sin."**

### ※ *The Talmud Teaches*
*His awe will then be upon your faces* The Jewish people have three distinguishing characteristics: They are merciful, shamefaced, and kind. They are shamefaced, as it says "His awe will then be upon your faces" (*Yevamot* 79a).

*His awe will then be upon your faces* This implies shame. "And you will not sin": this teaches us that shame leads to fear of sin. Others say: If a person is without shame, you can be sure that his ancestors did not stand at Mount Sinai (*Nedarim* 20a).

**(20:20) Do not make [images of what is] with me; gods of silver and gods of gold do not make for yourselves.**

### ✳ *The Midrash Teaches*
*Do not make . . . with Me* R. Akiva said: Do not do with Me as others do. When they are fortunate, they honor their gods; and when they meet with adversity, they curse them. But you, regardless whether good or ill comes your way, you should give thanks *(Mechilta)*.

NOTE: Afflictions are essentially good, because they atone for a person's transgressions.

**(20:21) Make an earthen altar for Me. You can sacrifice your burnt offerings, your peace offerings, your sheep, and your cattle on it. Wherever I allow My name to be mentioned, I will come to you and bless you.**

※ *The Talmud Teaches*
*an earthen altar*  R. Anan said: If a person is buried in Eretz Yisrael, it is as if he were buried beneath the altar that atones. For it says "Make an earthen altar for Me"; and concerning burial, it says "His earth, that is, the earth of the Land of Israel, will atone for His people" (Deuteronomy 32:43) (*Ketubot* 111a).

*I will come to you, and bless you*  From where do we know that even when a Jew sits by himself and is busy studying the Torah that the Shechinah is with him? From "Wherever I allow My name to be mentioned, I will come to you and bless you" (*Berachot* 6a).

**(20:22) When you make for Me an altar of stone, do not build it out of cut stone. Your sword will have been lifted against it, and you will have profaned it.**

✳ *The Midrash Teaches*
*Your sword will have been lifted against it*  R. Shimon b. Elazar says: The altar was created to lengthen a person's life, and the sword to shorten it. Therefore, the shortener may not be lifted against the lengthener (*Mechilta*).

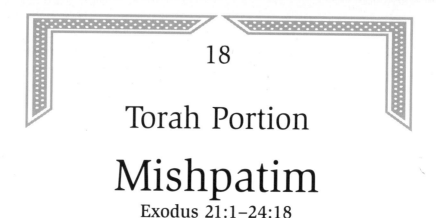

# 18

## Torah Portion

# Mishpatim

### Exodus 21:1–24:18

### CIVIL LAWS

**(21:1) These are the laws that you must set before them.**

✳ *The Talmud Teaches*
*that you must set before them* From where do we know that a teacher should explain the reasons of the laws to his students and not teach in an authoritarian way? From "These are the laws that you must set before them" so that they can be easily understood, rather than teach by rote (*Eruvin* 54b).

**(21:2) If you buy a Hebrew slave—one that was sold for robbery—he shall serve for six years, but in the seventh year he shall go free, for no charge.**

✳ *The Talmud Teaches*
*He shall serve for six years* How do we know that a runaway slave must make up the full six years of service? From "He shall serve six years." I might think that he must make up the years even if he was sick during the period; that's why it says "but in the seventh year he shall go free." He goes free, even if he was sick during his term of service (*Kiddushin* 17a).

✳ *The Maimonides Code of Law Teaches*
*free, for no charge* Even if he was sick and his master incurred great expense because of him, he owes nothing; for it says "He

shall go free, for no charge" (Maimonides, *Mishneh Torah*, Laws of Servants 2:12).

**(21:13) If he did not plan to kill his victim, but God caused it to happen, then I will provide a place where the killer can find refuge in one of the refuge cities.**

### ※ *The Talmud Teaches*
*If he did not plan to kill his victim*  R. Shimon b. Lakish expounded: About whom does this verse speak? About two men who killed: one inadvertently, the other deliberately. There were no witnesses against either one. God brings them together in one spot. The one who killed deliberately sits under a ladder; and the one who killed inadvertently climbs the ladder and falls on him, killing him. The one who killed deliberately is killed, and the one who killed inadvertently is exiled to one of the cities of refuge. Thus, even though they could not be convicted in court because there were no witnesses, God arranges that each gets the punishment he deserves (*Makkot* 10b).

NOTE: The Torah ordained that six cities of refuge were to be set aside as places of asylum, so that anyone who accidentally kills a person can escape there from the blood avenger (Numbers 35:9–34).

**(21:14) If a person plots against his neighbor to kill him intentionally, then you must even take him from My altar to put him to death.**

### ✳ *The Midrash Teaches*
*even from My altar*  It was taught: From where do we know that death penalties are carried out only when the *Bet Hamikdash* [Temple] is standing? From "Even take him from My altar to put him to death." If there is an altar, the death penalty is imposed; if not, it is not imposed *(Mechilta)*.

**(21:19) If the injured person gets up and can walk under his own power, the one who struck him shall be acquitted. Still, he must pay for the victim's loss of work, and must provide for complete cure.**

### ※ The Talmud Teaches

***The one who struck him shall be acquitted*** Now, would it enter your mind that the one who received the blows walks around in the street, and the one who struck him should be killed? That is impossible! Then why does the Torah expressly say, "The one who struck him shall be acquitted"? To teach us, by implication, that the one who struck is imprisoned until it can be determined whether the victim will recover. If the victim dies, he is killed; if he does not die, then "He must pay for the victim's loss of work, and must provide for a complete cure" (*Ketubot* 33b).

***He must provide for a complete cure*** It was taught in the yeshiva of R. Yishmael: "He must provide for a complete cure." From here, we derive that permission was granted by God to doctors to heal, and healing the sick person is not considered overriding God's will that made him sick. On the contrary, healing the sick is a religious duty (*Bava Kamma* 85a).

**(21:24) An eye for an eye; a tooth for a tooth; a hand for a hand; a foot for a foot.**

### ※ The Talmud Teaches

***An eye for an eye*** It was taught in the yeshiva of Chizkiah: It says "An eye for an eye" but not "an eye and life for an eye," which means that "an eye for an eye" must refer to monetary restitution. Now, if you assume that "an eye for an eye" means actual retaliation, and the offender's eye is to be taken out, it could sometimes happen that an eye and life would be taken for an eye, because the offender might die from having his eye removed. Therefore, "an eye for an eye" means that money-compensation must be paid to the injured party (*Bava Kamma* 84a).

**(21:37) If a person steals an ox or sheep and then slaughters and sells it, he must repay five oxen for each ox, and four sheep for each sheep.**

### ※ The Talmud Teaches

***five oxen for each ox*** R. Meir said: Notice how greatly the Torah values work. For if a thief stole and slaughtered an ox, taking the animal away from its work of plowing the field, he has to pay fivefold; whereas if he stole a sheep that he did not take from its work, because sheep are not fit for work, he has to pay only fourfold (*Bava Kamma* 79b).

*five oxen for each ox* R. Yochanan b. Zakkai said: Notice how important is the dignity of man in the eyes of God. For if the thief stole an ox that walks on its own feet and need not be carried while the thief poaches it, he pays fivefold; whereas for a sheep that he must carry on his back, he pays only fourfold, because by carrying the sheep he suffered loss of dignity (*Bava Kamma* 79b).

**(22:5) If a fire gets out of control and spreads through thorns, and the bound or standing grain or a field was consumed, the one who started the fire must make restitution.**

※ *The Talmud Teaches*
*If a fire gets out of control, . . . the one who started the fire must make restitution* God says: I must pay for the fire that I have lit. It was I who kindled a fire in Zion, as it says "He kindled a fire in Zion, and it consumed its foundations" (Lamentations 4:1); and it is I who will one day rebuild Zion by fire, as it says "I will be for Jerusalem a wall of fire all around, and for glory will I be in its midst" (Zechariah 2:9) (*Bava Kamma* 60b).

**(22:20) Do not hurt the feelings of a stranger or oppress him, for you were strangers in Egypt.**

※ *The Talmud Teaches*
*Do not hurt the feelings of a stranger [specifically, a convert]* The Rabbis taught: One who oppresses a convert violates three negative commandments: "Do not oppress him" (22:20); "do not oppress a stranger" (23:9); and "do not act toward him as a creditor" (22:24) (*Bava Metzia* 58b).

**(22:30) Be a holy people to Me. Do not eat flesh torn off in the field by a predator. Cast it to the dog.**

✳ *The Midrash Teaches*
**Cast it to the dog** Why to the dog? To teach that God does not hold back the reward from any creature. It says "But against all the children of Israel no dog shall growl" (11:7). And God says, "Give the dog its reward!" *(Mechilta).*

**(23:1) Do not accept a false report. Do not join forces with a wicked person to be a corrupt witness.**

✳ *The Midrash Teaches*
**Do not join forces with a wicked person** What is the circumstance of this case? The reference is to a case in which a crooked person said to someone, "That man owes me two hundred dinars, but I have only one witness. Come and join this witness, and you will get one hundred and I one hundred." In this regard, it says "Do not join forces with a wicked person to be a corrupt witness" *(Mechilta).*

NOTE: Two witnesses are needed to substantiate a claim.

**(23:5) If you see the donkey of someone you hate lying under its load, you might want to refrain from helping him, instead you must make every effort to help him unload.**

✳ *The Talmud Teaches*
**You must make every effort to help him unload** If the owner went and sat down doing nothing, telling the passerby, "Because it is your mitzvah, if you want to unload, go ahead and unload," the passerby is exempt, because it says "to help him." But if the owner is old or sick, the passerby is required to do the mitzvah of unloading the animal by himself (*Bava Metzia* 32a).

**(23:7) Keep away from anything false. Do not execute the innocent or the righteous, for I shall not exonerate the wicked.**

✳ *The Talmud Teaches*
**Keep away from anything false** How do we know that a judge who has concluded that the testimony of the witnesses is false

should not say: Because the witnesses give evidence, I will decide the case on the basis of their testimony, and let the guilt be on their heads? Because it says "Keep away from anything false."

How do we know that a disciple who sees his master making a mistake in the law should not say: I will wait until he finishes, and then I will prove him wrong and build up another verdict and have the judgment credited to me? Because it says "Keep away from anything false" (*Shevuot* 31a).

*Keep away from anything false* How do we know that if two litigants arrive for a court case, one dressed in rags, and the other wearing clothes worth a hundred *maneh,* that the second is told: Dress yourself as he is dressed or pay to dress him as you are dressed? From "Keep away from anything false" (*Shevuot* 31a).

## ✳ The Midrash Teaches
*Do not execute the innocent and the righteous* It was taught: If one man was pursuing another to kill him with a knife in his hand, and he was warned—if the witnesses looked away and then found the victim in the throes of death, with the knife dripping blood in the killer's hand, I might think that he could be convicted. No, he cannot be convicted on circumstantial evidence. That's why it says "Do not execute the righteous one"— that is, one who is theoretically "righteous"—because of lack of evidence *(Mechilta).*

**(24:7) They saw a vision of the God of Israel, and under His feet was something like a sapphire brick, like the essence of a clear blue sky.**

## ❈ The Talmud Teaches
*like a sapphire brick* R. Meir used to say: Why was the color blue chosen for the mitzvah of zizith, the tassels on the four corners of the tallith? Because blue resembles the color of the sea, and the sea looks like the color of the sky, and the sky is similar to the color of the throne of glory, for it says "The appearance of a blue sapphire stone in the likeness of a throne" (Ezekiel 1:26) (*Sotah* 17a).

**(24:11) Against the great men of the children of Israel God did not stretch out His hand—they had a vision of the Divine, yet they ate and drank.**

### ※ *The Talmud Teaches*

***They gazed at God, yet they ate and drank*** Rav used to say the following: The world to come is not like this world. In the world to come, there is no eating or drinking or begetting of children or business; there is no jealousy, hatred, or competition; the righteous will sit with their crowns on their heads and delight in the radiance of the Shechinah, as it says "They—the seventy elders of Israel—had a vision of the Divine, yet they ate and drank." Not in a physical sense, but the spiritual delight they derived from the radiance of the Shechinah is compared to the pleasure of eating and drinking (*Berachot* 17a).

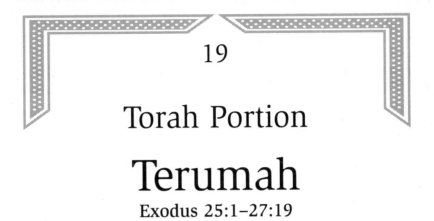

# 19

# Torah Portion

# Terumah

### Exodus 25:1–27:19

## THE FURNISHINGS OF THE SANCTUARY

**(25:8) Let them make a sanctuary for Me, then I will dwell among them.**

�֎ *The Talmud Teaches*
**Let them make a sanctuary for Me**  R. Tarfon said: You can see how highly labor is regarded, for God did not cause His Shechinah to rest upon Israel before they did work. As it says "Let them make a sanctuary for Me, then I will dwell among them" (*Avot d'Rabbi Natan* 11).

**(25:11) Cover it with a layer of pure gold on the inside and the outside, and make a gold crown all around its top.**

✖ *The Talmud Teaches*
**Cover it on the inside and the outside**  Rava interpreted this metaphorically to mean: Any Torah scholar whose inside is not like his outside—who is not sincere—is no scholar (*Yoma* 72b).

NOTE: A Torah scholar is compared to the ark of the covenant because it contained the tablets, which comprise the fundamentals of the Torah. The ark of the covenant was the gold-plated wooden chest that housed the two tablets of the Law given to Moses by God. The ark rested in the Holy of Holies inside the Tabernacle. Engraved on the tablets were the ten commandments.

### ✸ *The Jerusalem Talmud Teaches*
*Cover it on the inside and the outside*  They made three boxes: two of gold and one of wood. They placed the golden one inside the wooden one and the wooden one inside the golden one. Thus, they covered the wooden one with gold, in compliance with "Cover it on the inside and the outside with gold" (Jerusalem Talmud, *Shekalim* 6:1).

**(25:18) The cherubs shall be with wings spread upward, sheltering the cover of the ark with their wings; with their faces toward one another shall be the faces of the cherubs.**

### ✸ *The Talmud Teaches*
*With their faces toward one another*  And regarding the cherubs in Solomon's Temple, it says "They were standing up, facing the House"—away from each other (2 Chronicles 3:13). How can this be reconciled? The first verse, where the cherubs were facing each other, symbolic of the loving relationship between God and His people, applies to a time when Israel obeyed the will of God; the second, where the cherubs turned away from each other, was at a time when they did not obey the will of God (*Bava Batra* 99a).

**(25:22) I will meet with you there, and I will speak with you from atop the cover, from between the two cherubs that are on the ark of the testimonial tablets. In this manner I will give you instructions for the children of Israel.**

### ✸ *The Talmud Teaches*
*I will meet with you there*  At the outset, when Israel was faithful to God, God said, "I will meet with you there, and I will speak with you from atop the cover of the ark." Now, the height of the ark was nine handbreadths, and the height of the cover measured one handbreadth; ten handbreaths in all. Thus, the Shechinah descended to ten handbreadths from the ground. And regarding the Temple of Solomon, it says "The Temple that Solomon built for God, sixty cubits was its length, twenty its

width, and thirty cubits its height" (1 Kings 6:2). But later on, when Israel turned away from God, it says "Thus says God, 'The heaven is My Throne and the earth is My footstool; what house could you build for Me?'" (Isaiah 66:1), implying: Solomon's large Temple will not contain God's Presence, although the small ark did. This is borne out by the popular saying: When the love between myself and my wife was ardent, we found room to sleep on the blade of a sword; now that our ardor has cooled, a bed of sixty cubits is not large enough for us. When the love between God and Israel waned, even Solomon's vast Temple was not big enough to be a dwelling for the Divine Presence (*Sanhedrin* 7a).

**(25:40) Carefully observe the model that you will be shown on the mountain, and make the menorah in that manner.**

### ※ *The Talmud Teaches*
*The model that you will be shown on the mountain*  R. Yose b. R. Yehudah said: Moses was puzzled, wondering how to construct the ark, the table, and the menorah. So an ark of fire, a table of fire, and a menorah of fire came down from heaven and were shown to him. Moses saw these models and duplicated them, as it says "Carefully observe the model that you will be shown on the mountain" (*Bava Batra* 29a).

## THE TABERNACLE

**(26:15) Make beams for the tabernacle out of acacia wood standing up.**

### ※ *The Talmud Teaches*
*beams . . . standing up*  What is meant by "beams standing up"? It implies that the beams should stand in the direction the tree grew: upright, from root to top, and not upside-down or stacked sideways. Another interpretation: "Standing up" implies that the beams held up their gold covering, which was fastened to them with golden nails; thus, the beams made the covering stand. Another interpretation: So that you should not say: Now that the tabernacle is gone and hidden away, the beams will never again reappear. Therefore, it says expressly, "beams

standing," implying that they will stand for ever and to all eternity (*Sukkah* 45b).

**(27:18) The length of the courtyard of the tabernacle shall be a hundred cubits, and its width shall be fifty cubits, the pillars holding the hangings of twisted linen shall be five cubits high, and their bases shall be made of copper.**

### ✳ *The Talmud Teaches*
***The length of the courtyard*** If a person sells a courtyard, it is understood that he sells along with it the houses opening on the courtyard, as well as the pits, ditches, and caves attached to it, because in this regard it is comparable to the courtyard of the tabernacle, about which it says "The length of the courtyard shall be a hundred cubits, and its width shall be fifty cubits," and contained within that area are the holy of holies and the sanctuary, comparable to "houses" in this regard (*Bava Batra* 67a).

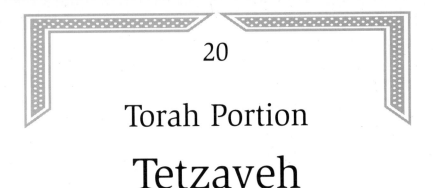

# 20

## Torah Portion

# Tetzaveh
### Exodus 27:20–30:10

## THE VESTMENTS OF THE *KOHANIM*

**(27:20) You, Moses, must command the children of Israel to take for you clear illuminating oil, made from hand-crushed olives, to keep the lamp constantly burning.**

�֎ *The Talmud Teaches*
*to take for you* R. Shmuel b. Nachmani said: It says "to take for *you*," which implies "the light of the menorah is meant to bring honor to Israel, and not to *Me*"; I do not need its light, says God (*Menachot* 86b).

*made from hand-crushed olives* It was taught: If you see olive oil in your dream, you may look forward to attaining the light of Torah scholarship. For it says "Let them take for you oil . . . made from olives," which was used in the menorah; and in the tabernacle, the menorah stood close to the ark that contained the tablets, which are the essence of the Torah. Thus, oil is associated with Torah knowledge (*Berachot* 57a).

**(28:10) Six of their names on one stone, and the names of the six remaining ones on the second stone, in the order that they were born.**

�֎ *The Talmud Teaches*
*Six of their names on one stone* The high priest had two precious stones on his shoulders, one on each shoulder. On them

were inscribed the names of the twelve tribes, six on one stone, six on the other. As it says "Six of their names on one stone and the six remaining ones on the second stone" (*Sotah* 36a).

**(28:30) Into the breastplate of judgment shall you place the *Urim* and *Tumim,* and they shall be on Aaron's heart when he comes before God; and Aaron shall bear the decision-making device for the children of Israel on his heart before God at all times.**

❋ *The Talmud Teaches*
*the Urim and Tumim* The Gemara asks: Why are they called *Urim* and *Tumim? Urim,* because their words shine forth; *urim* means "lights"; *Tumim* [because] *tumim* means "complete, because they fulfill their words" (*Yoma* 73b).

NOTE: The "*Urim* and *Tumim*" was a slip of parchment on which the ineffable name of God was written. It was inserted into the folds of the high priest's breastplate. Twelve precious stones on which the names of the tribes were engraved were attached to the front of the breastplate. When the *Urim* and *Tumim* were consulted, certain letters on the stones lit up. With divine inspiration, the high priest was able to combine the letters to spell out the answer.

❊ *The Jerusalem Talmud Teaches*
*the Urim and Tumim* They are called *Urim,* derived from *or,* "light," because they light the way for Israel, showing them what course to follow; *Tumim,* cognate to *tamim,* "whole," because they make the way "whole" before them. For when the children of Israel were "whole," that is, righteous, the *Urim* and *Tumim* would direct them along the proper path (Jerusalem Talmud, *Yoma* 7:3).

**(28:35) Aaron shall wear this robe when he performs the divine service. The sound of the bells that are attached to the hem of the robe shall be heard when he enters the sanctuary before God, and when he goes out, so that he not die.**

❊ *The Jerusalem Talmud Teaches*
*The sound of the bells shall be heard* R. Simon said: "Aaron

shall wear this robe when he performs the divine service, and the sound of the bells shall be heard when he enters the sanctuary." Let the sound of these bells come and atone for the person who killed inadvertently. For *sound* is associated with murder in the verse, "The 'sound' of your brother's blood" (Genesis 4:10) [referring to the blood of Abel, whom Cain murdered]. But a person who intentionally commits murder incurs the death penalty, and his death atones for his sin (Jerusalem Talmud, *Yoma* 7:5).

## CONSECRATION OF THE *KOHANIM*

**(29:1) This is what you, Moses, must do to consecrate Aaron and his sons as priests to Me: Take a young bull, and two unblemished rams.**

※ *The Talmud Teaches*
*This is what you . . . must do* R. Inyani b. Sasson said: The chapter about the priestly garments is followed by the sacrifices of the consecration of the priests. Why are these sections placed close together? To teach you that just as the sacrifices atone, so do the priestly garments atone. The robe atones for the spilling of blood, as it says "They slaughtered a goat and they dipped Joseph's coat in the blood" (Genesis 37:31). The pants atoned for illicit relations, as it says "Also make linen pants to cover their nakedness" (28:42). The turban atones for arrogance. Let an article placed on top of the head come and atone for the offense of haughtiness. The sash atones for the immoral thoughts of the heart, for the priest wore the sash on his chest in front of the heart, where thoughts originate. The breastplate atones for neglect of civil laws, as it says "Make a breastplate of judgment" (28:15). The *ephod,* the half-cape worn by Aaron and later by high priests when performing the service in the Tabernacle and Temple, atones for idolatry, as it says "There is no *ephod,* and, as a result, there is the sin of *terafim* [idol worship]" (Hosea 3:4). The robe to which the bells were attached atones for slander. Let an article of sound [the bells] come and atone for the sin of "the sound" of slander. The headplate atoned for brazenfacedness, for it says, regarding the plate, "It shall be on Aaron's forehead"; and concerning brazenness, it says "You had the forehead of a harlot" (Jeremiah 3:3) (*Zevachim* 88b).

**(29:43) I shall set My meeting there with the children of Israel, and the tabernacle will thus be sanctified by My honor.**

## ❈ *The Talmud Teaches*
***It will thus be sanctified by My honor [bichvodi]*** Don't read *bichvodi*, "by My honor," but *bichvudai*, "by My honored ones." This is what God said to Moses, but he did not know to whom "My honored ones" referred until the death of the two sons of Aaron. When the sons of Aaron died, Moses said to him, "Aaron, my brother, your sons died for no other reason than to sanctify the name of the Holy One, blessed be He." Now, Moses understood what God had meant by "My honored ones" (*Zevachim* 115b).

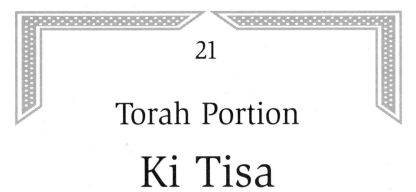

# 21

## Torah Portion

# Ki Tisa

### Exodus 30:11–34:35

## INSPIRED CRAFTSMEN

**(31:2) See, I have selected Betzalel son of Uri son of Chur, of the tribe of Judah, by name.**

✴ *The Talmud Teaches*
*See, I have selected Betzalel . . . by name*  R. Shmuel b. Nachmani said: The name Betzalel—which means "in the shadow of the Almighty"—was given to him to signify that he would become a person of great wisdom. How was his wisdom evident? When God said to Moses: Go and tell Betzalel to build Me a tabernacle, an ark, and vessels—in that order; first the building and then its contents (31:7)—Moses reversed the order and said to Betzalel: Make an ark, vessels, and a tabernacle—first the ark and then the tabernacle—as they are listed in *Parashat Terumah* (25:10–25:40). Betzalel said to Moses: As a rule, a person first builds a house, and then he brings the contents into it, but you say: Make an ark, vessels, and then a tabernacle. Where shall I put the vessels that you are telling me to make? Could it be that God told you: Make a tabernacle, an ark, and vessels? Replied Moses: You must have been "in the shadow of the Almighty," and that's how you knew (*Berachot* 55a)!

NOTE: Moses reversed the order, because the ark, which was the purpose for which the tabernacle was built, was uppermost in his mind.

**137**

**(31:3) I have filled him with a Godly spirit, with wisdom, understanding, and knowledge and with [the talent] for all kinds of craftsmanship.**

### ❋ The Talmud Teaches
*with wisdom, understanding, and knowledge* R. Yehudah said: Betzalel knew how to combine the letters with which heaven and earth were created (*Berachot* 31:3).

NOTE: The Torah is the blueprint of the universe. Thus, heaven and earth were created out of the Torah, which consists of words that are combinations of letters. Betzalel knew how to combine the appropriate letters to create a tabernacle that would have the proper degree of sanctity.

The Gemara asks: How do we know that Betzalel knew how to combine the letters? Because, when discussing the tabernacle, the Torah says "God has filled [Betzalel] with a Godly spirit of wisdom, understanding, and knowledge." And another verse says "God founded the world by wisdom; He established the heavens by understanding" (Proverbs 3:19). And it also says "By His knowledge He split the deep waters in order to make room for the world" (3:20). Thus, we see that wisdom, understanding, and knowledge were used to create the world; and Betzalel needed all three qualities in order to build the tabernacle.

## SHABBAT

**(31:13) Speak to the children of Israel and say to them: "However, you must observe My Sabbaths, for it is a sign between Me and you for all generations, to make you realize that I, God, am making you holy."**

### ❋ The Talmud Teaches
*However, you must observe My Sabbaths* R. Yose b. R. Yehudah said: From where do we know that saving a life overrides Shabbat? It says "However, you must observe My Sabbaths." I might think in all circumstances, even when a life is at stake; therefore, it says "However," to make the exception that saving a life sets aside Shabbat (*Yoma* 85b).

*to make you realize that I, God, am making you holy*  God
said to Moses: I have a wonderful gift in My treasure house, and
Shabbat is its name, and I want to give it to Israel. Go and let
them know that they are chosen to receive this gift. From here,
we know that if you give a gift to a friend, you must let him
know that you are the one who gave it (*Shabbat* 10b).

**(31:16) The children of Israel shall observe the Sabbath, to
make the Sabbath an eternal covenant for all generations.**

✳ *The Midrash Teaches*
*an eternal covenant*  R. Eliezer said: "To make the Sabbath an
eternal covenant": It is permitted to perform on Shabbat that by
which the covenant is sealed. What is that? Circumcision.

NOTE: It is forbidden to make a wound on Shabbat. However,
when a baby boy's eighth day of life comes out on Shabbat, the
circumcision must be performed, for the mitzvah of *milah* overrides the prohibition against causing a wound on Shabbat
(*Mechilta*).

**(31:17) Between Me and the children of Israel it is a sign for-
ever that in a six-day period God made heaven and earth,
and on the seventh day He rested and was refreshed.**

✖ *The Talmud Teaches*
*He rested and was refreshed*  R. Shimon b. Lakish said: God
places an additional soul in a person at the onset of Shabbat,
and it is taken from him after Shabbat ends (*Beitzah* 16a).

NOTE: Rashi explains the "additional soul" to mean a profound
sense of serenity that causes a person to be more relaxed.

## THE GOLDEN CALF

**(32:1) The people saw that Moses was late coming down
from the mountain, and the people gathered around Aaron
and said to him, "Rise up, make for us gods that will go before us, for this man Moses who brought us out from the
land of Egypt—we do not know what became of him!"**

## ✳ The Talmud Teaches

***Moses was late*** This is what happened: When Moses went up to heaven, he told the children of Israel: "I will return at the end of forty days, within the first six hours of the day." When at the end of forty days Moses had not yet come back, Satan came and caused a mix-up in the world. Said Satan to Israel, "Where is your teacher Moses?" "He has gone up to heaven," they answered. Said Satan, "The sixth hour has come, and he has not come back!"

NOTE: Moses meant forty full days and nights, not counting the day he went up, which was not a full day, because it did not include the previous night (*Shabbat* 89a).

**(32:9, 10) God said to Moses, "I have observed the people, and they are a stiff-necked people. Now do not try to stop Me when I unleash My wrath against them to destroy them. I will then make you into a great nation."**

## ✳ The Talmud Teaches

***I will then make you into a great nation*** R. Elazar said: When God said to Moses, "Now do not try to stop Me. . . . I will then make you into a great nation," Moses answered, "Master of the universe, now if a three-legged stool—meaning, a nation propped up by the merits of the three patriarchs—cannot stand before You, much less a one-legged stool—I myself! And what's more, I shall be put to shame before my ancestors. They will say, 'Look at this leader they appointed over themselves. He seeks glory for himself and does not ask mercy for them!'" (*Berachot* 32a).

**(32:16) The tablets were made by God and written with God's script engraved on the tablets.**

## ✳ The Talmud Teaches

***engraved on the tablets*** R. Elazar said: If the first tablets had not been broken, the Torah would never have been forgotten in Israel.

NOTE: Just as God's words were engraved on the tablets, so the Torah would have been indelibly etched on the consciousness of every Jew (*Eruvin 54a*).

### engraved [charut] on the tablets

R. Yehoshua b. Levi said: Do not read *charut,* "engraved," but *cheirut,* "freedom," for you can have no freer man than one who engages in the study of the Torah (*Avot* 6:2).

**(32:19) As he approached the camp and saw the calf and the dancing, Moses displayed anger, and threw down the tablets that were in his hand, shattering them at the foot of the mountain.**

### ▓ The Jerusalem Talmud Teaches

*as he approached the camp* But before he saw the calf and the dancing, he did not break them. R. Chilkiah said: This teaches us that you should not judge on the basis of guesswork, in this case, on the basis of hearsay, because God had told him, "The people . . . have bowed down to the calf" (32:8) (Jerusalem Talmud, *Taanit* 54:5).

**(32:31) Moses went back up to God, and he said, "The people have committed a terrible sin by making a golden idol."**

### ▓ The Jerusalem Talmud Teaches

*a golden idol* R. Levi said: Why doesn't the high priest serve on Yom Kippur in the golden garments? For the accuser—that is, gold—of which the calf was made does not become the defender—that is, the instrument of gaining atonement. Wearing the golden garments on Yom Kippur would be a paradox: Yesterday, "they sinned by making a golden idol," and today the high priest stands and serves in garments of gold (Jerusalem Talmud, *Yoma* 7:3)!

**(32:32) Now, if You would, please forgive their sin. If not, You can blot me out from the book that You have written.**

### ▓ The Talmud Teaches

*If not, You can blot me out* R. Kruspedai said: Three books are opened on Rosh Hashanah: one of the totally wicked, that is, people who have more sins than good deeds; one of the totally righteous people who have more good deeds than sins; and one for those in between. The totally righteous are inscribed and sealed immediately in the Book of Life; the totally wicked are inscribed and sealed immediately in the Book of Death; the sentence of the in-between people is left pending from Rosh Hashanah until Yom Kippur. If they deserve it, they are inscribed in the Book of Life; if they don't deserve it, they are inscribed in the Book of Death (*Rosh Hashanah* 16b).

**(33:20) God said to Moses, "You will not be able to see My face [that is, a complete perception of God] for no human can see My face and continue to exist."**

### ※ *The Talmud Teaches*
*No human can see My face* There are two contradictory verses: One verse says "For no human can see My face"; and another, "I saw the Lord sitting upon a high and lofty throne" (Isaiah 6:1). There is no contradiction, as it was taught: All the prophets saw their visions through a blurred glass, but Moses saw his visions through a clear glass (*Yevamot* 49b).

NOTE: All the prophets had prophetic visions in a dreamlike trance, thinking they saw Divinity, but they did not; but Moses was awake when he received a prophetic vision and understood that he could not see God (Rambam, *Yesodei Hatorah* 7:6).

**(34:27) God said to Moses, "Write these words down for yourself, since it is through these words that I have made a covenant with you and Israel."**

### ※ *The Talmud Teaches*
*for with these words* R. Yochanan said: The greater part of the Torah is oral tradition; the lesser, written, as it says "It is through [literally, 'by the mouth of'] these words that I have made a covenant with you" (*Gittin* 60a).

NOTE: The majority of the Torah laws, namely the Oral Torah, are derived from the Written Torah by means of the thirteen principles of exposition. Thus, the covenant was made on the basis of the Oral Law, which is the greater part of the Torah (*Gittin* 60a).

**(34:29) Moses came down from Mount Sinai with the two tablets of the testimony in his hand. As Moses descended from the mountain, he did not realize that the skin of his face had become luminous when God had spoken to him.**

### ※ *The Talmud Explains*
***Moses did not realize*** R. Chama said: If someone makes a gift to his neighbor, he does not have to let him know that he has done so, for it says "Moses did not realize that the skin of his face had become luminous when God had spoken to him." So you see that Moses received the gift of radiance from God, and he was not aware of it. However, this applies only when the recipient eventually would find out about it, as in the case of Moses. He was bound to discover that his face was luminescent. But if the recipient would never know that he received the gift, he should be notified (*Shabbat* 10b).

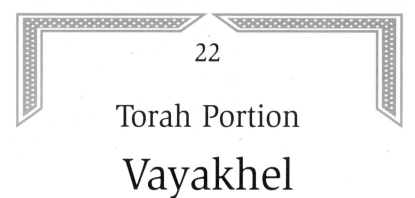

# 22

# Torah Portion

# Vayakhel

### Exodus 35:1–38:20

## THE GIFTS FOR THE TABERNACLE

**(35:1) Moses assembled the entire assembly of the children of Israel and said to them, "These are the things that God has commanded you to do."**

✳ *The Midrash Teaches*
*Moses . . . said to them* The verses that follow deal with Shabbat. Why mention Shabbat again? After all, it has been discussed before. It is appropriate to mention it here, because it says "Let them make Me a sanctuary" (25:8). I might think that they are allowed to build the tabernacle even on Shabbat. Therefore, it says "You may do work during the six weekdays"—you are to build it on weekdays, but not on Shabbat. The building of the tabernacle does not override the laws of Shabbat *(Mechilta)*.

**(35:22) The men came with the women; everyone whose heart motivated him brought bracelets, nose rings, rings, body ornaments—all sorts of gold ornaments—every man who raised up an offering of gold to God.**

�✳ *The Talmud Teaches*
*Everyone whose heart motivated him* It was taught: It says "You must fulfill what has crossed your lips" (Deuteronomy

23:24). This tells us that you must fulfill a pledge you articulated with your lips. From where do we derive the law that you must fulfill a pledge you resolved in your thoughts? From "everyone whose heart motivated him brought" (*Shevuot* 27b).

**(35:27) The leaders brought the *shoham* stones and other precious stones for the *ephod* and the breastplate.**

### �֍ *The Talmud Teaches*
**The leaders brought** R. Natan said: When Moses was busy with the work of the tabernacle, he did not want to consult the leaders of the tribes of Israel. Because God had shown Moses a fiery image of all the vessels and explained everything in detail, it would be unseemly for him to ask the advice of the leaders. The leaders said, "Woe to us that we had no part in the work of the tabernacle!" So they got up and added a large gift of their own, as it says "The leaders brought the *shoham* stones" (*Avot d'Rabbi Natan* 11).

NOTE: "*Shoham* stones" is variously translated as onyx, sardonyx, or lapis lazuli, all precious gems.

### ✳ *The Midrash Teaches*
**The leaders brought** R. Natan said: Why were the leaders the first to contribute at the dedication of the altar, while at the construction of the tabernacle they did not contribute at the beginning? At the construction of the tabernacle, the leaders smugly said: Let the community donate whatever they will donate, and whatever will be lacking we will complete. But when the community contributed everything that was needed, as it says "The materials were more than enough" (36:7), the leaders said, "What is there left for us to contribute?" So "they brought the *shoham* stones . . ." Therefore, at the dedication of the altar, they were the first to contribute. And because they were tardy at the construction of the tabernacle, a letter *yud* is missing from their title; for in this passage the word *nesi'im*, "leaders," is written without the first *yud*, as a sign of disapproval (*Sifrei, Vayakhel*).

NOTE: Omitting the letter *yud* is just as disparaging as describing in an official document a governor as "gov" or a doctor as "doc."

**(35:30) Moses said to the children of Israel, "See, God has selected Betzalel son of Uri son of Chur, of the tribe of Judah."**

### �֍ *The Talmud Teaches*
*See, God has selected Betzalel* You should not appoint a leader unless you first consult the community, as it says "See, God has selected Betzalel son of Uri." What transpired? God said to Moses: Moses, do you consider Betzalel to be suitable for this task? Moses replied: Master of the universe! If You consider Betzalel suitable, then I surely consider him suitable! Said God to him: Nevertheless, go and tell the people, and see what they have to say. He went and asked Israel: Do you consider Betzalel suitable? They replied: If God and you consider him suitable, then surely we consider him suitable (*Berachot* 55a)!

**(36:3) In Moses' presence they took the entire donation that the children of Israel had brought to complete the work on the sacred task. But they continued to bring him free-willed gifts morning after morning.**

### ✖ *The Talmud Teaches*
*morning after morning* What is implied by the phrase "morning after morning"? Did they bring gifts only in the morning? R. Shmuel b. Nachmani said: It means that they brought gifts of the substance that descended for them every morning, namely, the manna. This teaches us that along with the manna that fell every morning, there came down precious stones and pearls, and these they donated (*Yoma* 75a).

**(37:24) Of a talent of pure gold did he make the menorah and all its utensils.**

### ✖ *The Jerusalem Talmud Teaches*
*Of a talent of pure gold* Rav Yehudah taught: When Solomon made the menorah for the Temple, he took a thousand talents

of gold; placed them in a crucible; and after the refining process, it was reduced to one talent, in fulfillment of "Of a talent of pure gold did he make it" (Jerusalem Talmud, *Shekalim* 6:3).

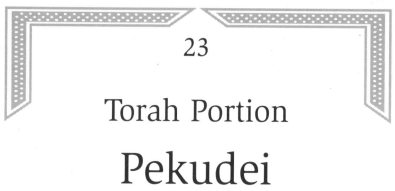

# 23

## Torah Portion

# Pekudei

### Exodus 38:21–40:38

### ERECTING THE TABERNACLE

**(38:21) These are the accounts of the tabernacle—the tabernacle of testimony—which were calculated on Moses' order by the Levites under the authority of Ithamar, son of Aaron the priest.**

◎ *The Code of Jewish Law Teaches*
***These are the accounts*** From here, we derive that, although reliable overseers of charity are not closely supervised, still, it is good that they give an accounting; as we find with Moses our teacher, who gave an account of the contributions to the tabernacle, as it says "These are the accounts of the tabernacle" (*Bach, Yoreh Dei'ah* 257).

**(38:22) Betzalel, son of Uri son of Chur, of the tribe of Judah, did everything that God had commanded Moses.**

▨ *The Jerusalem Talmud Teaches*
***everything that God had commanded Moses*** It does not say "everything that Moses had commanded him" but "everything that God commanded Moses," to teach us that even with respect to those things that Betzalel did not hear from his teacher, his thinking corresponded with what was said to Moses on Sinai (Jerusalem Talmud, *Pe'ah* 1:1).

NOTE: The underlying thought is that if you do something sincerely for the sake of God, heaven helps you to arrive at the truth.

**(40:18) Moses set up the tabernacle. He did this by putting down its bases, placing the beams in them, and fastening them together with crossbars. He then set up the pillars.**

### ※ The Talmud Teaches
*Moses set up the tabernacle* Rebbi said: It says "Moses set up the tabernacle. He did this by putting down its . . . bases. . . . He then set up the pillars." From the fact that Moses himself completed the erection of the tabernacle and did not let others take over, we derive the rule that when it comes to holy things, we must move up and not move down. It would have been demeaning if others had completed it (*Menachot* 99a).

NOTE: It is for this reason that, for example, we are not allowed to sell a Torah scroll and buy books with the proceeds.

**(40:35) Moses could not enter the tent of meeting for the cloud rested upon it, and the glory of God filled the tabernacle.**

### ※ The Talmud Teaches
*Moses could not enter* R. Elazar asked: Here it says "Moses could not enter the tent of meeting for the cloud rested upon it." But another verse says "Moses went into the cloud" (24:18). How can the two be reconciled? It teaches us that God took hold of Moses and brought him into the cloud, shielding him from the immense *kedushah* (holiness) that pervaded the cloud (*Yoma* 4b).

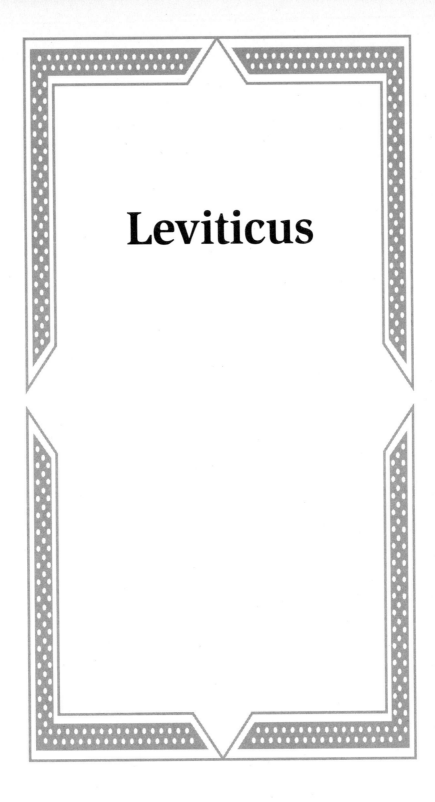

# Leviticus

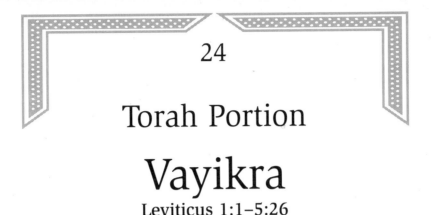

# 24

## Torah Portion

# Vayikra

### Leviticus 1:1–5:26

## THE OFFERINGS

**(1:1) God called to Moses, and spoke to him from the communion tent, saying . . .**

**�֎ *The Talmud Teaches***
***God called to Moses, and spoke to him*** Why is it that God called before He spoke? The Torah wants to teach us good manners—that a person should not say something to a friend on impulse, blurting out the message he wants to convey. He should first tell him that he wants to speak to him, so that the friend can mentally prepare himself (*Yoma* 4b).

***saying*** R. Menassiah Rabbah said: How do we know that when a person tells something to a friend, the friend must keep the message confidential until he is told, "Go ahead and relate it to others"? From the word *leimor,* "saying."

NOTE: Rashi explains that *leimor* is seen as a contraction of *lo emor,* "do not tell" (*Yoma* 4b).

**(1:2) Speak to the children of Israel and say to them: When one of you brings an animal as an offering to God, the sacrifice must be taken from the cattle, sheep, or goats.**

✳ **The Talmud Teaches**
*from the cattle* This includes persons who are like cattle, that
is, who do not fulfill the commandments. Based on this, the
Rabbis declared: We accept sacrifices from the transgressors
among the Jews, so that they will be encouraged to repent, but
we do not accept sacrifices from a heretic or from a person who
offers a wine libation to idols or from one who desecrates Shabbat (*Chullin* 5a).

**(1:3) If the sacrifice is a burnt offering, that is, an offering
that was completely burned, taken from the cattle, it must
be an unblemished male. He shall bring it voluntarily to the
entrance of the communion tent, before God.**

✳ **The Talmud Teaches**
*He shall bring it voluntarily* It says "He shall bring it." This
teaches us that a person who by law is required to bring a burnt
or peace offering is forced to offer it. You might think that he is
coerced to bring it against his will. That's why it says *lirtzono:*
He should offer it "voluntarily." But how can a person be compelled to do something voluntarily? He is pressured until he
says, "I want to bring the offering."

NOTE: In his heart, every Jew wants to do the mitzvoth; it is his
evil impulse that deters him. By compelling him, we allow his in-
nate good impulse to gain the upper hand, so that when he says,
"I want to bring the offering," he really means it (*Arachin* 21a).

**(1:9) He shall wash its innards and its legs with water. The
priest shall thus burn the entire animal on the altar as a
completely burnt fire offering, a satisfying aroma to God.**

✳ **The Talmud Teaches**
*a fire offering, a satisfying aroma* It says regarding the burnt
offering of cattle "A burnt fire offering, a satisfying aroma to
God." Concerning the meal offering, it says likewise "a fire
offering, a satisfying aroma to God" (2:2). This teaches you that
no matter whether a person offers much or little, it is all the
same, as long as he directs his heart toward heaven.

NOTE: A poor man brings a meal offering; a rich man brings a bull. However, if a rich man brings a poor man's meal offering instead of a bull, he has not fulfilled the mitzvah properly (*Menachot* 110a).

**(2:1) When a soul [that is, a person] offers a meal offering to God, his offering shall be of fine flour. He shall pour oil on it and place frankincense on it.**

### ※ *The Talmud Teaches*
**When a soul [nefesh]** R. Yitzchak said: Why is the meal offering different in that the term *nefesh,* "soul," is used in connection with it? God said: Who is it that usually brings a meal offering? A poor man, because he cannot afford to bring an animal. I consider his meal offering as if he had offered his soul (*Menachot* 104b).

**(5:1) This is the law if a person sins in any of the following ways: If he accepted an oath to give evidence in court where he was a witness who saw or knew something, and he does not testify, he must bear his guilt.**

### ※ *The Talmud Teaches*
**Who saw or knew something** R. Yose Hagelili said: How do we know that the verse speaks only of a money claim? It says "Where he was a witness who saw or knew something." The verse deals with testimony that can be established by seeing without knowing and by knowing without seeing. How is that possible? If a claimant said to a debtor, "I counted out a hundred *zuz* for you in front of So-and-so and So-and-so, but I did not tell them whether it was a gift or a loan or a repayment of a debt," and the debtor replies, "If they testify that they saw you counting out the money, I will pay you," this is "seeing without knowing" whether the money was a gift or a loan. If the claimant says to the debtor, "You admitted that you owe me a hundred *zuz* in front of So-and-so and So-and-so; they did not *see* the transaction; they only heard your admission and therefore *know* that you owe me the money." This is "knowing without seeing" (*Shevuot* 33b).

*If he does not testify, he must bear his guilt* It was taught in the Mishnah: How are the witnesses intimidated so that they do not stray from the truth in capital cases? They are told: Perhaps what you say is based only on conjecture or hearsay. You should know that you are held responsible for the blood of the accused and the blood of his potential descendants until the end of time. And in case you say: If so, why should we testify at all and worry about the responsibility? You should know that it says "If he does not testify, he must bear his guilt" (*Sanhedrin* 37a, b).

**(5:17) If a person sins and commits one of all the commandments of God that may not be done, without knowing for sure, and became guilty, he still bears responsibility.**

### ※ *The Talmud Teaches*

*without knowing . . . he still bears responsibility* The verse speaks of a person who had in front of him forbidden fat and permitted fat. If he ate the forbidden fat, thinking that he was eating permitted fat, he must bring an *asham taluy,* a "guilt-offering in case of doubt." When R. Akiva came to this verse, he wept, saying: If in the case of a person who had the intention of eating permitted fat but instead ate forbidden fat, the Torah says "He still bears responsibility," surely a person who intended to eat forbidden fat and actually ate forbidden fat bears responsibility. The fact that a person is held responsible even for unintentional sins should cause all souls to agonize (*Kiddushin* 81b).

**(5:21) If a person sins and commits a treachery against God by lying to his neighbor. It can involve an article left for safekeeping, a loan, robbery, or by defrauding his neighbor.**

### ✳ *The Midrash Teaches*

*and commits treachery against God* R. Akiva said: Why does it say, "he commits treachery against God"? When a person gives a loan, he asks for a receipt. By contrast, if someone leaves an article for safekeeping, he does not usually ask for a receipt and deposits it without witnesses, so that no one but

God knows about the transaction. Therefore, when the guardian denies receiving it, he denies it to the "One who knows." That's why it says "He commits a treachery against God" *(Torat Kohanim)*.

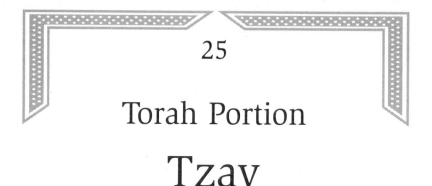

# 25

## Torah Portion

# Tzav

### Leviticus 6:1–8:36

## OFFERINGS

**(6:1, 2) God spoke to Moses, saying, "Command Aaron and his sons, saying: This is the law of the burnt offering. The burnt offering shall remain on the altar's flame all night until morning, so that the fire of the altar should be kept aflame on it."**

✳ *The Midrash Teaches*
**Command** The word *command* implies "prodding the priests to be zealous when offering the burnt sacrifice." R. Shimon said: Such prodding is needed especially in the case of a burnt offering, from which no benefit can be expected *(Torat Kohanim)*.

NOTE: Unlike other sacrifices from which the priests receive certain portions, burnt offerings are consumed completely on the altar, so that the priests do not benefit from them at all. This may cause them to be careless about the burnt offering; hence, they arc urged to be zealous.

**(6:6) There shall be a constant fire kept burning on the altar, without being extinguished.**

▨ *The Talmud Teaches*
**a constant fire** From where do we derive that the fire for lighting the menorah in the tabernacle is taken from the outer altar?

From: "A constant fire shall be kept burning on the altar," meaning, the constant fire of which I spoke to you with regard to the menorah, about which it says "To keep the lamp constantly burning" (Exodus 27:20), it must be taken only from the top of the outer altar (*Yoma* 45b).

NOTE: The term *constant* in regard to the menorah and the altar forms the connection between the two.

**(7:12) If the peace offering is offered as a thanksgiving offering, then he shall offer it along with unleavened loaves mixed with oil, flat matzos saturated with oil, and loaves made of boiled flour mixed with oil.**

✳ *The Talmud Teaches*
**then he shall offer it** Why was it necessary to say, "then he shall offer it"? It refers to the case where a person sets aside an animal as a thanksgiving offering and it was lost, so he set aside another one in its place; and then the first one was found, so that now both animals are standing in front of him to be offered as thank offerings. From where do we derive that only one of these two offerings, either the original animal or what was brought in its place, requires loaves? From "then he shall offer it." I might think that the other animal also required loaves; to teach you otherwise, it says "then he shall offer *it,*" implying only one of these two thank offerings is offered with loaves but not both (*Menachot* 79b).

## INSTALLATION OF THE *KOHANIM*

**(8:34) God has commanded that whatever was done on this day of the installation of the *kohanim* must be done all seven days to atone for you.**

✳ *The Talmud Teaches*
**Must be done all seven days to atone for you** Seven days before Yom Kippur, the high priest was removed from his wife, to preclude the chance of his becoming ritually unclean, which would disqualify him to perform the Yom Kippur service. Similarly, seven days before the burning of the red cow, the priest

who is to burn it is removed from his wife. From what verse is this derived? From "God has commanded that whatever was done on this day must be done all seven days to atone for you." "Must be done" alludes to the matter of the red cow; "to atone for you" alludes to the service of Yom Kippur (*Yoma* 2a).

NOTE: A person who became ritually unclean through contact with a dead body is purified by having the ashes of a red cow sprinkled on him. The law of the red cow, described in Numbers 19, is the most unfathomable ordinance in the Torah. Even King Solomon in his wisdom despaired of learning the secret meaning of this ritual.

**(8:35) At their installation, Moses said to Aaron and his sons, "Remain at the communion tent's entrance day and night for seven days. You will thus keep God's charge and not die, since this is what I was commanded."**

### ⚜ *The Jerusalem Talmud Teaches*

*for seven days* Where in the Torah do we find an allusion to the seven-day mourning period? R. Yaakov said: From "Remain at the communion tent's entrance day and night for seven days. You will thus keep God's charge." Just as God mourned for His world for seven days before he brought the Flood, so should you mourn for your brothers for seven days. And how do you know that God mourned for the world for seven days before he brought the Flood? For it says "Seven days passed, and the flood waters came on the earth in the days of Noah" (Genesis 7:10). But do we then mourn before a person has died, yet God mourned seven days before the people perished in the Flood! A human being who does not know what the future holds mourns only after death has occurred; God, who knows what the future holds, mourns before death has set in (Jerusalem Talmud, *Moed Katan* 3:5).

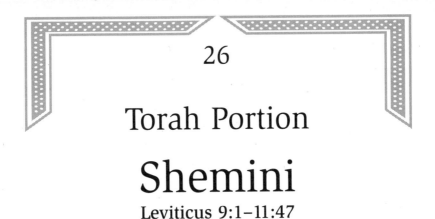

26

# Torah Portion

# Shemini

Leviticus 9:1–11:47

## INAUGURATION OF THE TABERNACLE

**(9:22) Aaron lifted his hands toward the people and blessed them. He then descended from having performed the sin offering, the burnt offering, and the peace offering.**

***The Talmud Teaches***

***Aaron lifted his hands*** From this, we learn that the priests lift their hands for the priestly blessing (*Sotah* 38a).

## THE DEATH OF NADAV AND AVIHU

**(10:2) Thereupon fire came forth from before God, and it consumed them, so that they died before God.**

EXPLANATION: At the peak of the joyous inauguration service, Nadav and Avihu, Aaron's sons, brought an unauthorized incense offering.

***The Talmud Teaches***

***and it consumed them*** Their souls were burned, but their bodies remained intact (*Sanhedrin* 52a).

**(10:3) Moses said to Aaron, "This is exactly what God meant when He said, 'I will be sanctified through those close to Me, and I will thus be glorified.'" Aaron remained silent.**

### ❋ *The Talmud Teaches*

***Aaron remained silent*** Moses said to Aaron: Aaron, my brother, your sons died only to sanctify the name of God. When Aaron realized that his sons were the favored ones of God, he was silent; and he was rewarded for his silence in that subsequently God spoke directly to him (*Zevachim* 115b).

**(10:6) Moses said to Aaron and to his remaining sons, Elazar and Ithamar, "Do not let your hair grow long, and do not tear your garments, otherwise you will die, bringing divine wrath upon the entire community. As far as your brothers are concerned, let the entire family of Israel mourn for the ones whom God burned."**

### ❋ *The Talmud Teaches*

***Do not let your hair grow long*** From where do we derive that a mourner may not cut his hair? Because Scripture says about the sons of Aaron that they were not to let their hair grow long, we infer that all other mourners may not take a haircut (*Moed Katan* 14b).

***and do not tear your garments*** A mourner must tear his garments. Because Scripture says about the sons of Aaron that they should not tear their garments, we can infer that all other mourners must tear their garments (*Moed Katan* 15a).

## LAWS OF KASHRUTH

**(11:1, 2) God spoke to Moses and Aaron, telling them to speak to the children of Israel, saying: Of all the creatures in the world, these are the animals you may eat.**

### ❋ *The Talmud Teaches*

***These are the animals you may eat*** The word *these* teaches us that God took hold of one of each species of animal and showed it to Moses, telling him: This you may eat; this you may not eat (*Chullin* 42a).

***These are the animals you may eat*** Literally: "This is the living thing that you may eat." The implication is: An animal that can continue to live, that is, a healthy animal, you may eat; but an animal that cannot continue to live, you may not eat. From here, it is derived that a *tereifah* animal is not considered living (*Chullin* 42a).

NOTE: *Tereifah* means literally an animal torn by a wild beast; the term applies to any animal suffering from a fatal disease and whose meat is forbidden even if it has been ritually slaughtered. For this reason, after the slaughter, the *shochet* (ritual slaughterer) must subject the animal's inner organs, particularly the lungs, to a minute examination. The discovery of the slightest sign of a diseased organ renders the animal *nevelah*, "forbidden as food."

**(11:4) However, this is what you may not eat from the cud-chewing animals or that have split hooves: The camel shall be unclean to you although it brings up its cud, since it does not have a split hoof.**

### ※ The Talmud Teaches
**The camel** The Ruler of the universe knows that there is no animal that chews the cud and yet is unclean except the camel and the other animals listed in this verse. For this reason, it and the other animals listed were singled out by Scripture (*Chullin* 59b).

NOTE: This is proof of the divine origin of the Torah, for no human being could say with certainty that these are the only species in the world that chew the cud but do not have split hooves. Indeed, no other species have ever been found with these characteristics.

**(11:7) The pig shall be unclean to you although it has a split hoof, because it does not chew its cud.**

### ※ The Talmud Teaches
**The pig** The Ruler of the universe knows that there is no other animal that has split hooves and yet is unclean, except the pig, because it does not chew its cud; therefore, it was singled out by Scripture (*Chullin* 59b).

**(11:19) These are the flying animals that may not be eaten: The stork *[chasidah]*, the heron, the hoopoe, and the bat.**

### *The Talmud Teaches*

***The stork [chasidah]*** R. Yehudah said: "Why is the stork called *chasidah*, 'the kind one'"? Because it shows kindness to its fellow storks by sharing its food with them (*Chullin* 63a).

NOTE: Remarks the *Chidushei Harim:* This being so, why is the stork included among the unclean birds? Because it is kind only to its fellow storks. Kindness should be extended to all living creatures, not restricted to your own kind.

**(11:21) Only this may you eat from among all flying teeming creatures that walk on four legs; one that has jumping legs above its legs with which to hop on the ground.**

***from among all flying teeming creatures*** You may not eat an unclean flying teeming creature, but you are allowed to eat what an unclean flying creature gives forth from its body. And what is that? Bees' honey, which is the nectar from flowers the bee collects but is not part of the bee itself (*Bechorot* 7b).

**(11:42) Thus, you may not eat any creature that crawls on its belly, or any small animal with four or more feet that breeds on land, for they are an abomination.**

### *The Talmud Teaches*

***any creature that crawls on its belly [gachon]*** The phrase, "that crawls on its belly" refers to the snake; "any creature" includes snails and the like (*Chullin* 67b).

***its belly*** The *vav* in the word *gachon*, "belly," marks the midpoint of the letters of the Torah; there are as many letters in the Torah after the *vav* as before it (*Kiddushin* 30a).

NOTE: It is interesting to note that this *vav*, a letter that is part of God's name, is found in *gachon*, "the belly" of the snake, the only animal that was cursed. Perhaps this is an indication that a spark of holiness exists even in the lowliest creature, and that by doing *teshuvah* and clinging to the Torah, a person who is mired in the abyss of sin can reach the highest level of *kedushah.*

**(11:43) Do not make yourselves detestable [by eating] any small creature that swarms. Do not defile yourselves with them, because it will make you unclean.**

### ✳ The Talmud Teaches
**because it will make you unclean** A transgression makes a person spiritually insensitive, as it says "Do not defile yourselves, because it will make you unclean." Do not read *venitmeitem,* "because it will make you unclean," but *venitamtem,* "because it will make you spiritually insensitive" (*Yoma* 39a).

**(11:44) For I am God your Lord, and since I am holy, you must also make yourselves holy and remain sanctified. Therefore, do not defile your souls by eating any small animal that crawls about on the land.**

### ✳ The Talmud Teaches
**You must also make yourselves holy and remain sanctified** The Rabbis taught: If a person sanctifies himself a little by resisting things that stand in the way of morality, he becomes greatly sanctified; the fight against evil becomes gradually easier. If he sanctifies himself below, he is sanctified from on high; if he sanctifies himself in this world, he becomes sanctified in the world to come; for if a person tries to purify himself, he is helped from above (*Yoma* 39a).

# 27

## Torah Portion

# Tazria

### Leviticus 12:1–13:59

## LAWS OF PURITY

**(12:1, 2) God spoke to Moses, telling him to speak to the children of Israel, relating the following: When a woman conceives and gives birth to a boy, she shall be ritually unclean for seven days, just as she is during the time of separation when she has her period.**

※ *The Talmud Teaches*
***When a woman conceives and gives birth*** For a child born through cesarean section, there is no need for its mother to observe the prescribed days of uncleanness or the days of cleanness, nor does she have to bring an offering. Why so? Because it says "If a woman conceives and gives birth"—only if she gives birth by the passageway through which she conceived (*Niddah* 40a).

***She shall be ritually unclean*** A Tanna [teacher of the Mishnah] recited before Rav: If a woman miscarries a fetus with a shapeless body or a shapeless head, you might think that she is ritually unclean because of its birth; therefore, it says "If a woman conceives and gives birth, she shall be ritually unclean. And on the eighth day, the child's foreskin shall be circumcised," which implies that only a child that is fit to undergo the *brit*, "covenant," of the eighth day causes uncleanness in his mother; but these are excluded because they are not fit to undergo the *brit* of the eighth day (*Niddah* 24b).

***She shall be ritually unclean for seven days*** The students asked R. Shimon b. Yochai: Why did the Torah mandate that a woman after childbirth should bring a sacrifice? He replied: When she crouches to give birth, she swears impulsively that she will never again have intercourse with her husband. The Torah ordained therefore that she should bring a sacrifice. And why did the Torah ordain that if she gives birth to a boy, the woman is clean after seven days; and if she gives birth to a girl, she is clean after fourteen days? When she has a boy, with whom all are happy, she regrets her oath not to have intercourse after seven days; but when she has a girl, and everyone is disappointed, she regrets her oath only after fourteen days (*Niddah* 31b).

**(12:3) On the eighth day, the child's foreskin shall be circumcised.**

✖ *The Talmud Teaches*
***On the eighth day*** Why did the Torah ordain circumcision on the eighth day and not before? So that the guests at the *brit milah* feast should not enjoy themselves while the baby's father and mother are not in a happy mood, because they are forbidden to have relations until after the seven days of uncleanness due to birth (*Niddah* 31b).

***On the eighth day*** Even if it falls on Shabbat (*Shabbat* 132a).

NOTE: The commandment of *milah* sets aside the prohibition of causing a wound on Shabbat.

The whole day is valid for *milah,* as it says "On the eighth *day,* the child's foreskin shall be circumcised," but the zealous are quick to do the mitzvoth, doing it in the morning (*Pesachim* 4a).

Circumcision is not performed until sunrise, as it says "On the eighth day, the child's foreskin shall be circumcised" (*Megillah* 20a).

*the child's foreskin shall be circumcised* The circumcision of the foreskin of a child that is certain to survive sets aside Shabbat if Shabbat is the eighth day but not the circumcision of a child whose survival is doubtful and not the circumcision of a hermaphrodite, that is, an individual having both male and female sexual characteristics, or one born at twilight, or the circumcision of a child born circumcised, in which case "letting the blood of the covenant" is not done on Shabbat (*Shabbat* 132b).

NOTE: "Letting the blood of the covenant" involves drawing a few drops of blood.

## THE LAWS OF *TZARAAT* (LEPROSY)

**(13:45) When a person has the mark of the leprous plague, his clothing must have a tear in it [like a mourner], he must go without a haircut, and he must cover his head down to his lips. "Unclean! Unclean!" he must call out.**

### ✳ *The Talmud Teaches*
*"Unclean! Unclean!" he must call out* This teaches us that he must make his suffering known to the people, so that they will pray for him (*Moed Katan* 15a).

Rava said to Rabbah b. Mari: What is the source of the popular saying that poverty follows the poor? He said: You derive it from here, "'Unclean! Unclean!' he must call out." Meaning, in addition to suffering the misery of the leprosy, the leper is forced by law to make it public (*Bava Kamma* 92a, b).

**(13:46) As long as the person has the leprous mark, he shall remain unclean. Because he is unclean, he must remain alone, and his place shall be outside the camp.**

### ✳ *The Talmud Teaches*
*He must remain alone* Why is the leper singled out to live in isolation? Because his affliction is a punishment for slander, which causes husbands to be separated from their wives and friends from one another. Therefore, it is fitting that he be punished through isolation from society (*Arachin* 16b).

NOTE: The ultimate purpose of "a punishment that fits the crime" is to make the sinner aware of what he did and what it has brought on him. Such reflection should lead him to repent.

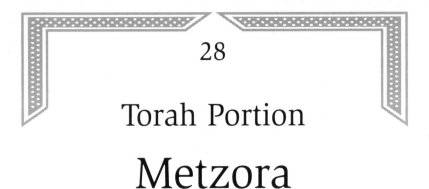

# 28

# Torah Portion

# Metzora

### Leviticus 14:1–15:33

## PURIFICATION OF A LEPER

**(14:1, 2) God spoke to Moses, saying: This is the law concerning the leper when he is purified; he shall be brought to the priest.**

※ *The Talmud Teaches*
***This is the law concerning the leper*** Resh Lakish said: What is meant by "This is the law concerning the leper [*metzora*]"? It means: This shall be the law for a person who slanders, *motzi shem ra* (*Arachin* 15b).

NOTE: The word *metzora*, "leper," is seen as a contraction of *motzi shem ra*, "slanderer." Thus, the law of the slanderer is that he shall be punished with leprosy.

**(14:4) The priest shall then order that for the person undergoing purification there be taken two live kosher birds, some crimson wool, and a hyssop branch.**

※ *The Talmud Teaches*
***two . . . birds*** R. Yehoshua b. Levi said: In what way is the leper singled out that the Torah said about him, "He should bring two live kosher birds" so that he will become pure again?

God said: His affliction came in punishment for the chatter of gossip and slander; his purification comes about by offering chirping twittering birds (*Arachin* 16b).

**(14:35) The owner of the house that has a leprous mark shall come and tell the priest, saying, "It looks to me as if there is something like a leprous mark in the house."**

### � The Talmud Teaches
**The owner of the house** It was taught: The plague of leprosy comes because of selfishness, as it says "The owner of the house shall come," which was expounded in the yeshiva of R. Yishmael: This refers to a person who keeps his house for himself. He is unwilling to lend his utensils to others, claiming that he does not have any. God exposes him when he is compelled to empty out his house because of the leprous mark on it (*Arachin* 16a, *Yoma* 11b).

### ✳ The Midrash Teaches
**And he shall tell the priest, saying** The superfluous word *saying* teaches that the priest will make a careful investigation as to what brought the plague on his house. The priest shall tell the owner words of reproof: "My son, the marks of plague come only because of slander" *(Torat Kohanim).*

### ✖ The Talmud Teaches
**There is something like a leprous mark in the house** He says, "There is something like a leprous mark" but not "There *is* a leprous mark." Even if he is a Torah scholar and knows for sure that it is a leprous mark, he should not say unequivocally, "It is a leprous mark" but tentatively, "It looks to me as if there is something like a leprous mark in the house," because a person should make it a habit to say, "I am not sure" (*Nega'im* 12:5).

**(14:36) The priest shall give orders that the house be emptied before any priest comes to see the mark, so that everything in the house will not become unclean. Only then shall a priest come to see the house.**

※ *The Talmud Teaches*
*the house be emptied* Leprous marks come because of theft, as
it says "The priest shall give orders that the house be emptied."
This is expounded: The thief took in property that did not
belong to him—the priest will come and scatter his property
(*Arachin* 16a).

## MENSTRUATION

(15:19) When a woman has a discharge, it can consist of any
blood that emerges from her body. For seven days she is then
in a state of *niddah* [ritual uncleanness], because of her
monthly period, and anyone touching her shall be unclean
until evening.

※ *The Talmud Teaches*
*For seven days she is then in a state of niddah* R. Meir used
to say: Why did the Torah ordain that the uncleanness of menstruation should last for seven days? Because being in constant
contact with his wife, a husband might come to dislike her.
Therefore, the Torah mandated: Let her be *niddah,* even after
seeing the slightest bloodstain, for seven days, during which
intercourse is forbidden in order that she shall be beloved by
her husband as when she entered beneath the bridal canopy
(*Niddah* 31b).

(15:31) You, Moses and Aaron, must warn the children of Israel
about their impurity, so that their impurity not cause them to
die if they defile My tabernacle that I have placed among them.

※ *The Talmud Teaches*
*You must warn the children of Israel* Where is the marking of
graves alluded to in the Torah? Mar Zutra answered: In "You
must warn the children of Israel about their impurity," that is,
by marking their graves, so that they will be recognized as
places of uncleanness (*Moed Katan* 5a).

*You must warn the children of Israel about their impurity*
This is a warning to the children of Israel to separate from their
wives before the onset of their monthly period (*Shevuot* 15b).

***You must . . . warn*** It was taught: R. Yochanan said: If a person does not separate from his wife before the onset of her monthly period, even if he will have sons like the sons of Aaron, they will die. For it says "You must warn the children of Israel about their impurity," which is followed by "A woman who has her monthly period" (15:33), which in turn is followed by "After the death of the two sons of Aaron" (16:1).

## ✳ *The Midrash Teaches*

***if they defile My tabernacle that I have placed among them*** This teaches us that although the Jewish people may be unclean, the Shechinah is among them *(Torat Kohanim)*.

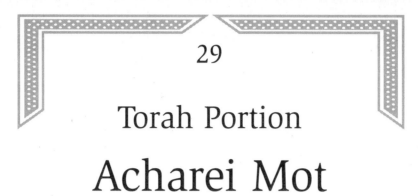

# 29

# Torah Portion

# Acharei Mot

### Leviticus 16:1–18:30

## THE YOM KIPPUR SERVICE

**(16:1) God spoke to Moses right after the death of Aaron's two sons who brought an unauthorized offering before God and died.**

✵ *The Jerusalem Talmud Teaches*
*right after the death* Why is their death mentioned in connection with Yom Kippur? To teach that just as Yom Kippur atones for the Jewish people, so does the death of the righteous provide atonement for the Jewish people (Jerusalem Talmud, *Yoma* 1:1).

**(16:13) There, before God, in the holy of holies, he shall place the incense upon the fire, so that the smoke from the incense cover the ark-cover over the tablets of the testimony. Then He will not die.**

✵ *The Talmud Teaches*
*There, before God, in the Holy of Holies, he shall place the incense upon the fire* This tells us that he should not prepare the incense outside and then bring it in—as opposed to the view of the Sadducees, who said that he must prepare the incense outside and then bring it in (*Yoma* 53a).

NOTE: The Sadducees were a heretical sect that rejected the Oral Torah. They denied the immortality of the soul, bodily resurrection after death, and they did not believe in punishment in the hereafter. After the destruction of the Temple in 70 C.E., the Sadducees quickly disappeared from history.

**(16:16) All this shall be an eternal law for you. Each year on the tenth day of the seventh month, you must afflict yourselves, and not do any work. This is true both for the native born and the proselyte who joins you.**

### ✳ *The Talmud Teaches*
*You must afflict yourselves* The Torah does not say how we are to afflict ourselves. You might think that a person should afflict himself by sitting in the sun on a hot day. To teach you otherwise, the verse continues, "and do not do any work." Just as the prohibition of work means passively abstaining from work, so too the command to afflict yourself means a passive kind affliction, namely, denying yourself food and drink. The Torah does not demand self-affliction by specific activity such as sitting in the sun on a hot day (*Yoma* 74b).

**(16:30) For on this day of Yom Kippur He will provide atonement for you; from all your sins before God will you be cleansed.**

### ✳ *The Midrash Teaches*
*For on this day . . . will you be cleansed* Even when there are no offerings and no he-goat, that is, when the Temple is not standing, the day—Yom Kippur—affords atonement (*Torat Kohanim*).

### ✳ *The Talmud Teaches*
*He will provide atonement for you* R. Yishmael expounded: If a person transgressed a commandment and repented, his repentance holds off the punishment; and Yom Kippur atones, as it says "For on this day He will provide atonement for you" (*Yoma* 86a).

### *from all your sins before God*
R. Elazar b. Azariah expounded: From here we derive that for transgressions against God, Yom Kippur atones, but for transgressions between man and his neighbor, Yom Kippur does not atone until he appeases his neighbor (*Yoma* 85b).

**(18:4) Keep My decrees and laws, which man shall carry out, and by which he shall live—I am God.**

### ✳ *The Talmud Teaches*
***which man shall carry out*** R. Meir used to say: From where do we know that even a Gentile who studies the Torah and lives by the moral principles of the Torah is equal in status to the high priest? From "which man shall carry out." It does not say "priests, Levites, and Israelites shall carry out" but "man," which shows that even a Gentile who studies the Torah and lives by its moral standards is like the high priest (*Bava Kamma* 38a).

***by which he shall live*** From where do we derive that the need to preserve life supersedes the observance of Shabbat? Rav Yehudah said: From "Keep My decrees and laws which man shall carry out and by which he shall live"—He shall live by them, and not die by observing them (*Yoma* 85b).

***and by which he shall live*** With regard to all transgressions in the Torah, if a person is told: Transgress or you will be killed, he should transgress and save his life. The exceptions are the three cardinal sins: idolatry, forbidden sexual relations, and murder, and cases where the violation of commandments would cause desecration of God's name. In these cases, one should give up his life rather than transgress (*Sanhedrin* 74a).

## FORBIDDEN SEXUAL RELATIONS

**(18:6) No person shall approach a close relative to commit a sexual offense. I am God.**

### ✳ *The Talmud Teaches*
***No person shall approach*** From this verse, the Sages derived that a man should not be alone with a woman in an inn—even with his sister and with his daughter. He should not walk and talk with a woman in the marketplace—even with his wife—because of what people might say (*Avot d'Rabbi Natan* 2).

**(18:22) Do not lie with a male as you would with a woman, since this is an abomination.**

❋ *The Talmud Teaches*
**an abomination [to'evah]** What is meant by *to'evah*, "abomination"? It is a contraction of the phrase *to'eh atta bah;* by committing homosexuality, a person deviates from the ways of nature (*Nedarim* 51a).

NOTE: *Pesikta Zutreta* comments: Such a person ranks lower than an unclean beast, for a male beast mates only with a female.

**(18:27) The people who lived in the land before you did all these abominations and defiled the land.**

❋ *The Talmud Teaches*
**all these abominations** R. Chama b. Chanina said: An arrogant person is like one who engaged in all of the forbidden relations. For it says about an arrogant person "Every haughty person is an abomination to God" (Proverbs 16:5); and regarding forbidden relations, it says "The people did all these abominations." Both arrogance and forbidden sexual relations are characterized as abominations (*Sotah* 4b).

**(18:28) Do not cause the land to vomit you out when you defile it, as it vomited out the nation that was there before you.**

❋ *The Talmud Teaches*
**Do not cause the land to vomit you out** Because of the sin of forbidden relations, exile comes to the world. God sends the Jewish people into exile, and other people come and take over their land, for it says "The people who lived in the land before you did all these abominations—incest, adultery, and homosexuality—and defiled the land," and it says "Do not cause the land to vomit you out when you defile it, as it vomited out the nation that was there before you," proof that engaging in illicit sexual relations is punished by exile (*Shabbat* 33a).

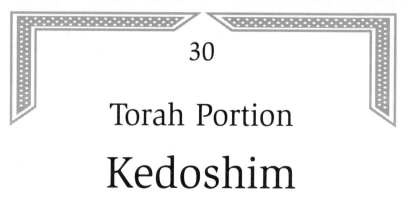

# 30

## Torah Portion

# Kedoshim
### Leviticus 19:1–20:27

## FUNDAMENTAL MORAL LAWS

**(19:1, 2) God spoke to Moses, telling him to speak to the entire assembly of the children of Israel and say to them: You must be holy, since I am your God and I am holy.**

✴ *The Midrash Teaches*
***Speak to the entire assembly*** This chapter was stated in the presence of the entire people and not just to the leaders. And why so? Because many of the major doctrines of the Torah are contained in this portion, such as "You must love your neighbor as you love yourself" (19:18) *(Torat Kohanim)*.

***You must be holy*** You become holy by keeping away from the incestuous relations mentioned in the previous portion.

***since I am holy*** If you sanctify yourselves, I consider it as if you had sanctified Me *(Torat Kohanim)*.

**(19:3) Every person must respect his mother and father, and keep My Sabbaths. I am God your Lord.**

▓ *The Talmud Teaches*
***his mother and father*** R. Shimon said: In most places in the Torah, the father is mentioned before the mother, as in "Honor your father and your mother" (Exodus 20:12). This may lead

you to believe that a son must honor his father more than his mother. To teach you otherwise, it says "Every person must respect his mother and father," where the mother is mentioned before the father, to teach you that both are equal. But the Sages have said that although biblically the father and mother are equal, rabbinically the father comes before the mother in every respect, because both the son and his mother are required to honor the father (*Keritot* 28a).

***Every person must respect his mother and father*** It says "Every person must respect his mother and father," and it says "God your Lord you shall respect, Him you shall serve" (Deuteronomy 10:20). In both passages, the word *respect* is used. The Torah equates the respect you owe your parents with the respect you must show God (*Kiddushin* 30b).

***Every person must respect his mother and father*** It was taught: Why does the mother precede the father? Rebbi said: It is obvious to God that a son respects his father more than his mother, because he teaches him Torah; therefore, to compensate for the imbalance, God placed the respect a son owes his mother before that of the father (*Kiddushin* 31a).

***Every person must respect*** The Rabbis taught: What is meant by *respect?* Not to stand in your father's place nor sit in his place nor side with his opponents in a Torah debate (*Kiddushin* 31a).

***and keep My Sabbaths*** It was taught: You might think that the respect a son owes his father and mother overrides Shabbat, and in the case when the father orders the son to desecrate Shabbat, he must obey him; therefore, it says "Every person must respect his father and mother, and keep My Sabbaths; I am God your Lord"—he should not obey his father when he tells him to desecrate Shabbat, because the son as well as his father and mother are required to honor Me (*Yevamot* 8b).

**(19:14) Do not curse a deaf man. Do not place a stumbling block before the morally blind. You must fear your God. I am God.**

### ✳ *The Talmud Teaches*

**Do not curse a deaf man** Is it then forbidden to curse only a
deaf man? Surely, cursing anyone is forbidden! Why then does
it say, "Do not curse a deaf man"? Scripture is speaking of the
most hapless among your people. You are forbidden to curse
even the deaf man who cannot hear the curse and does not feel
angered or embarrassed by it. Surely, therefore, it is forbidden
to curse those who are aware of what is being done to them
(*Sanhedrin* 66a).

### ✳ *The Midrash Teaches*

**Do not place a stumbling block before the blind** In addition
to its literal meaning, what is meant by "before the blind"?
Don't give bad advice to an unsuspecting person, particularly
if the adviser stands to benefit from the other's error. If he asks
you for advice, don't give him advice that is not suitable for
him. Don't tell him, "Leave early in the morning," so that he
may be assaulted by robbers; "leave in the afternoon," so that
he may be overcome by heat. And don't say, "I am giving him
good advice," because in general this would indeed be good
advice, only for this particular person it is unsuitable, for you
know your true intentions, and God knows what you really had
in mind. And so it says "You must fear God who knows your
innermost thoughts" *(Torat Kohanim)*.

### ✳ *The Talmud Teaches*

**Do not place a stumbling block before the blind** R. Natan said:
From where do we know that you should not offer a cup of
wine to a Nazirite [that is, a person who took a vow not to
drink wine], or a limb torn from a living animal to a Gentile?
Because it says "Do not place a stumbling block before the
blind," for you would cause the Nazirite and the Gentile to
stumble into sin (*Pesachim* 22b).

NOTE: The prohibition against eating a limb torn from a living
animal is one of the seven Noahide commandments, the seven
universal laws that are binding on all mankind.

### ✳ *The Talmud Teaches*

**Do not place a stumbling block before the blind** It was taught:
Scripture is alluding also to a father who strikes his grown-up

son. For the son may react in a disrespectful manner and thereby transgress the commandment of "Honor your father and mother." Thus, by striking his son, the father is causing his son to stumble (*Mo'ed Katan* 5a).

**(19:15) Do not pervert justice. Do not give special consideration to the poor, nor show respect to the great. Judge your people fairly.**

✳ *The Midrash Teaches*
*Do not give special consideration to the poor* A judge should not say that because the wealthy man is obligated to help the poor one, it is proper for a judge to rule in favor of the poor litigant so that he will be supported in dignity. The Torah insists that justice be rendered honestly; charity may not interfere with it. For it says "Do not give special consideration to the poor" *(Torat Kohanim)*.

*Do not show respect to the great* The judge should not say: He is a wealthy man; he comes from a prominent family; how can I humiliate him by ruling against him? That's why it says "Do not show respect to the great" *(Torat Kohanim)*.

✵ *The Talmud Teaches*
*Judge your people fairly* The Rabbis taught: "Judge your people fairly"—that one of the litigants should not be allowed to sit and the other made to stand; one allowed to speak and the other told to cut it short *(Shevuot* 30a).

**(19:16) Do not go around as a gossiper among your people. Do not stand idly by when your neighbor's life is in danger. I am God.**

✵ *The Talmud Teaches*
*Do not go around as a gossiper* From where do we know that the judge should not say to a litigant: *I* found you innocent, but my fellow judges found you guilty. What can I do? They were the majority and outvoted me. It is derived from: "Do not go around as a gossiper" *(Sanhedrin* 30a).

***Do not stand idly by when your neighbor's life is in danger***
From where do we know that if someone threatens to kill your neighbor that it is your duty to save his life by killing the attacker who is threatening his life? From the verse "Do not stand idly by when your neighbor's life is in danger" (*Sanhedrin* 73a).

**(19:17) Do not hate your brother in your heart. You must admonish your neighbor, and not bear sin because of him.**

### ✳ *The Talmud Teaches*
***You must admonish your neighbor*** How far should you go in admonishing people? Rav said: Until they beat you up for reprimanding them (*Arachin* 16b).

***and do not bear sin because of him*** I might think that you should admonish him even if his face turned white for shame for being humiliated publicly. That's why it says "Do not bear sin because of humiliating him" (*Arachin* 16b).

**(19:18) Do not take revenge nor bear a grudge against the children of your people. You must love your neighbor as you love yourself. I am God.**

### ✳ *The Talmud Teaches*
***Do not take revenge nor bear a grudge*** It was taught: What is revenge and what is bearing a grudge? If someone said, "I won't lend you my tool because you refused to lend me yours," that is taking revenge. If you answer, "I will lend you money. I am not like you who refused me when you could have lent me your tool," that is bearing a grudge (*Yoma* 23a).

***You must love your neighbor as you love yourself*** When a heathen asked Hillel to teach him the Torah in the shortest possible way, he answered, interpreting this verse as follows: Do not do to your neighbor that which you would hate to have done to you. This is the essence of the whole Torah; everything else is only the explanation and elaboration of this principle. Now, go and learn it (*Shabbat* 31a).

### ❋ *The Jerusalem Talmud Teaches*

**You must love your neighbor as you love yourself** R. Akiva said: "You must love your neighbor as you love yourself"—this is a fundamental principle in the Torah (Jerusalem Talmud, *Nedarim* 9:4).

**(19:26) Do not eat over the blood. Do not act on the basis of omens.**

### ❋ *The Talmud Teaches*

**Do not act on the basis of omens** Acting on the basis of omens is, for instance, if a person says: Today is an unlucky day, because a piece of bread fell out of my mouth; because my stick fell out of my hand; because my child is calling me from behind; a raven croaked as I passed; there was a snake on my right and a fox on my left, or he says to the tax collector: It will bring me bad luck if you start with me. Or he believes that it is bad luck to pay out money early in the morning or on the first of the month or to start the week with paying, just after the conclusion of Shabbat.

Further, it says there, "Do not act on the basis of omens"— like those who see portents in black cats, fish, birds, and so on (*Sanhedrin* 66a).

**(19:29) Do not prostitute your daughter to lead her to lewdness. You will then not make the land sexually immoral, and the land will not be filled with perversion.**

### ❋ *The Talmud Teaches*

**Do not prostitute your daughter** R. Eliezer said: This refers to a person who marries off his daughter to an old man. R. Akiva said: It refers to a person who delays marrying off his daughter after she has reached the age of maturity. Both cases lead her to promiscuity (*Sanhedrin* 76a).

**(19:30) Keep My Sabbaths and revere My sanctuary. I am God.**

### ❋ *The Talmud Teaches*

**Keep My Sabbaths** It was taught: You might think that the building of the Temple sets aside the observance of Shabbat and that you are allowed to build the Temple even on Shabbat; to teach you otherwise, it says "Keep My Sabbaths and revere My sanctuary"—you are all required to honor Me, and the building of the sanctuary does not supersede the laws of Shabbat (*Yevamot* 6a).

### You shall thus fear your God
You might think that you may close your eyes as if not to see the approaching elder; that's why it says "Stand up . . . you shall thus fear your God"—you should bear in mind that God knows your innermost thoughts; He knows whether you avoided seeing the elder (*Kiddushin* 32b).

**(19:33) When a convert dwells among you, do not hurt his feelings.**

### ※ *The Talmud Teaches*
*When a convert dwells among you* Righteous converts are included in the Amidah prayer with the righteous of the Jews; for it says "Give respect to an elder" (19:32) followed by "When a convert dwells among you" (*Megillah* 17b).

*Do not hurt his feelings* The Torah speaks here of hurting someone with something you say. For example: If a convert is coming to study Torah, you should not say to him, "Shall the mouth that ate unclean and forbidden foods, abominable and creeping things, come to study the Torah that was uttered by the mouth of the Almighty?" If he is a descendant of converts, you should not say to him, "Remember the deeds of your ancestors" (*Bava Metzia* 58b).

**(20:26) You shall be holy to Me, for I, God, am holy, and I have separated you from among the nations to be Mine.**

### ✳ *The Midrash Teaches*
*I have separated you* R. Elazar b. Azariah said: From where do we know that you should not say: I don't want to eat the meat of a pig because I dislike it, but you should say: I *do* want to eat it, but what can I do? My Father in heaven has decreed that I

may not eat pig's meat. We know it from the verse "I have separated you from the nations to be Mine" *(Torat Kohanim)*.

NOTE: R. Samson Raphael Hirsch comments: The purpose of our being separated from the nations is so that every moment a Jew abstains from sin becomes a homage to God.

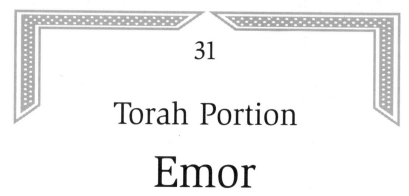

# 31

## Torah Portion

# Emor

### Leviticus 21:1–24:23

## LAWS OF THE *KOHANIM*

**(21:1) God said to Moses: Say to Aaron's descendants, the priests, and tell them: Let no priest defile himself by contact with the dead among his people.**

⚜ *The Talmud Teaches*
*Let no priest defile himself by contact with the dead among his people* The prohibition applies only when the corpse is "among its own people," but when a *kohen* finds an abandoned corpse in a place where no one else can attend to it, he may not leave it but must bury it (*Yevamot* 114a).

**(21:8) You shall keep the *kohen* holy, since he presents the food offering to God. He must be holy, since I am God—I am holy, and I am making you holy.**

⚜ *The Talmud Teaches*
*You shall keep the* **kohen** *holy* It was taught in the yeshiva of R. Yishmael: "You shall keep the *kohen* holy"—the rest of the nation must recognize the sanctity of priests by showing them respect and giving them precedence. That is why a *kohen* is called to the Torah first and has priority in leading the assemblage in Grace after Meals (*Gittin* 59b).

**(22:18) God spoke to Moses, telling him to speak to Aaron, to his sons and to all the children of Israel, saying to them: This is the law if any person, whether of the family of Israel or of the proselytes who join them, offers an animal that can be presented to God as a burnt offering to fulfill a general or a specific pledge.**

※ *The Talmud Teaches*
*if any person . . . offers an animal*  Including Gentiles. Even heathens can bring free-will offerings in the Temple along with Jews (*Menachot* 73b).

*that can be presented to God as a burnt offering*  The offerings of non-Jews are limited to *olah*, a "burnt offering" that is completely consumed by fire. Even if the Gentile wants to bring a *shelamim*, "peace offering," which the bringer eats with his family outside the Temple, it is offered as an *olah* (*Menachot* 73b).

NOTE: R. Samson Raphael Hirsch explains why the Gentile's peace offering is treated as an *olah* and consumed by fire on the altar. The Gentile has the idea of giving himself entirely to God. He does not comprehend the specifically Jewish concept that the true divine service is found in the joyful, moral enjoyment of the earthly material human life that is expressed in the *shelamim* offering.

## THE FESTIVALS

**(23:2, 3) There are special times that you must celebrate as sacred holidays to God. The following are My special times: You may do work during the six weekdays, but the seventh day is a day of complete rest, a holy convocation, you shall not do any work, it is a Sabbath for God wherever you may live.**

✳ *The Midrash Teaches*
*You may do work during the six weekdays*  Why does the chapter of the festivals begin by mentioning Shabbat? To teach

us that whoever desecrates the festivals is considered as having desecrated Shabbat, and whoever keeps the festivals is considered to have kept Shabbat *(Torat Kohanim)*.

**(23:10) Speak to the children of Israel and say to them: When you come to the land that I am going to give you, and you reap its harvest, you must bring an *omer* of your first reaping to the priest.**

### ※ *The Talmud Teaches*
**When you come** R. Yehudah said: Why did the Torah command us to bring an *omer* (measure) on Passover? Because Passover is the time when God judges the grain crop. Therefore, God said: Bring the *omer* for Me on Passover, so that I will bless the grain in the fields *(Rosh Hashanah 16a)*.

NOTE: The *omer* offering consists of a measure—about two quarts—of the first reaping of barley that was offered on the second day of Passover, the sixteenth of Nisan. Before the bringing of the *omer*, new cereals of that year's crop were forbidden for use.

**(23:24) Speak to the children of Israel and say: The first day of the seventh month—Tishri—shall be a day of rest for you. It is a sacred holiday for remembrance and sounding of *teruah*, blowing the shofar.**

### ※ *The Talmud Teaches*
*a remembrance and sounding of teruah (sounding of the ram's horn)* It was taught: The present verse says "A remembrance of *teruah*," and another verse says "A day of *teruah* shall there be for you" (Numbers 29:1). How can the verses be reconciled? The Gemara answers: The first applies to Rosh Hashanah that falls on Shabbat, when the shofar is not blown, but is "remembered" in verses; the second applies to Rosh Hashanah that falls on a weekday, when we do blow the shofar *(Rosh Hashanah 32a)*.

**(23:32) Yom Kippur is a Sabbath of Sabbaths to you, and a day when you must fast; on the ninth of the month in the**

evening—from evening to evening—must you keep this holiday.

### ✖ *The Talmud Teaches*
*On the ninth of the month* Now, do we then fast on the ninth of the month? Why, we fast on the *tenth!* But this teaches you that if you eat and drink on the ninth, Scripture considers it as if you fasted on the ninth and the tenth (*Berachot* 8b).

**(23:40) You shall take for yourselves on the first day [of Sukkot] the fruit of a citron tree, the branches of date palms, twigs of a plaited tree, and brook willows; and you shall rejoice before the Lord your God for seven days.**

### ✖ *The Talmud Teaches*
*You shall take* The Rabbis taught: It says *ulekachtem*, "you shall take," which may be seen as a combination of *ulekach*, "take," and *tam*, "whole," implying that the taking must be complete. Which means that if one of the four species is missing, it invalidates all of them because the bundle is incomplete. Implied also is that the four species must be perfect; if the tip of any of them is broken, all are invalidated (*Sukkah* 34b).

NOTE: The present verse commands the taking of the four species on Sukkot. They are a citron, *etrog;* a palm branch, *lulav;* three myrtle twigs, *hadassim;* and two willow twigs, *aravot.* The *lulav, hadassim,* and *aravot* are bound together and held in the right hand; the *etrog* is held in the left hand when the blessing is recited. The *lulav* bundle is taken in hand by every Jew, every day of Sukkot, except on Shabbat.

### ✳ *The Maimonides Code of Law Teaches*
*And you shall rejoice* Although it is a mitzvah to rejoice on all the festivals, on Sukkot there was an extra measure of rejoicing in the Temple, for it says "And you shall rejoice before the Lord your God seven days" (Rambam, *Hilchot Lulav* 3:11).

**(23:42) During these seven days you must live in *sukkot*, every native in Israel must live in *sukkot*.**

※ *The Talmud Teaches*
**You must live in sukkot** A *sukkah* that is higher than twenty ells is unfit for the mitzvah of *sukkah*. From where do we know this? Rava said: It says "During these seven days, you must live in *sukkot*." The Torah is telling you: For seven days, you should leave your permanent home and live in a temporary dwelling. Up to twenty ells, a person builds a structure as a temporary home, but no one builds a structure higher than twenty ells to use as a temporary home (*Sukkah* 2a).

NOTE: A *sukkah* is a temporary dwelling or booth in which we dwell during the festival of Sukkot. The temporary quality of a *sukkah* comes to the fore mainly in its roof or cover, called *s'chach*. Anything that grows from the ground and has been cut off qualifies as material for *s'chach*.

**You must live in sukkot** Similar to the way you live in your permanent home. During all the seven days of Sukkot, you should make the *sukkah* your permanent home and your house a temporary dwelling. How so? If you have beautiful vessels and beautiful spreads, you should take them into the *sukkah*. Also, you eat, drink, and learn in the *sukkah* (*Sukkah* 28b).

## THE MENORAH

**(24:3) Aaron shall light the menorah consistently with this oil. It shall burn before God, from evening to morning, outside the cloth partition in the communion tent. This shall be an eternal law for all your generations.**

※ *The Talmud Teaches*
**outside the cloth partition in the communion tent** Does God then need the light of the menorah? Surely, during the forty years that the Jews traveled in the wilderness, they traveled only by His spiritual light! Rather, it means that the light of the menorah is evidence to mankind that the Shechinah rests in Israel. What was the evidence? Rav said: It was the western lamp of the Menorah into which the same quantity of oil was poured as into the other lamps, and yet he would begin lighting all the other lamps with it and end with it (*Shabbat* 23b).

NOTE: Half a *log* of oil (about six fluid ounces) was poured into each lamp; and by morning, they were burned out except for the western lamp. The following evening, the *kohen* cleaned out the old wicks, poured in fresh oil, and lit the menorah again; yet the western lamp was still burning. This miracle was evidence that the Shechinah rested in Israel.

## PENALTIES

**(24:22) There shall be one law for you, it shall be for the convert and native alike, for I, the Lord, am your God.**

### *The Talmud Teaches*

***There shall be one law for you*** R. Chanina said: According to the Torah, both capital cases and monetary litigations require a thorough examination of the witnesses about the day, the hour, and the accompanying circumstances. Why then did the Sages contravene the Torah, saying that in monetary litigations, no such thorough cross-examination is needed? In order not to "bolt the door to borrowers" (*Sanhedrin* 3a).

NOTE: "Bolting the door to borrowers" means that people would be reluctant to lend money for fear that they would be unable to collect if the creditor denied the loan; and in the ensuing rigorous cross-examination, the testimony of the witnesses would be rejected on a technicality. That's why in monetary litigations the Sages dispensed with the exhaustive examination of the witnesses.

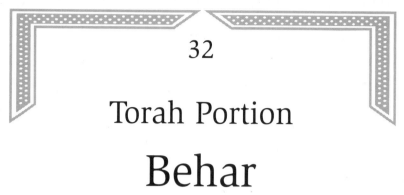

# 32

## Torah Portion

# Behar

### Leviticus 25:1–26:2

## THE SABBATICAL YEAR

**(25:1) God spoke to Moses on Mount Sinai, saying . . .**

❋ *The Midrash Teaches*
***God spoke to Moses on Mount Sinai, saying*** In this portion, the laws of *shemittah*—the Sabbatical Year—are outlined in great detail. Why are we told in this verse that the laws of *shemittah* were given at Mount Sinai? Were not all the laws given at Sinai? By associating the laws of *shemittah* with Mount Sinai, the Torah teaches us that just as the mitzvah of *shemittah* was given in the Torah with all its rules and details, so were all laws revealed on Sinai with all their rules and particulars, even though the Torah mentions them only in general terms *(Torat Kohanim).*

NOTE: For example, the Torah says that we should make zizith, but it does not specify how many threads and knots the zizith must contain. These details were taught in the Oral Torah, which Moses received on Sinai.

**(25:11) It shall also be a Jubilee Year for you—this fiftieth year—insofar as you may not sow, harvest crops growing of their own accord, nor gather grapes from unpruned vines during that year.**

✳ *The Talmud Teaches*
*It shall also be a Jubilee Year—this fiftieth year*  You count
the fiftieth year as the Jubilee Year and not the fifty-first year
(*Rosh Hashanah* 9a).

NOTE: This means that the Jubilee Year is not part of the *shemittah* cycle; you do not count the fiftieth year both as the Jubilee
and as the first of the next *shemittah* cycle. Accordingly, every
forty-ninth year, there are two consecutive Sabbatical Years,
the forty-ninth, which is the *shemittah* year, and the fiftieth,
which is the Jubilee Year. Thus, the fifty-first year is the first year
of the new *shemittah* cycle.

## KINDNESS TO OTHERS

**(25:17) You shall not wrong one another. You shall fear your
God, since it is I who am God, your Lord.**

✳ *The Talmud Teaches*
*You shall fear God*  About things that you know in your heart to
be wrong—although they do not appear to be wrong to others—
it says "You shall fear God," who knows your innermost
thoughts (*Kiddushin* 32b).

NOTE: For example: arousing false hopes in a merchant by asking the price of an article that you have no intention of buying.
Only you and God know what you had in mind.

**(25:35) When your brother becomes impoverished and loses
the ability to support himself in your community, you must
come to his aid. Help him survive, whether he is a convert
or sojourner.**

✳ *The Midrash Teaches*
*When your brother becomes impoverished and loses the abil-
ity to support himself*  Do not allow him to slide down into
indigence. It is like the load on an animal's back. As long as it is
up there, a single person can grab it and set it right. Once it has
fallen to the ground, not even five can get it back again *(Torat
Kohanim)*.

## ✳ *The Talmud Teaches*

**Whether he is a convert or a sojourner [ger vetoshav]** *Ger* refers to a *ger tzedek,* a "righteous convert," one who accepts all the mitzvoth; *toshav,* a "sojourner," refers to a non-Jew who has not entirely adopted Jewish nationality. He renounced idolatry and accepted the seven Noahide laws of the duties of mankind in general. He thereby acquired the right to live in the Land of Israel *(Torat Kohanim).*

**(25:36) Do not take interest and increase from him. Fear your God, and let your brother live with you.**

## ✳ *The Talmud Teaches*

**Let your brother live with you** If two men are traveling through a desert, and one has a pitcher of water, and there is not enough water to slake the thirst of two people, so that if both drink, both will die; but if one drinks, he can reach the nearest village and survive. Ben Petirah taught: It is better that both should drink and die, rather than that one should watch his friend perish. Until R. Akiva came and taught: It says "Let your brother live with you," which implies that your life takes precedence over your fellow's life *(Bava Metzia* 62a).

NOTE: "With you" denotes that your fellow takes second place to you.

**(25:38) I am God your Lord, who brought you out of Egypt to give you the land of Canaan, and to be a God for you.**

## ✳ *The Talmud Teaches*

**to be a God for you** You should always live in the Land of Israel, even in a city where the majority are Gentiles, rather than outside the Land of Israel, even in a city where the majority are Jews. For whoever lives in the Land of Israel is considered to have a God, and whoever lives outside the Land of Israel is considered as though he worshipped idols. For it says "To give you the land of Canaan, and to be a God to you" *(Ketubot* 110b).

**(25:55) For the children of Israel are servants to Me, they are My servants, whom I have taken out of the land of Egypt—I am God your Lord.**

### ✳ *The Talmud Teaches*

***For the children of Israel are servants to Me*** It says if the
Hebrew slave does not want to go free after serving for six
years, "his master shall pierce his ear with an awl" (Exodus
21:6). R. Yochanan b. Zakkai used to explain this verse with an
allegory: Why was the ear singled out from all the other limbs
in the body to be pierced? God said: The ear that heard My
voice on Mount Sinai when I proclaimed, "For the children of
Israel are servants to Me, they are My servants," and not servants of servants—the master himself is a servant, namely, a
servant of God—and yet this man went and acquired a master
for himself, when he had the opportunity to go free—this ear
should be pierced (*Kiddushin* 22a)!

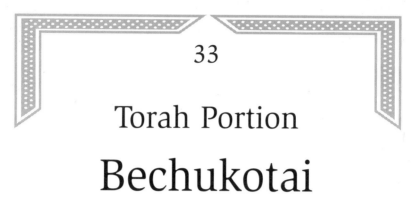

# 33

## Torah Portion

# Bechukotai

### Leviticus 26:3–27:34

## REWARD FOR OBEDIENCE

**(26:3) If you follow My laws and are careful to keep My commandments . . .**

✷ *The Talmud Teaches*
*If you follow My laws* In the verse, "If you follow My laws," the word *if* is used in the sense of a plea, that is, "if only you would follow My laws," as in the verse, "If only My people would listen to Me . . . then I would subdue their enemies at once" (Psalms 81:14, 15), or as in the verse, "If only you would heed My commands! Then your prosperity would flow like a river" (Isaiah 48:18) (*Avodah Zarah* 5a).

**(26:4) I will provide your rains at the right time, so that the land will bear its crops, and the trees of the field will provide fruit.**

✷ *The Midrash Teaches*
*I will provide your rains at the right time* It says "*your* rains" and not the rains of all the other countries. There will be abundance in the Land of Israel and hunger in all the other countries, so that they will come and buy grain and produce from you, bringing you prosperity *(Torat Kohanim).*

## ※ *The Talmud Teaches*

*at the right time* What is "the right time"? It means that the
earth will not be drenched with rain nor will it be parched, but
the rain will come just in the right amount. Overabundant rain
makes the earth muddy, so that it yields no fruit. Another explanation: "At the right time" means that it will rain only at times
when it will not inconvenience people, namely on Wednesday
night and Friday night (*Taanit* 22b).

NOTE: Rashi explains that on Wednesday night people used to
stay indoors because of a demon that roamed the streets on that
night, and on Friday night everyone stayed at home to enjoy
Shabbat.

**(26:5) You will have so much that your threshing season will
last until your grape harvest, and your grape harvest will last
until the time you plant. You will have your fill of food, and
you will live securely in the land.**

## ✳ *The Midrash Teaches*

*You will have your fill of food* The point is not that a person
will eat a lot and be satisfied, but rather that he will eat little and
"have his fill of food." As it says "He will bless your bread
and your water" (Exodus 23:25) *(Torat Kohanim)*.

**(26:8) Five of you will be able to chase away a hundred, and
a hundred of you will pursue ten thousand, as your enemies
fall before your sword.**

## ✳ *The Midrash Teaches*

*A hundred of you will pursue ten thousand* Is that the right
proportion? If five defeat one hundred, it takes five hundred—
not one hundred—to defeat ten thousand! The answer is: There
is no comparison between many who observe the Torah and
few who observe it; the power of the many grows exponentially
*(Torat Kohanim)*.

## THE *TOCHACHAH:*
## REPROOF FOR DISOBEDIENCE

**(26:14) But this is what will happen if you do not listen to Me, and do not keep all these commandments.**

✻ *The Midrash Teaches*
*If you do not listen to Me* I might think that this passage refers to disobedience of what is written in the Torah. That cannot be the intent, for the passage continues, "and do not keep all these commandments," which would be redundant. How then am I to understand "If you do not listen to Me"? It means: If you do not listen to the interpretations of the Sages who derive the details of the mitzvoth from Scriptural verses *(Torat Kohanim)*.

**(26:37) They will stumble over one another as if chased by the sword, even when there is no one pursuing. You will have no means of standing up before your foes.**

✻ *The Talmud Teaches*
*They will stumble over one another* Literally, "a man over his brother": One man will fall because of the sin of his brother, which teaches us that all Jews are responsible for one another *(Sanhedrin* 27b).

**(26:42) I will remember My covenant with Jacob, also My covenant with Isaac, and I will remember also My covenant with Abraham. I will remember the land.**

✻ *The Midrash Teaches*
*I will remember My covenant with Jacob* Why are Abraham and Isaac qualified by the word *also* but not Jacob? The word *also* suggests that Abraham and Isaac rank below Jacob. To teach us that the children of Jacob were flawless *(Torat Kohanim)*.

NOTE: Unlike Abraham who had a wayward son Ishmael and Isaac who had the wicked son Esau, all of Jacob's children were righteous.

*My covenant with Isaac* Why is the term *remember* mentioned with respect to Abraham and Jacob but not with respect to

Isaac? Because God does much more than merely remember Isaac. God constantly sees his ashes heaped on the altar *(Torat Kohanim)*.

NOTE: The Midrash is referring to the ashes of the ram that Abraham offered as a burnt offering instead of Isaac. God constantly views these ashes as heaped upon the altar on which Isaac willingly let himself be bound at the binding of Isaac. The term remember does not apply to something you see in front of your eyes. That's why the word *remember* is not used with regard to Isaac.

**(26:44) Thus, even when they are in their enemies' land, I will not grow so disgusted with them, nor so tired of them that I would destroy them and break My covenant with them, since I am the Lord their God.**

### ※ *The Talmud Teaches*
*I will not grow so disgusted with . . . them* Shmuel expounded: "I will not grow so disgusted with them"—this refers to the times of the Greek occupation of the Land of Israel; "nor so tired of them"—this refers to the times of the Roman emperor Vespasian whose forces destroyed the Second Temple; "that I would destroy them"—in the days of Haman; "and break My covenant with them"—during the long exile that followed the destruction of the Temple; "for I am the Lord their God"—I will protect them during the times of Gog and Magog, the climactic war that will usher in the end of days and the messianic era *(Megillah* 11a).

**(27:34) These are the commandments that God gave Moses for the children of Israel at Mount Sinai.**

### ※ *The Talmud Teaches*
*These are the commandments* The passage, "*These* are the commandments" implies only these and no others. From this, we derive that a prophet is not permitted to innovate any new law from this point on *(Shabbat* 104a).

✳ *The Midrash Teaches*
*at Mount Sinai* This teaches us that all mitzvoth with their details and inferences were stated on Sinai *(Torat Kohanim)*.

# Numbers

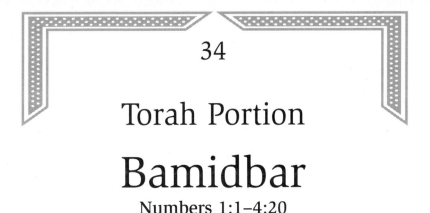

# 34

# Torah Portion

# Bamidbar

### Numbers 1:1–4:20

## THE ASSIGNMENT OF THE LEVITES

**(1:51) When the tabernacle is ready to set out, the Levites shall take it down, and when it is to be pitched, the Levites shall set it up. Any non-Levite who comes close shall die.**

### ※ *The Talmud Teaches*

*Any non-Levite who comes close shall die* The story is told about a non-Jew who came to Hillel and asked, "Would you make me a convert on condition that I be appointed high priest?" Hillel told him, "First, go and study the Torah and the laws of priesthood." He went and started to learn. When he came to the verse, "Any non-Levite who comes close shall die," he asked, "To whom does this verse apply?" "Even to David, king of Israel," Hillel replied.

NOTE: Hillel chose David as an example because David was a descendant of Ruth, who was a convert; yet even though he was a king, he was included in the prohibition. In light of this, the convert would understand that he had no prospect of becoming a high priest (*Shabbat* 31a).

**(2:17) The communion tent and the camp of the Levites shall journey in the middle of the other camps. The people shall travel in the same order as they camp. Each person shall be in his place, according to each one's banner.**

## ❖ The Jerusalem Talmud Teaches

**The people shall travel in the same order as they camp** How did the children of Israel travel in the desert? R. Chama b. Chanina and R. Hoshaya differ on this. One says: In a boxlike formation: Judah in the east, Reuben in the south, Ephraim in the west, and Dan in the north. The other says: In a straight column: Judah, followed by Reuben, Ephraim, and Dan. The one who says "In a boxlike formation" bases himself on "They shall travel in the same order as they camp," and they camped in that configuration. The one who says "In a straight column" bases himself on the fact that Dan is referred to as "the rear guard of all the camps" (10:25); thus, Dan was at the end of the procession (Jerusalem Talmud, *Eruvin* 5:1).

**(3:1) These are the offspring of Aaron and Moses on the day God spoke with Moses at Mount Sinai.**

## ❖ The Talmud Teaches

**These are the offspring of Aaron and Moses** [The verse announces the listing of the offspring of both Aaron and Moses but gives only the names of Aaron's sons.] R. Shmuel b. Nachmani said: [Moses was the one who taught Torah to Aaron's sons, and] whoever teaches his fellow's son Torah is regarded by Scripture as if he had fathered that son. For it says "These are the children of Aaron and Moses," and the next verse reads, "These are the names of Aaron's sons" (*Sanhedrin* 19b).

NOTE: Because Moses taught Torah to Aaron's sons, he is considered their spiritual father.

**(3:4) Nadav and Avihu died before God when they offered an unauthorized fire before God in the wilderness of Sinai, and they had no children; but Elazar and Itamar ministered during the lifetime of Aaron their father.**

## ❖ The Talmud Teaches

**They had no children** The Shechinah does not rest on less than a group of twenty-two thousand Jews. Suppose Israel comprised twenty-two thousand less one person, and one individual did not get married, does he not by the fact that he did not have a

child push away the Shechinah from Israel? For he could bring
the twenty-two thousandth into the world. Abba Chanan said:
He deserves a harsh punishment, for it says Nadav and Avihu
died, "and they had no children," because they did not get married. From this, we can infer that if they had children, they
would not have died (*Yevamot* 64a).

**(3:38) Camping to the east, in front of the tabernacle, shall
be Moses and Aaron and his sons, those who keep charge of
the sanctuary as a trust for the Israelites. Any unauthorized
person who includes himself shall die.**

�֍ *The Talmud Teaches*
*Any unauthorized person who includes himself shall die*
What is meant by "unauthorized person"? It cannot be meant
in the literal sense, for that has already been stated (3:10). It
must refer then to a person who is unauthorized to perform a
particular service. For example: If a Levite whose service was
singing took on the assignment of guarding the gate, he incurred the death penalty at the hand of heaven (*Arachin* 11b).

**(4:3) The census of the children of Kehat shall include those
from thirty to fifty years old, all who enter service to work
in the communion tent.**

✖ *The Talmud Teaches*
*From thirty . . . years* And elsewhere, it says "From twenty-
five years and up, the Levites shall participate in the work force
in the tabernacle" (8:24). How can the two passages be reconciled? Like this: At the age of twenty-five, a Levite enters the
work force as a trainee; and at the age of thirty, he begins to
perform the service. This is the premise for the saying: If a student does not make progress in his studies after five years, he
never will (*Chullin* 24a).

NOTE: Rashi explains that the work of the Levites entailed dismantling and raising the communion tent, chanting the hymns,
and playing the instruments that accompany the bringing of the
sacrifices.

# 35

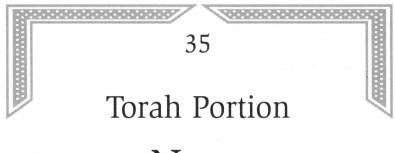

# Torah Portion

# Naso

Numbers 4:21–7:89

## PURIFYING THE CAMP

**(5:1, 2) God spoke to Moses saying: Instruct the children of Israel to send out of the camp everyone who has a leprous mark or a male discharge, and all who are ritually defiled by the dead.**

*The Talmud Teaches*

***to send out of the camp*** R. Yose said: It is not the place that honors the person who lives there; it is the person who honors the place. We find an illustration of this in connection with the tabernacle in the wilderness. As long as it remained pitched, the Torah commanded, "to send out of the camp everyone who has a leprous mark or a male discharge"; but once the curtain of the tabernacle was rolled up to be transported to a new site, both those with a male discharge and a leprous mark were permitted to enter the camp, for it was the Shechinah dwelling in the tabernacle that honored the camp (*Taanit* 21b).

## OFFERINGS

**(5:10) Every man's sacred offering shall be his; only that which a man gives to the priest belongs to him.**

*The Talmud Teaches*

***shall be his*** When a Jew sets aside part of his possessions as priestly gifts, the gift is his in the sense that he retains the right

to decide which *kohen* should receive it. R. Yochanan said: If someone keeps for himself the gifts that he is required to turn over to the priests, God will punish him by depriving him of his prosperity and leaving him with nothing more than the small amount that he should have given away to God's servants, as it says "Every man's holy things shall be his." R. Nachman b. Yitzchak said: Whoever has priestly gifts and gives them to the *kohen* will become wealthy, as it says figuratively "Whatever a man gives to the *kohen* will belong to the giver" (*Berachot* 63a).

✳ *The Midrash Teaches*
**Every man's sacred offerings shall be his** I might think that the *kohen* could forcibly seize the priestly gifts. That's why it says "Every man's sacred offerings shall be his": The owner shall have the option of giving the gifts to whichever *kohen* he wishes. No *kohen* can demand it from him *(Sifrei)*.

## THE SUSPECTED ADULTERESS

**(5:12) Speak to the children of Israel and say to them: Any man whose wife shall go astray and commits an act of disloyalty against him . . .**

❊ *The Talmud Teaches*
**Speak to the children of Israel** R. Yochanan said: Why does the section dealing with the *sotah*, "the suspected adulteress," follow immediately after the section of the priestly gifts? To tell you that if someone has priestly gifts or tithes and does not give them to the *kohen*, he will end up suspecting his wife of infidelity and need the services of a *kohen* to administer the ordeal of the bitter waters that the *sotah* has to submit to (*Berachot* 63a).

**(5:18) The priest shall stand the woman before God and uncover her hair, and upon her palms he shall place the meal-offering of remembrance—it is a meal-offering of jealousy. In the priest's hand shall be the bitter waters that cause curse.**

✳ *The Midrash Teaches*
**The priest shall . . . uncover her hair** R. Yishmael said: "The priest shall . . . uncover her hair." This teaches us that the

married daughters of Israel cover their hair. And although there
is no proof for this, there is an allusion to it, for it says "And
Tamar, after she was raped by Amnon, placed a cloth on her
head" (2 Samuel 13:19) *(Sifrei)*.

### ✸ The Jerusalem Talmud Teaches
**The bitter waters that cause curse** R. Tanchuma said: The numeric value of *hame'arerim,* "that cause curse" [5 + 40 + 1 +
200 + 200 + 10 + 40 = 496], equals the total of her 248
organs and the 248 organs of her partner in adultery (Jerusalem
Talmud, *Sotah* 2:2).

**(5:19) The priest shall administer an oath to the woman, say-
ing to her, "If no man has lain with you, and you have not
committed adultery so as to be defiled to your husband, you
shall be unharmed by these bitter waters that cause curse."**

### ✸ The Talmud Teaches
**If no man has lain with you** It was taught: Helena, the queen
of Adiabene, a small kingdom in northern Mesopotamia [now
Iraq], had a golden tablet made on which was inscribed the
oath of the *sotah,* so that when the scribe would write it out on
parchment, he would copy it from the tablet, and there would
be no need to take out a Torah scroll from which to copy it. And
what was written on it? "If a man has lain with you"; "if no
man has lain with you"; "if you have committed adultery"; "if
you have not committed adultery" (*Yoma* 37b).

**(5:24) The priest shall then make the woman drink the bit-
ter waters that cause curse, and waters that cause curse shall
come into her.**

### ✸ The Talmud Teaches
**The waters . . . shall come into her** Why is it written twice,
here and again in verse 22? To teach that just as the waters test
her, so do they test her partner in adultery, when they are
administered to her. When she is found guilty, the waters will
have the same effect on him as they do on her; his thigh
will also rupture, and his belly will also blow up. And just as
she is forbidden to her husband, so is she forbidden to her partner in adultery (*Sotah* 27b).

**(5:27) When the woman drinks the water, if she has been defiled and untrue to her husband, the waters that cause curse will enter her body to poison her, causing her belly to blow up and her thigh to rupture. The woman will be a curse among her people.**

✳ *The Midrash Teaches*
***The woman will be a curse*** When people will curse someone, they will use her as an example, saying, "What happened to this *sotah* should happen to you!" *(Sifrei).*

▓ *The Jerusalem Talmud Teaches*
***among her people*** When adultery became commonplace, the bitter waters became ineffective. For it says "The woman will be a curse among her people"—only when the people are moral but not when they are promiscuous (Jerusalem Talmud, *Sotah* 9:9).

NOTE: When the majority is promiscuous, she is one of them; and people will not utter curses by naming her.

**(5:28) However, if the woman is pure and has not been defiled to her husband, she will remain unharmed and will become pregnant.**

▒ *The Talmud Teaches*
***She will become pregnant*** If she used to have difficult childbirths, she will give birth in comfort; if she had only girls, she will now give birth to boys; if her babies were short, she will have tall ones; if she used to give birth to swarthy children, she will have fair children *(Sotah* 26a).

**(5:31) If the husband is free of guilt, then the wife has to bear her guilt.**

▒ *The Talmud Teaches*
***If the husband is free of guilt*** If the husband is free from every sexual misbehavior, the waters are effective in testing his wife; when the husband is not free of immoral behavior, the waters do not test his wife. Therefore, when adultery became widespread, the bitter waters became ineffective *(Sotah* 47b).

NOTE: R. Samson Raphael Hirsch comments: God's laws of morality grant men in no way greater license for sexual irregularities than they do for women.

## THE NAZIRITE

**(6:1, 2) God spoke to Moses, telling him to speak to the children of Israel and say to them: This is the law when a man or woman expresses a Nazirite vow of abstinence to God.**

### ※ *The Talmud Teaches*
***Speak to the children of Israel*** Rebbi said: Why is the section of the *nazir* placed immediately after the section of the *sotah*? To teach that whoever sees a *sotah* in her degradation should abstain from wine, because wine dulls the mind, leading him to commit adultery (*Sotah* 2b).

NOTE: A *nazir*, or "Nazirite," is a person who took a vow to attain a higher degree of holiness. He must abstain from drinking wine; he must let his hair grow; and he may not come into contact with the dead. Ordinarily, the Nazirite vow is for a term of thirty days.

***expresses a Nazirite vow of abstinence to God*** Shimon Hatzaddik said: Once a man from the south came to me. He had beautiful eyes, a handsome appearance, and his thick locks were arranged in jet-black ringlets. He had taken the Nazirite vow and came to bring his sacrifice and to shave his head, which a *nazir* must do at the end of his Nazirite term. So I asked him, "What prompted you to become a *nazir* and to destroy your beautiful hair?" He replied, "Back home, I was a shepherd. Once, while drawing water from the well, I gazed at my reflection in the water. At that moment, my evil impulse took hold of me and tried to make me lose my share in the world to come by filling me with pride. But I said to my lust, 'Good-for-nothing! Why are you proud of something that is destined to become dust, worms, and maggots? I swear, I will become a *nazir* so that I will be forced to shave off this beautiful head of hair for the sake of heaven!'" Continued Shimon Hatzaddik: "Then I got up, kissed him on his head and said to him, 'May there be many more Nazirites like you in Israel. You became a *nazir* for the right reason, namely, to subdue your evil impulse; not in order to flaunt your piety. Of Nazirites like you, it says 'If a man or woman expresses a Nazirite vow of abstinence to God'" (*Nedarim* 9b and *Nazir* 4b).

**(6:11) On the eighth day, the *nazir* must bring two turtle doves. The priest shall prepare one turtle dove as a sin offering and one as a burnt offering to atone for him for having sinned against the soul; and he shall sanctify his head on that day.**

※ *The Talmud Teaches*
*for having sinned against the soul* R. Elazar Hakappar said: It says that the *nazir* has to "atone for having sinned against the soul." Against which soul has the *nazir* sinned? Against his own soul, because he tormented himself by abstaining from wine. And we can draw a logical inference from this: If a person who torments himself only in regard to wine is called a sinner, how much more so is a person called a sinner if he mortifies himself by denying himself all enjoyment. Thus, anyone who fasts as an ascetic practice is called a sinner (*Nedarim* 10a).

## THE PRIESTLY BLESSING

**(6:23) Speak to Aaron and his sons, saying: This is how you must bless the children of Israel. Say to them . . .**

※ *The Talmud Teaches*
*This is how you must bless* It was taught: R. Yehoshua b. Levi said in the name of Bar Kappara: Why does the section dealing with the priestly blessing follow immediately after the section of the *nazir*? In order to teach you that, just as the *nazir* is forbidden to drink wine, so is the *kohen* who is about to recite the priestly blessing forbidden to drink wine. From here, we derive that a *kohen* who is intoxicated may not raise his hand to bless the congregation, because his mind is confused (*Taanit* 26b).

*This is how you must bless the children of Israel*
This tells me only about the children—literally: "the sons"—of
Israel. From where do I derive that converts, women, and servants are included in the blessing? From "Say to them"—to *all*
of them (*Sotah* 38a).

**(6:24) May God bless you and keep you.**

✳ *The Midrash Teaches*
*May God bless you* With the explicit blessing: "Blessed will you
be in the city, and blessed in the field. Blessed will be the fruit of
your . . . womb. . . . Blessed will you be when you come and
blessed when you go" (Deuteronomy 28:3 and following) *(Sifrei)*.

*and keep you* May He keep for you the covenant of your forefathers, as it says "God your Lord will keep for you the covenant
and the love with which He made an oath to your forefathers"
(Deuteronomy 7:12) *(Sifrei)*.

**(6:25) May God illuminate His countenance for you, and be
gracious to you.**

✳ *The Midrash Teaches*
*May God . . . illuminate* "Illuminate" refers to the light of the
Torah, as it says "For the mitzvah is a lamp, and the Torah,
light" (Proverbs 6:23) *(Sifrei)*.

*and be gracious to you* Let him be gracious to you in granting
your requests. An alternative view: Let Him grant you grace in
the eyes of men, as it says "He granted Joseph grace in the eyes
of the overseer of the prison" (Genesis 39:21) *(Sifrei)*.

**(6:26) May God bestow favor on you, and establish peace for
you.**

✳ *The Talmud Teaches*
*May God bestow favor on you* R. Avira expounded: The ministering angels said to God: Master of the universe! It is written
in Your Torah "The awesome God who does not bestow favor,
and who does not take bribes" (Deuteronomy 10:17). Is that so?

Aren't You showing favor to Israel? For it says "May God bestow favor on You"? Replied God: Why shouldn't I show favor to Israel! Look, I wrote in the Torah, "When you eat and are satisfied, you must bless God your Lord" (Deuteronomy 8:10). I said they should bless only when they are satiated, but they are so stringent that even when they eat as little as the size of an olive or an egg, they recite Birkat Hamazon, Grace after Meals (*Berachot* 20b).

✳ *The Midrash Teaches*
*and grant you peace* This is the peace of Torah, as it says "God gives strength—the Torah—to His people; God blesses His people with peace" *(Sifrei).*

(6:27) **The priests will link My name with the children of Israel, and I will bless them.**

✳ *The Talmud Teaches*
*They will link My name with the children of Israel* R. Yehoshua b. Levi also said: Every *kohen* who blesses is blessed himself, for it says "I will bless those who bless you" (Genesis 12:3).

R. Yehoshua b. Levi also said: From where do we know that God yearns to hear the priestly blessing? From "The priests will link My name with the children of Israel, and I will bless them" (*Sotah* 38b).

NOTE: Maharsha explains: God could bless Israel Himself, but He designated the *kohanim* to bless, because He yearns to hear their blessing.

*and I will bless them* R. Yishmael said: We learned that the *kohanim* bless the Jewish people, but who blesses them? However, "and I will bless them" teaches us that although the *kohanim* bless the Jewish people, God blesses the *kohanim* (*Chullin* 49a).

## THE DEDICATION OF THE TABERNACLE

(7:1) **On the day that Moses finished erecting the tabernacle, he anointed it and sanctified it along with all utensils.**

He also anointed the altar and all its utensils and thus sanctified them.

### ✺ The Jerusalem Talmud Teaches

**On the day that Moses finished erecting the tabernacle** It does not say, "On the day that Moses erected the tabernacle." This teaches us that on each of the seven days of dedication, Moses set up the tabernacle and took it apart, but on the eighth day, the first of Nisan, he set it up and did not take it apart, as it says "On the day that Moses finished erecting the tabernacle"—meaning, on the day that the process of setting it up and dismantling it came to an end (Jerusalem Talmud, *Yoma* 1:1).

**(7:9) He did not give any wagons to the sons of Kehat; since they had the responsibility for the most sacred articles, which they had to carry on their shoulders.**

### ✺ The Talmud Teaches

**He did not give any wagons to the sons of Kehat** Rava expounded: Why was David punished in that Uzzah died because of him? Because he called the words of the Torah "songs." For David said, "Your statutes were songs to me" (Psalms 119:54). God said to him: The Torah is so exalted and profound; how could you call it "songs"! I will make you stumble on something even schoolchildren know. For it says "Moses did not give any wagons to the sons of Kehat, since they had the responsibility for the most sacred articles, which they had to carry on their shoulders," and yet you, David, brought the ark on a wagon rather than have it carried, and this error resulted in Uzzah's death (*Sotah* 35a).

NOTE: When David transported the ark to Jerusalem, he placed it on a wagon pulled by oxen. At one point, it seemed that the ark would fall to the ground. Not realizing that the ark was so holy that it carried itself, Uzzah impulsively grasped it to steady it. God became angry at Uzzah for not respecting the holiness of the ark, "and he died there for the blunder he had made" (2 Samuel 6:6–8). David was upset with himself for failing to make the necessary precautions to avoid such a mishap.

**(7:89) When Moses came into the communion tent to speak with God, he would hear the Voice speaking with him from between the two cherubs on the ark cover over the ark of testimony. God thus spoke with him.**

***The Talmud Teaches***

***He heard the Voice speaking with him*** It does not say "speaking *to him*" but "speaking *with him,*" which denotes a closer and more exclusive conversation. This teaches us that Moses heard the Voice, but not all of Israel heard it (*Yoma* 4b).

# 36

# Torah Portion

# Beha'alotecha

Numbers 8:1–12:16

## THE MENORAH

(8:4) This is the workmanship of the menorah, hammered-out gold, from its base to its flower it is hammered out; according to the vision that God showed Moses, so did he make the menorah.

※ *The Talmud Teaches*
*This is the workmanship of the menorah* Moses had difficulty grasping the structure of the menorah because of its many details and ornaments until God showed him a model of the menorah, pointing at it with His finger. For it says "*This* is the workmanship of the menorah." "This" implies that God pointed it out to him (*Menachot* 29b).

## TRAVELING THROUGH THE WILDERNESS

(10:25) Then journeyed the banner of the camp of the children of Dan, the rear guard of all the camps, according to their legions. Heading that legion was Achiezer son of Amishaddai.

※ *The Jerusalem Talmud Teaches*
*The rear guard of all the camps* Why was the tribe of Dan the rear guard of all the camps? Because it was the most numerous of the tribes. It traveled last, so that if someone up front had

lost something, they would return it to him. Because they occupied a wide area at the end of the column, it was more likely for them to find it (Jerusalem Talmud, *Eruvin* 5:1).

**(10:33) The children of Israel marched the distance of a three-day journey from God's mountain. The ark of God's covenant traveled three days ahead of them to find them a place to settle.**

### ✺ *The Talmud Teaches*
***They marched from God's mountain*** What is meant by "God's mountain"? R. Chama b. R. Chanina said: This is Mount Sinai, and "They marched from God's mountain" alludes to the fact that three days after leaving Mount Sinai, they strayed from God, complaining about the monotony of the manna and the lack of meat (11:4) (*Shabbat* 116a).

## COMPLAINTS

**(11:8) The people would stroll and gather the manna. They would then grind it in a hand mill and crush it in a mortar, cooking it in a pan and making it into cakes. It tasted like an oil wafer—*leshad hashamen.***

### ✺ *The Talmud Teaches*
***It tasted like an oil wafer [leshad]*** R. Abbahu said: What is the meaning of *leshad*? Just as a nursing infant tastes many flavors in the breast, *shad*, depending on what the mother has eaten, so did the Jewish people find many tastes in the manna they ate (*Yoma* 75a).

**(11:10) Moses heard the people weeping in their family groups near the entrance of their tents. God became very angry, and Moses also considered it wrong.**

### ✺ *The Talmud Teaches*
***Weeping in their family groups*** The word *family* alludes to the underlying reason for their complaints. They were frustrated over the family laws that prohibited illicit relations (*Shabbat* 130a).

**(11:20) God is going to give you meat for a full month; you will eat it until it is coming out of your nose and making you nauseated. This is because you rejected God now that He is among you, and you whined before Him, saying, "Why did we ever leave Egypt."**

### ※ *The Talmud Teaches*
*for a full month* And later, in verse 33, it says "The meat was still between their teeth when the people began to die," implying that they died as soon as they began to eat it; so they did not eat meat for an entire month. How can these verses be reconciled? The ordinary people died immediately; the wicked ones continued to suffer for an entire month (*Yoma* 75b).

**(11:22) Moses said: Even if all the cattle and sheep were slaughtered, could there be enough for them? If all the fish in the sea were caught, would it be sufficient?**

### ※ *The Talmud Teaches*
*if all the fish in the sea were caught* From here, we derive that fish are not slaughtered; merely catching them is sufficient for eating them (*Chullin* 27b).

**(11:26) Two men remained in the camp, the name of one was Eldad, and the name of the other was Medad, and the spirit rested upon them; they were among those registered, but they had not gone out to the tent, and they prophesied in the camp.**

### ※ *The Talmud Teaches*
*Two men remained in the camp* When God told Moses, "Assemble seventy of Israel's elders" (11:16), Eldad and Medad said, "We are not worthy of such a high appointment"; and that is why they remained in the camp. So God said: "Because you have humbled yourselves, I will add glory to your greatness." And what glory did God add to their greatness? The seventy elders prophesied at that moment but did not keep the spirit of prophecy, but Eldad and Medad prophesied and did not lose their prophetic inspiration. From where do we know this? Regarding the others, it says "They gained the gift of prophecy

but did not keep it" (11:25), but with regard to Eldad and Medad, it says "They are prophesying" (11:27); they continued prophesying (*Sanhedrin* 17a).

**They prophesied in the camp**  What did they prophesy? They said, "Moses will die, and Joshua will bring Israel into the Land" (*Sanhedrin* 17a).

NOTE: R. Samson Raphael Hirsch comments: No man, not even a Moses, may be considered as indispensable. Moses dies, and the destiny of the nation still gets fulfilled.

**(11:28) Joshua son of Nun, the servant of Moses since his youth, spoke up. "My lord Moses," he said, "stop them!"**

### ※ *The Talmud Teaches*
**My lord Moses, . . . stop them**  R. Levi said: Whoever utters a word of religious law in the presence of his teacher will die childless. For it says Eldad and Medad were prophesying in the camp, whereupon "Joshua son of Nun, the servant of Moses since his youth, spoke up. 'My lord Moses,' he said, 'stop them!'" Joshua, in effect, told Moses what to do, and this smacks of impudence. [He was punished for that in that he had no children,] for elsewhere it says "Nun his son, Joshua his son" (1 Chronicles 7:27). The genealogy ends here, because Joshua was childless (*Eruvin* 63b).

**Stop them!**  What did Joshua mean by "Stop them!"? How was Moses going to stop them from prophesying? Joshua said to Moses: Put them in charge of communal work, and they will stop prophesying by themselves (*Sanhedrin* 17a).

NOTE: Tosafot explains: Communal work involves drudgery, sorrow, grief, and bickering; and prophecy can be attained only in a spirit of happiness. Communal work will put an end to their prophesying.

**(11:33) The meat was still between their teeth, not yet chewed, when the wrath of God flared against the people, and God struck a very mighty blow against the people.**

*The Talmud Teaches*
**The meat was still between their teeth** R. Chisda said: If you ate meat, you may not eat dairy. R. Acha b. Yosef asked R. Chisda: What is the halachah with respect to meat between the teeth? Do you have to remove it before you are going to eat dairy? He answered, "The meat was still between their teeth," implying that particles that are lodged between the teeth are still called "meat." Therefore, you must wait six hours—according to other authorities, three hours—between meat and dairy (*Chullin* 105a).

## MIRIAM STRICKEN WITH LEPROSY

**(12:1) Miriam and Aaron began speaking against Moses because of the Cushite woman he had married, for he had married a Cushite woman.**

※ *The Talmud Teaches*
*because of the Cushite woman he had married* Was her name then Cushite? Surely, her name was Zipporah! But just as a Cushite, that is, an Ethiopian woman, stands out for the color of her skin, so did Zipporah stand out for her kind deeds. Similarly, it says "To Me, O children of Israel, you are just like the Cushites—Ethiopians—declared God" (Amos 9:7). Wasn't their name Israel? But just as a Cushite—Ethiopian—is different with his skin, so are the children of Israel different in their conduct from all other nations (*Mo'ed Katan* 16b).

**(12:13) When Miriam was stricken with leprosy, Moses cried out to God, "O God, please heal her!"**

※ *The Talmud Teaches*
*O God, please heal her!* The Rabbis taught: A certain student who once led the service in the presence of R. Eliezer cut his prayer very short. The others said to R. Eliezer, "Look how he rushes through his prayer!" Replied R. Eliezer, "Is his prayer shorter than that of Moses our teacher who pleaded, 'O God, please heal her!'?" (*Berachot* 34a).

**(12:15) Miriam remained quarantined outside the camp for seven days, and the people did not move on until Miriam was able to return home.**

### ※ *The Talmud Teaches*

*and the people did not move on* A person is treated as he treats others. Miriam waited for the infant Moses when his mother had placed him in a box near the bank of the Nile, as it says "His sister stood herself at a distance to see what would happen to him" (Exodus 2:4). And Israel waited for her in the desert, as it says "And the people did not move on until Miriam was able to return home." And the compensation is even greater; for Miriam waited only one hour, whereas Israel waited for her for seven days (*Sotah* 9b, 11a).

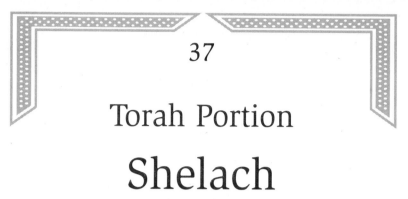

# 37

# Torah Portion

# Shelach

## Numbers 13:1–15:41

### DISPATCHING THE SPIES

**(13:16) These are the names of the men Moses sent to explore. However, Moses gave Hoshea son of Nun the new name Joshua (Yehoshua).**

※ *The Jerusalem Talmud Teaches*
*Moses gave Hoshea . . . the new name Yehoshua* R. Hoshaya taught: The *yud* that was taken from our mother Sarah when her name was changed from Sarai to Sarah (Genesis 17:15) bowed down before God and complained: Master of the universe! You have deleted me from the name of this righteous woman! God appeased the *yud,* saying: Until now you were the last letter of a woman's name. I assure you, the day will come when you will be the first letter of a man's name. This came true in the verse, "Moses called Hoshea son of Nun *Yehoshua*"; where the *yud* was placed in front of the name Hoshea, changing it to *Yehoshua* (Jerusalem Talmud, *Sanhedrin* 2:6).

**(13:22) They went up on the south side, and he arrived at Hebron, where there were Achiman, Sheshai, and Talmai, the offspring of the giant. Hebron had been built before Tzo'an in Egypt.**

※ *The Talmud Teaches*
*They went up on the south side, and he arrived at Hebron* It should have said "*they* arrived at Hebron"! Rava said: This

teaches us that Caleb separated himself from the conspiracy of the spies and prostrated himself on the graves of the patriarchs in Hebron, praying that they should save him from the plot of spies. As proof that Caleb alone went to Hebron, the Gemara cites the passage "God said, 'My servant Caleb, since he had a different idea . . . I will bring him to the land to which he came, that is, Hebron, and his descendants will possess it'" (14:24) (*Sotah* 34b).

**(13:23) They arrived at the Valley of Eshkol and cut from there a vine and a cluster of grapes which two men carried on a pole. They took also some pomegranates and figs.**

✳ *The Talmud Teaches*
*a cluster of grapes which two men carried on a pole* From the fact that they carried it on a pole, don't I know that it was carried by two men? Why then does the verse state the obvious? It means that two men carried the cluster on two poles. R. Yitzchak said: It means that there were a number of poles. Ten spies carried fruit: Eight carried clusters of grapes; one carried pomegranates; the other, figs. Joshua and Caleb did not carry anything, either because they were the most distinguished among them or because they were not a party to the plan of the spies (*Sotah* 34a).

NOTE: The spies brought the fruit in order to discourage the people, suggesting that the inhabitants of the land were just as gigantic as these enormous fruits.

## THE SLANDEROUS REPORT

**(13:27, 28) They gave the following report: "We came to the land where you sent us, and it is indeed flowing with milk and honey, as you can see from its fruits, but the people that dwell in the land are powerful."**

✳ *The Talmud Teaches*
*It is indeed flowing with milk and honey* The spies began by giving a true description of the land, but then they changed their story. R. Yochanan set forth a general rule: Any slander

that does not have a kernel of truth will not endure, because people will see through the lie. That's why the spies opened their slanderous report with a true statement (*Sotah* 35a).

**(13:30) Caleb hushed the people toward Moses. "We must go forth and occupy the land," he said. "We can do it."**

### �֎ *The Talmud Explains*

*Caleb hushed the people toward Moses* What is meant by "toward Moses"? Rabbah said: Caleb won the people over with words, rousing their curiosity to hear what he had to say about Moses. This is what happened. Joshua began to say good things about the Land of Israel. So the people cried out: This person who has no children to inherit a share of the land, he should speak to us? Caleb said to himself: If I begin to speak in the same vein as Joshua, they'll heckle me, interrupt me, and won't let me speak. So he used a different tactic, telling them, "Is this the only thing Amram's son has done to us!" Hearing how he sneeringly referred to Moses as "Amram's son," the people thought that he was about to make derogatory remarks about Moses, so they kept quiet. Once Caleb had their attention, he told them, "Why, he brought us out of Egypt, split the Red Sea for us, and gave us manna to eat. If he would tell us: Prepare ladders and climb up to heaven, shouldn't we listen to him? We must go forth and conquer the land," he said. "We can do it!" (*Sotah* 35a).

**(13:31) "We cannot go forward against those people!" replied the men who had gone with Caleb. "They are stronger than we!"**

### ✖ *The Talmud Teaches*

*They are stronger than we* R. Chanina b. Papa said: The spies made a shocking statement when they said, "We cannot go forward against those people. They are stronger than we [*mimenu*]!" The word *mimenu* can mean both "than we" and "than He." They did not mean to say, "They—the people of Canaan—are stronger than *we!*" but "They are stronger than *He.*" They implied: What good are all the miracles Moses performed until now? The owner of the house himself cannot remove his belongings from there, meaning, God, the Owner of the land, is helpless against the Canaanites. He will never be able to expel them; they are too strong for *Him!* Which is blasphemy (*Sotah* 35a).

**(13:32) They began to speak badly about the land that they had explored. They told the children of Israel, "The land that we crossed to explore is a land that devours its inhabitants. All the people we saw there were huge!"**

✳ *The Talmud Teaches*
*A land that devours its inhabitants* Rava expounded: God said: I intended this as a favor for the spies, but they interpreted it in a bad sense. I intended it for their good, because wherever the spies came, the prominent people of that locality died, so that everyone should be busy with their funeral, and they would not have time to inquire about the spies, so that the spies would be able to return unharmed. Some say that not all the prominent people died but that Job [the foremost sage of that time], died, and all were busy with his funeral. But the spies interpreted it in a negative sense, saying, "Wherever we went, we saw people going to a funeral. It is a land that devours its inhabitants" (*Sotah* 35a).

**(13:33) There we saw the giants, the sons of Anak, descendants of the giants. We felt like tiny grasshoppers, and so we looked to them.**

✳ *The Talmud Teaches*
*and so we looked to them* How could they know what the Canaanites were thinking? When the Canaanites made the meals to comfort the mourners after the funerals, they sat down to eat under a cedar tree; and when the spies saw them, they climbed the trees and sat there. They overheard them say, "We are seeing people in the trees that look like grasshoppers" (*Sotah* 35a).

**(14:1) And the whole community broke into loud cries, and the people wept all through that night.**

✳ *The Talmud Teaches*
*The people wept all through that night* Rabbah said: That night was the night of Tishah beAv. God said: Now you are crying for

nothing, for you believe the lies of the spies, but I will set aside this day for you as a day of weeping for generations to come (*Taanit* 29a).

NOTE: Tishah beAv, the Ninth of Av, is the day on which both Temples were destroyed. The day is observed as a mournful fast.

**(14:37) The people who spread the evil report about the land died in a plague before God.**

❋ *The Talmud Teaches*
*who spread the evil report about the land* R. Elazar b. Parta said: Look how much damage evil speech can do. Consider this: If the spies, who spoke evil only of the trees and stones in the Land of Israel, were punished so harshly, how much worse is it if someone maligns his neighbor (*Arachin* 15a).

## MOSES' PLEA

**(15:24) If such a sin is committed inadvertently by the community because of their leadership, the entire community must prepare one young bull for a burnt offering as an appeasing fragrance to God, along with its prescribed grain offering as libation. They must also present one goat for a sin offering.**

❋ *The Talmud Teaches*
*If such a sin is committed inadvertently by the community because of their leadership* Literally: "eyes of the community." It happened during a drought that the Office of the *Nasi*—the political and religious leader of the community—proclaimed a fast, but no rain fell. Thereupon, Oshaiah, the youngest of the scholars in the yeshiva, expounded the verse "If a sin is committed unintentionally by the community because of their leadership" [literally, "eyes of the community"], meaning, if the court rendered an erroneous ruling, and the community acted on this ruling, they are required to bring an offering. Said Oshaiah: The "eyes of the community" can be compared to a bride. If her eyes are beautiful, she does not need to be examined for imperfections; you may assume that she is pure, because the eyes are

the windows of the soul. But if her eyes are not beautiful, then she needs to be examined; an implied criticism of the *Nasi*, who is considered "the eye of the community." As if to say: It is because of the shortcomings of the *Nasi* that it does not rain (*Taanit* 24a).

**(15:31) Since he has denigrated God's word and violated His commandment, that person shall be utterly cut off spiritually and his sin is upon him.**

### ❈ *The Talmud Teaches*
*He has denigrated God's word* This refers to a person who says that the Torah is not from heaven, that is, that it is not "God's word." Even if he said that the entire Torah is from heaven except for this verse that was not said by God but by Moses on his own; and what's more, even if he said, except for this one inference, this one *kal vachomer*, "logical deduction," this one parallel—this too is an example of "He has denigrated God's word" (*Sanhedrin* 99a).

*his sin is upon him* This teaches us that if he repents before he dies, death wipes out his sin, meaning, he shall be cut off spiritually only if his sin is still upon him but not if he repents (*Shevuot* 13a).

## ZIZITH

**(15:39) It shall be zizith for you, that you may see it and remember all the commandments of God so as to do them. You will then not stray after your heart and eyes, which in the past have led you to immorality.**

### ❈ *The Talmud Teaches*
*That you may see it* It was taught in the name of R. Meir: It does not say, "That you may see *them*," that is, the zizith, but "You shall see *oto*," that is, "Him": This teaches us that fulfilling the mitzvah of zizith is comparable to beholding the Presence of the Shechinah. For *techeilet*—the thread of sky-blue wool of the zizith—resembles the color of the sea; the color of the sea resembles heaven; heaven resembles the color of sapphire; and

sapphire resembles the color of the throne of glory, as it says "They saw a vision of the God of Israel, and under His feet was something like a sapphire brick, like the essence of a clear blue sky" (Exodus 24:10). Hence, the benefit of the *techeilet* thread is that by looking at it we connect with the higher world of the throne of glory (*Chullin* 89a).

NOTE: The blue dye for the thread in the zizith was taken from the blue blood of an amphibian known as *chilazon*. Because today the identity of this animal is not known, the mitzvah is fulfilled with white threads.

## ✻ The Midrash Teaches
*after your hearts and eyes* This teaches us that the eyes follow the heart. But shouldn't it be that the heart follows the eyes; first you see a desirable object, and then you long for it? This is not so, for are there not blind people who perform all the abominations in the world? *(Sifrei)*.

## ❁ The Jerusalem Talmud Teaches
*after your hearts and eyes* R. Levi said: The heart and the eye are the two agents of sin. And so it is written, "Give your heart to Me, My son; let your eyes watch My ways" (Proverbs 23:26). God is saying, in effect: If you give Me your heart and your eyes, I know that you belong to Me (Jerusalem Talmud, *Berachot* 15).

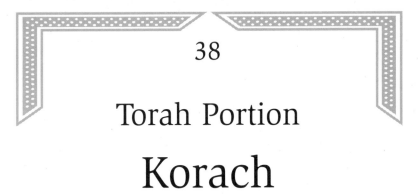

## 38

# Torah Portion

# Korach

## Numbers 16:1–18:32

### KORACH'S REBELLION

**(16:1) Korach son of Yitzhar son of Kehat and great-grandson of Levi took [the right to himself] together with Datan and Abiram, sons of Eliav, and On son of Pelet, sons of Reuben.**

�֍ *The Talmud Teaches*
*Korach . . . took* What did he take? Resh Lakish said: He took—that is, he made—a bad deal for himself (*Sanhedrin* 109b).

NOTE: According to the Midrash, the wealthy Korach spent a great deal of money to bribe and wine and dine his fellow conspirators in an attempt to make them join his rebellion. It turned out to be a very bad investment.

**(16:4) When Moses heard, he fell on his face.**

✷ *The Talmud Teaches*
*When Moses heard* What news did Moses hear that caused him to fall on his face? R. Shmuel b. Nachmani said: He heard that the people suspected him of adultery, as it says "They forewarned their wives concerning Moses in the camp" (Psalms 106:16). This teaches us that every husband formally warned his wife against secluding herself with Moses because they suspected their wives of committing adultery with him. And so it

says "And Moses took the tent and pitched it outside the camp" (16:25) in order to avoid further suspicion (*Sanhedrin* 110a).

**(16:15) Moses became very angry. He prayed to God, "Do not accept their offering. I did not take a single donkey from them! I did not do any of them any harm!"**

*The Talmud Teaches*

***not . . . a single donkey*** The Rabbis taught: King Ptolemy of Egypt once gathered seventy-two sages of Israel and placed them in seventy-two separate chambers, telling each one, "Write for me a Greek translation of the Torah of Moses your teacher." God guided the thoughts of each of them, and all of them independently arrived at a common decision about how to translate certain words in the Torah, which, if translated literally, might anger Ptolemy. And so they all wrote, "I—Moses—have not taken one 'desired object' of theirs," instead of "a single donkey of theirs," so that Ptolemy should not insinuate that Moses did not take a donkey but did take other things from them (*Megillah* 9a).

**(16:30) But if God creates something entirely new, making the earth open its mouth and swallow them and all that is theirs, so that they descend to the depth alive, then it is these men who are provoking God.**

*The Talmud Teaches*

***But if God creates something entirely new*** Rava expounded: Moses said to God: If Gehinnom (Hell) has already been created, so that Korach and his group can be sent there, fine. And if it has not yet been created, then let God create it! The Gemara asks: To what purpose did Moses make such a request? If you say that he wanted God actually to create Gehinnom—that cannot be, for "There is nothing new under the sun!" Rather, Moses was praying for God to move the entrance of Gehinnom close to the spot where Korach and his party were standing. God answered Moses' prayer, and when the earth opened up under the rebels, they descended directly into Gehinnom (*Sanhedrin* 110a).

**(16:33) They and all that was theirs descended alive to the pit; the earth covered them over, and they were lost to the community.**

### ⚑ *The Jerusalem Talmud Teaches*
*and all that was theirs*  R. Berechiah said: Even their names that were engraved on their treasure chests flew away. R. Yose b. R. Chanina said: Even a needle that someone had borrowed from them was swallowed up with them, as it says "They and all that was theirs descended alive to the pit" (Jerusalem Talmud, *Sanhedrin* 10:1).

### ⚑ *The Talmud Teaches*
*the earth covered them up*  R. Akiva said: The party of Korach is not destined to rise up from the ground, for it says "The earth covered them over"—in this world; "and they were lost to the community"—for the world to come. R. Eliezer disagreed: About them, it says "God deals death and brings to life; casts down into the pit and raises up" (1 Samuel 2:6); as they fell into the abyss, they repented, which earned them a share in the world to come (*Sanhedrin* 108a).

## AARON HALTS THE PLAGUE

**(17:12, 13) Aaron took the pan as Moses had told him, and he ran to the middle of the assembled masses, where the plague had already begun to kill people. He offered the incense to atone for the people. He stood between the dead and the living, and the plague was checked.**

### ⚑ *The Talmud Teaches*
*He offered the incense*  When Moses went up to heaven, all the angels became his friends; and each angel taught him a concept as a gift. And even the Angel of Death revealed a secret to him, namely, that the offering of incense would halt the spread of a plague, for it says "He offered incense to atone for the people." Then it says "He stood between the dead and the living, and the plague was checked." Now, how did Moses know that the incense would halt the plague, if not for the fact that the Angel of Death himself had told him? (*Shabbat* 89a).

NOTE: After the death of Korach and his followers, the people complained against Moses and Aaron, saying, "You have killed the people of God" (17:6). Thereupon, God threatened to destroy the entire community. Moses then told Aaron to offer incense to make atonement for them.

## REDEMPTION OF THE FIRSTBORN

**(18:15) The first fruits of the womb that must be presented to God, among man or beast, shall be the *kohen*'s, but you shall surely redeem the firstborn of man and the firstborn of an unclean animal.**

✳ *The Talmud Teaches*
**but you shall surely redeem**  Literally: "redeem you shall redeem." It was taught: The father must redeem his son by performing the mitzvah of *pidyon haben* (redemption of the firstborn). If the father did not do so, the son must redeem himself when he becomes thirteen years old, for it says twice, "redeem you shall redeem" (*Kiddushin* 29a).

*and the firstborn of an unclean animal*  I might think that the firstborn of horses and camels are also included and must be redeemed. That's why it says "Every firstling donkey must be redeemed" (Exodus 13:13)—to specify that only the firstborn of a donkey must be redeemed, and not the firstborn of horses and camels (*Bechorot* 5b).

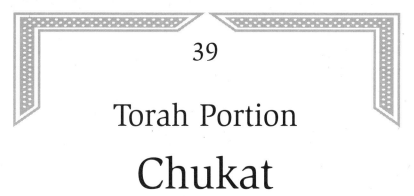

# 39

# Torah Portion

# Chukat

Numbers 19:1–22:1

## THE RED COW

**(19:2) This is the decree of the Torah [that] God has commanded, saying: Speak to the children of Israel and have them bring you a red cow, complete, which is without blemish, and which has never had a yoke on it.**

✳ *The Midrash Teaches*
**complete**  Complete in its redness. But perhaps the verse means that the cow should be complete in the sense of being free from blemishes? This cannot be, for the verse continues, "which is without blemish." Thus, "complete" does not refer to the cow but to its redness; in fact, if it has two or more hairs that are not red, the cow is invalid (*Parah* 2:5) *(Sifrei Zuta)*.

**(19:14) This is the Torah: When a man dies in the tent—anything that comes into the tent or was originally in the tent shall be unclean for seven days.**

✖ *The Talmud Teaches*
**When a man dies in the tent**  Resh Lakish said: From where do we know that the words of Torah remain firmly rooted in a person and his descendants only if he makes sacrifices for it? Because it says "This is the Torah, when a man dies in the tent," meaning, he mortifies himself and does not overindulge in worldly pleasures *(Berachot 63b)*.

**When a man dies in the tent**  R. Yonatan said: A person should never miss a lecture in the bet midrash [house of study] or skip Torah study even on his deathbed, for it says "This is the Torah, when a man dies in the tent"—even when lying on his deathbed, a person should engross himself in the study of the Torah (*Shabbat* 83b).

## MIRIAM'S DEATH

**(20:1) In the first month [that is, Nisan of the fortieth year] the entire community of the children of Israel came to the desert of Tzin, and the people stopped in Kadesh. It was there that Miriam died and was buried.**

### ※ *The Talmud Teaches*
**It was there that Miriam died**  R. Ammi said: Why does the Torah place the report of Miriam's death immediately after the chapter of the red cow, whose ashes are used in purifying a person who was contaminated by contact with a corpse? What is the connection? To tell you that just as the red cow brings about atonement, so does the death of the righteous atone for their generation (*Mo'ed Katan* 28a).

**It was there that Miriam died**  R. Elazar said: It says here, "It was there, *sham*, that Miriam died," and it says regarding Moses, "Moses died there, *sham* . . . by the mouth of God" (Deuteronomy 34:5) meaning, a very gentle, painless death, not through the Angel of Death. We infer from the fact that the word sham occurs in connection with the death of both Moses and Miriam that, just as Moses died by "the mouth of God"— that is, a kiss—so did Miriam die by a kiss. And why doesn't the Torah say expressly that she died "by the mouth of God"? Because it would be disrespectful to use the phrase "by the mouth of God" in connection with a woman. And from here we derive that neither the Angel of Death nor worms and maggots had an effect on her body (*Bava Batra* 17a).

## MOSES STRIKES THE ROCK

**(20:2) The people did not have any water, so they began demonstrating against Moses and Aaron.**

※ *The Talmud Teaches*
*The people did not have any water* R. Yose b. R. Yehudah said: The well that accompanied Israel on their wanderings through the wilderness was given to them in the merit of Miriam, and when she died, it disappeared, as it says "It was there that Miriam . . . died. . . . and the people did not have any water" (*Taanit* 9a).

(20:8) **God spoke to Moses, saying, "Take the staff and gather the entire community, you and Aaron your brother, and speak to the rock before their eyes that it shall give its waters. You shall bring forth for them water from the rock and allow the community and their cattle to drink."**

※ *The Talmud Teaches*
*Allow the community and their cattle to drink* From here, we derive that the Torah is mindful of the possessions of Israel. For the miracle of providing water in the desert was performed also out of consideration for the survival of the cattle (*Menachot* 76b).

(20:12) **God then said to Moses and Aaron: Because you did not have enough faith in Me to sanctify Me in the presence of the children of Israel, therefore you shall not bring this assembly to the land that I have given them.**

NOTE: Instead of speaking to the rock, as God directed him to do, Moses angrily struck it twice with his rod, whereupon a huge amount of water gushed forth. His sin was that he struck rather than spoke.

※ *The Talmud Teaches*
*Because you did not have enough faith in Me* The Jewish people had two good leaders: Moses and David. Moses said: Let my sin be recorded candidly, and so it says point-blank, "You did not have enough faith in Me." David asked that his sin with Bathsheba should not be recorded, and so it says "Happy is he whose transgression is forgiven, whose sin is covered over" (Psalms 32:1).

The difference in the requests of Moses and David is analogous to the appeals of two women who were given stripes by the court. One of them had committed adultery; the other, a minor violation of the laws of the Sabbatical Year. The latter said to the judges: I beg of you, please tell everyone why I am receiving these lashes, so that people should not say that I was punished for the same sin as the other woman. So they announced: This woman has received lashes because of a violation of the laws of the Sabbatical Year (*Shabbat* 86b).

NOTE: Similarly, the children of Israel committed the grave sin of accepting the bad report of the spies; their punishment was that they would die during the forty years of wandering in the desert. By comparison, Moses' sin of striking the rock was relatively minor. Yet he too was destined to die in the desert. That's why Moses asked that his transgression be spelled out plainly.

**(20:13) These are the Waters of Dispute [Mey Merivah] where the children of Israel disputed with God, and where He was sanctified through them.**

### ※ The Talmud Teaches

**These are the Waters of Dispute** R. Chama b. R. Chanina said: The Waters of Dispute are the waters the Pharaoh's astrologers saw and about whose interpretation they erred. They saw in the stars that the future savior of Israel, Moses, would be smitten through water. So they advised Pharaoh accordingly, and hoping to kill the Jewish savior, Pharaoh declared, "Every boy who is born must be cast into the Nile" (Exodus 1:22). They did not realize, however, that it was not literally by water but rather on account of the Waters of Merivah, where Moses struck the rock rather than speaking to it, that Moses was destined to be smitten. Thus, the astrologers did see the omen that Moses would be defeated through water, but they misinterpreted it (*Sanhedrin* 101b).

**where they disputed with God** R. Chama b. R. Chanina said: Whoever picks a quarrel with his teacher is like one who picks a quarrel with the Divine Presence, for it says "These are the Waters of Dispute, where the children of Israel disputed with God" (*Sanhedrin* 101b).

NOTE: The children of Israel quarreled with Moses and Aaron. But the verse says that they quarreled with God, implying that quarreling with their teacher Moses was equivalent to quarreling with God.

**(21:1) When the Canaanite king of Arad who lived in the Negev heard that the children of Israel had come by the route of the spies, he attacked them and took some captives.**

✳ *The Talmud Teaches*
*When the Canaanite king of Arad . . . heard* What report did he hear that gave him courage to launch an attack? He heard that Aaron had died, and that the clouds of glory that surrounded and protected Israel, and which had come in the merit of Aaron, had vanished. He then thought that he had permission to attack Israel. That's why it says "The people realized, *vayiru,* that Aaron had died" (20:29). And R. Avahu explains: Do not read vayiru, "they saw; they realized." Read instead, vayeira'u, "they became visible." When the protective cover of the clouds of glory departed, the people became visible and exposed, and the Canaanites pounced on them (*Taanit* 9a).

**(21:5) The people spoke out against God and Moses, "Why did you take us out of Egypt to die in the desert? There is no bread and no water, and we are getting disgusted with this insubstantial food."**

✳ *The Talmud Teaches*
*against God and Moses* Moses said to Israel: You are an ungrateful people. You showed your thanklessness when you said about the miraculous gift of the manna, "We are getting disgusted with this insubstantial food." The manna was so wondrously light that it was absorbed entirely in their organs, making it unnecessary for them to defecate—and for this they complained (*Avodah Zarah* 5a)!

**(21:8) [When the people spoke out against God and Moses, God punished them by letting loose poisonous snakes against them that killed many people. The people repented, and when Moses prayed for them,] God said to Moses, "Make**

**yourself the image of a venomous snake, and place it on a
pole. Everyone who is bitten shall look at it and live."**

### �֎ *The Talmud Teaches*
*shall look at it and live* Now, can a snake kill or can it keep
alive? Of course, it cannot. The Torah wants to tell you that
when Israel looked upward and humbled themselves to their
Father in heaven and repented, they were healed; otherwise,
they perished (*Rosh Hashanah* 29a).

## THE BATTLE WITH THE AMORITES

**(21:14) It is therefore told in the book of God's wars: Et and
Hev in the rear, and in the streams of Arnon.**

### ✻ *The Talmud Teaches*
*Et and Hev in the rear* If you see the crossing of the valley of
Arnon, you must give praise and thanks to God because a great
miracle happened there. But how do we know that a miracle
occurred when the Jews crossed the streams of the mountains
of Arnon? Because it says "It is therefore told in the book of
God's wars: Et and Hev in the rear." The Gemara explains the
phrase as follows: "Et and Hev in the rear." There were two lep-
ers, one named Et and the other Hev, who were following in the
rear of the camp of Israel. When the children of Israel were
passing the streams of Arnon, the Amorites came and dug caves
in the mountains that were close to one another, and the road
passed through the valley, and lay there in ambush. The Amorites reckoned: When the Jews pass below in the narrow valley,
they will be at our mercy, and we will kill them with arrows
and stones thrown from above. The Amorites did not know that
the ark that was traveling in front of the nation leveled the
mountains in their path. When the ark came to the place where
the Amorites were lying in ambush, the two mountains moved
together, and the promontories on one side pushed into the
caves on the other side, crushing the Amorites, so that their
blood flowed into the streams of Arnon. But the children of
Israel did not see the blood in the streams behind them. When
Et and Hev came trailing the camp and saw blood coming from

between these two mountains, they realized what had happened. They went and told the children of Israel, who broke out into song. And that is the incident that is referred to in the verse "The outpouring of the blood into the streams at the foot of the mountain which inclined toward the habitation of Or, and leans toward the borders of Moab" (21:15) (*Berachot* 54a, b).

**Et and Hav in the rear**  R. Chiya b. Abba said: Even a father and a son, or a teacher and his student, who study Torah together become enemies of each other, arguing about Torah issues, and one not wishing to accept the other's line of reasoning, yet they do not move away from there until they come to love each other. For it says "Therefore, it is said in the book of the wars of God: *Et vaheiv besufah*—A war that is fought while learning together the Book of God ends in love." Don't read *besufah* but *besofah*, "in the end," and *hav* suggesting *ahavah*, "love." A dispute about Torah will end in love (*Kiddushin* 30b).

40

# Torah Portion

# Balak

Numbers 22:2–25:9

## BALAK AND BALAAM

**(22:7) The elders of Moab and Midian went to Balaam with magical devices in hand, conveying to him Balak's message, asking him to come and curse the Jews.**

*The Talmud Teaches*

***The elders of Moab and Midian*** Midian and Moab had never been at peace with each other. Why then did they suddenly unite? This can be explained by a parable of two watchdogs that were with a flock of sheep, and the dogs were fiercely hostile to each other. When one day a wolf attacked one of the dogs, the other said: If I don't help my fellow, today the wolf will kill him, and tomorrow he will come and attack me. So the two of them went and killed the wolf. Said R. Papa: This is the meaning of the popular adage: The weasel and the cat, which are natural enemies, made a feast from the fat of an unlucky victim. Similarly, Moab and Midian set aside their long-standing hostility to make common cause against their mutual enemy, the Jews (*Sanhedrin* 105a).

**(22:8) "Spend the night here," Balaam replied to Balak's emissaries, "and when God speaks to me, I will be able to give you an answer." The Moabite dignitaries remained with Balaam.**

※ *The Talmud Teaches*
*The Moabite dignitaries remained with Balaam* And where did the Midianite dignitaries go? Once Balaam said to the Moabite and Midianite emissaries: "Spend the night here, and when God speaks to me, I will be able to give you an answer," the Midianites said: Is there any father who hates his own son? Of course not! They reasoned that because Balaam had to get permission from God to curse the Jews, God, who is the Father of the Jews, would never allow this. [So they despaired and went home] (*Sanhedrin* 105a).

**(22:20) That night, God appeared to Balaam and said to him, "If the men have come to summon you, set out and go with them. But only do exactly as I instruct you."**

※ *The Talmud Teaches*
*Set out and go with them* R. Nachman said: Audacity succeeds even against the opposition of heaven. For at first, it says "God told Balaam, 'Do not go with them'" (22:12), and in the end God said, "Set out and go with them." For Balaam to ask a second time, seeing that God disapproved of his going, that showed impudence (*Sanhedrin* 105a).

*Set out and go with them* Rabbah b. R. Huna said: From here, we derive that heaven guides a person along the way he wants to follow. For it says "God said to Balaam, 'Do not go with them,'" and then it says "If the men have come to summon you, set out and go with them." Thus, once Balaam decided to resist God's will, God steered him on the path he had chosen (*Makkot* 10b).

**(22:21) When Balaam got up in the morning, he saddled his female donkey and went with the Moabite dignitaries.**

※ *The Talmud Teaches*
*he saddled his female donkey* It was taught in the name of R. Shimon b. Elazar: Hatred sets aside the rules of conduct imposed by high position, as you can see from the case of Balaam. For it says "When Balaam got up in the morning, he saddled his

female donkey." [Driven by his hatred of the Jews and his intense desire to curse them, he was glad to do the menial job of saddling his donkey himself, which was unbefitting his high position] (*Sanhedrin* 105b).

**(23:5) God placed a message in Balaam's mouth and said, "Go back to Balak, and declare exactly what I have told you."**

※ *The Talmud Teaches*
*God placed a message in Balaam's mouth* Literally: "God placed a thing in Baalam's mouth." What was this thing? R. Elazar said: It was an angel who would not let Balaam speak when he tried to curse the Jews. R. Yonatan said: It was a hook that pulled his mouth shut whenever he tried to utter a curse, preventing him from speaking (*Sanhedrin* 105b).

**(23:9) Balaam declared, "I see this nation from mountaintops, and gaze on it from the heights. It is a nation dwelling alone and not counted among the other nations."**

※ *The Talmud Teaches*
*It is a nation . . . not counted among the other nations* A heretic once said to R. Avina: It says "David said, 'Who is like Your people, like Israel, a unique nation on earth'" (2 Samuel 7:23). What's so special about the Jewish people? he asked. You are also included among the nations of the world; you are no better than we are! For it says "All the nations are like nothing before Him" (Isaiah 40:17), including the Jewish people! Replied R. Avina: One of your people, the heathen prophet Balaam, has already testified about us. He said, "It is a nation that is not counted among the other nations," so you see, the phrase "All the nations are like nothing before Him" does not include the Jewish people (*Sanhedrin* 39b)!

**(23:29) Balaam said to Balak, "Build me seven altars here, and prepare for me here seven bulls and seven rams."**

※ *The Talmud Teaches*
*Build me seven altars here* Rav Yehudah said in the name of Rav: A person should always occupy himself with Torah and

mitzvoth, even if he does it for ulterior motives, because from doing it for selfish reasons, eventually he will do it for the sake of heaven. What is the source for this adage? Let's see. Balak, king of Moab, offered forty-two sacrifices. His purpose certainly was not for the sake of heaven, for he did it in order to entice God to allow Balaam to curse Israel. Nevertheless, he merited that Ruth should come forth from him. And Ruth was the ancestor of Solomon, about whom it says "Solomon offered up a thousand burnt offerings on that altar" (1 Kings 3:4) (*Sotah* 16a).

NOTE: The forty-two sacrifices Balak offered consisted of seven bulls and seven rams he offered in verse 23:1, in 23:14, and in the present verse; and three occasions times fourteen sacrifices equals forty-two sacrifices.

## BALAAM'S BLESSINGS

**(24:2) When Balaam raised his eyes, and saw Israel dwelling according to its tribes, the spirit of God came over him.**

### ※ *The Talmud Teaches*
*Balaam . . . saw Israel* What did he see? He saw that their tent openings were not facing each other, so that they could not peek into each other's tents. Admiring their modesty and decency, Balaam declared, "People such as these deserve to have the Shechinah rest upon them" (*Bava Batra* 60a).

**(24:5) Balaam proclaimed, "How good are your tents, Jacob, your dwelling places, Israel."**

### ※ *The Talmud Teaches*
*How good are your tents, Jacob* R. Yochanan said: From the blessings of that wicked man, Balaam, you can figure out what he intended to say if he had not been restrained by God. He wanted to curse the Jews that they should not have any synagogues or study halls, but he was forced to say, "How good are your tents, Jacob." For tents are symbolic of synagogues and yeshivas. He wanted to say: May the Shechinah not rest on the Jews, but he was forced to say, "How good are your dwelling places, Israel," which symbolize the Temple. He meant to say:

May Israel's kingdom not endure, but he was forced to say, "They stretch out like streams" (24:6), meaning, their kingdom will stretch forth like a stream. He meant to say: May they have no olive orchards and vineyards, but he was forced to say, "Like gardens by a river" (24:6). He tried to say: May their fragrance, that is, fame, not spread, but instead he was forced to say, "like fragrant aloes planted by God" (24:6). He tried to say: May they have no kings of impressive stature, but he was forced to say, "like cedars by the water." He wanted to say: May they not have a king who is succeeded by a king, but he was forced to say, "May water flow from his wells," for an enduring dynasty. He meant to say: May their king not rule over other nations, but he was forced to say, "and his seed in abundant waters," a metaphor for the conquest of many nations. He wanted to say: May their kingdom not be strong, but he was forced to say, "May his king be greater than Agag," a reference to Saul's triumph over Agag, king of Amalek. He intended to say: May their kingdom not inspire fear, but he was forced to say, "May his kingdom be exalted" (24:8).

R. Abba b. Kahana said: All of Balaam's blessings eventually reverted into the curse he had in mind, except for the curse regarding synagogues and study halls. For it says "God your Lord transformed his curse to a blessing for you, since God your Lord loves you" (Deuteronomy 23:6). The passage says *curse*, not *curses*, that is, only one intended curse, namely, the one regarding synagogues and study halls remained a blessing (*Sanhedrin* 105b).

**(24:6) They stretch forth like streams, like gardens by the river; they are like aloes planted by God, like cedars by the water.**

### ※ *The Talmud Teaches*
**Like streams . . . like aloes** *Ahalim* (aloes, a plant of the lily family) similar to *ohalim*, "tents." R. Chama b. R. Chanina said: Why are tents mentioned in conjunction with streams? To teach you that, just as immersion in streams brings a person up from uncleanness to purity, so do the tents of Torah, that is, yeshivas, lift a person from the scale of guilt to the scale of merit; which means that the Torah has the power to transform a person's shortcomings into merits (*Berachot* 16a).

*like cedars by the water* R. Shmuel b. Nachmani said: What is meant by the verse, "Wounds inflicted by a loved one are faithful, while the kisses of an enemy are deceitful" (Proverbs 27:6)? The curse with which the prophet Achiya the Shelonite cursed Israel, because of the sins of King Jeroboam, was better than the blessing with which the wicked Balaam blessed them. Achiya the Shelonite cursed Israel, comparing them to a reed, for it says "God will strike Israel until it sways like a reed in water" (1 Kings 14:15). Just as a reed grows in a watery place, and its stem grows back when it is cut, and it has many roots, and even if all the winds of the world come and blow on it, they cannot budge it from its place, but it always sways back and forth in harmony with the winds, and as soon as the winds subside, the reed again stands upright in its place, so too the Jewish people will overcome all adversities. However, the wicked Balaam blessed them by comparing them with a cedar. A cedar does not stand in a watery place; it has only a few roots; its trunk does not grow back once it is cut; and if the south wind blows at it, it uproots it and turns it upside down. Thus, Achiyah's curse was better than Balaam's blessing (*Taanit* 20a).

**(24:16) Balaam declared: It is the word of the one who hears God's sayings and knows the knowledge of the Highest One; who sees a vision of the Almighty while fallen in a meditative trance with mystical insight.**

※ *The Talmud Teaches*
*Who knows the knowledge of the Highest One* How could this be true? He could not even figure out what his donkey wanted when it edged over to the side, crushing his foot against the wall (Numbers 32:25), then how could he know the knowledge of the Most High! So what does this mean? It comes to teach us that Balaam knew how to pinpoint the exact instant when God gets angry, and he wanted to curse the Jews at precisely that moment, to bring God's anger down on them (*Berachot* 7a).

**(24:21) When Balaam saw the Keni he proclaimed his parable and said, "You live in a fortress and have placed your nest in a cliff."**

### �֎ *The Talmud Teaches*

***When Balaam saw the Keni*** Balaam said to Jethro, "Keni—one of Jethro's names—were you not with us in giving that advice to Pharaoh to kill the newborn Jewish boys? Who then placed you among 'the mighty ones of the world'?" [This was] a reference to the Sanhedrin whose members included Jethro's descendants. R. Chiya b. Abba explained: Three persons were involved in advising Pharaoh to kill the newborn Jewish boys: Balaam, Job, and Jethro. Balaam, who advised Pharaoh to drown the Jewish babies, was killed (Numbers 31:8). Job, who remained silent and did not protest, was punished with harrowing agony. As for Jethro, who protested against the plan and then fled to avoid being killed, his descendants were privileged to sit in the chamber of the hewn stone in the Temple, as members of the Sanhedrin (*Sanhedrin* 106a).

## ZIMRI CHALLENGES MOSES

**(25:6) They were crying at the entrance of the tent of meeting, when an Israelite, Zimri, brought forth a Midianite woman to his brothers before the eyes of Moses and the entire Israelite community.**

### �֎ *The Talmud Teaches*

***They were crying*** Why were they crying? Because Zimri had said to Moses: Son of Amram, is this Midianite woman forbidden or permitted? And if you say she is forbidden, who permitted you to marry Jethro's daughter, Tzipporah, when Jethro was a Midianite sheik? At that moment, Moses forgot the *halachah* regarding intimacy with a heathen woman, and all the people burst into tears.

NOTE: He forgot that he married Tzipporah before the Torah was given. At that time, Jews were permitted to intermarry with non-Jews. However, at the giving of the Torah, Tzipporah, along with all Jews, entered into the covenant with God (*Sanhedrin* 82a).

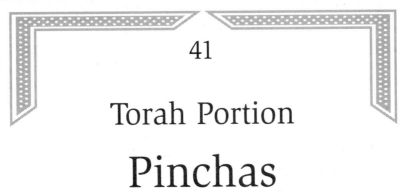

# 41

# Torah Portion

# Pinchas

## Numbers 25:10–30:1

## ETERNAL PRIESTHOOD FOR PINCHAS

**(25:10) Pinchas, son of Elazar and grandson of Aaron the priest, was the one who zealously took up My cause among the Israelites and turned My anger away from them, so that I did not destroy them in My vengeance.**

### ✳ *The Talmud Teaches*

*Pinchas, son of Elazar and grandson of Aaron* Why does the Torah point out that Pinchas was Aaron's grandson? After Pinchas avenged God by killing Zimri, the other tribes vilified him, accusing him of wanton murder, saying, "Look at this descendant of Jethro who sacrificed calves for idol worship, and he went and killed Zimri, a leader of the tribe of Simon." The Torah, therefore, went out of its way to specify Pinchas's descent, "Pinchas, son of Elazar and grandson of Aaron the priest"; and Aaron was the epitome of "a lover of peace" (*Sanhedrin* 82b).

NOTE: Pinchas's maternal grandfather was Jethro, a Midianite priest.

**(25:13) This shall be for him and his descendants a covenant of eternal priesthood. It is given to him because he zealously took up God's cause and made atonement for the children of Israel.**

✳ *The Talmud Teaches*
***This shall be for him and his descendants*** If a *kohen* performed the service in the Temple, thinking that he is a qualified *kohen*, and later discovered that he is the son of a divorced woman or the son of a *chalutzah*, and therefore unfit to perform priestly services, how do we know that his service is retroactively valid? Rav Yehudah said in the name of Shmuel: Because it says concerning Pinchas "This shall be for him and his descendants a covenant of eternal priesthood"—this includes both fit and unfit offspring (*Kiddushin* 66b).

NOTE: A *kohen* is forbidden to marry a divorced woman or a *chalutzah*, a woman who has been freed from a levirate marriage. A son of such a forbidden union is unqualified to perform the Temple service. What is a *levirate marriage?* If a husband dies childless, his widow should marry one of his brothers. This is known as a levirate marriage. In case the brother does not want to go through with the marriage, the *chalitzah* ritual severs the bond between them (Deuteronomy 25:5–10).

**(25:15) The name of the Midianite woman who was killed was Kozbi the daughter of Tzur, who was the head of a Midianite tribe.**

✸ *The Jerusalem Talmud Teaches*
***who was the head of a Midianite tribe*** Balaam said to Balak: The God of these people hates immorality. If you make your daughters available to Israel for immoral purposes, you can rule them, because their God will be angry with them. Said Balak: But will our daughters listen to us? Replied Balaam: Start with the daughters of your tribal leaders first, and the others will follow suit. That's why it says "Kozbi the daughter of Tzur, who was the head of a Midianite tribe" to show that Kozbi was a Midianite chieftain's daughter (Jerusalem Talmud, *Sanhedrin* 10:2).

**(26:11) The sons of Korach did not die.**

✳ *The Talmud Teaches*
***The sons of Korach did not die*** A place was set up high for them in Gehinnom, where they sat and sang songs in praise to God for their salvation (*Sanhedrin* 110a).

NOTE: They did *teshuvah,* which is evident in Psalm 88, "A song of psalms by the sons of Korach," which includes verses like "I was reckoned with those who descend to the pit" and "You placed me in the lowest of pits, into utter darkness, into shadowy depths" (88:5, 7) (*Sanhedrin* 110a).

## TZELOFCHAD'S DAUGHTERS

**(27:1) The daughters of Tzelofchad, son of Chefer, son of Gilead, son of Machir, son of Menasseh, of the family of Joseph's son Menasseh drew near to present a petition. The names of the daughters were Machlah, Noah, Choglah, Milkah, and Tirzah.**

### ✖ *The Talmud Teaches*
**The daughters of Tzelofchad drew near** The names of Tzelofchad's daughters are listed in different order in Numbers 36:11. Here, where they petitioned Moses on a matter of law, they are listed according to wisdom; but when the Torah relates their marriages, they are listed by age, because the older daughter usually gets married before the younger. This is in line with R. Ammi's way of thinking, who said: At a yeshiva where law is being studied, you should show preference to wisdom when making the seating arrangements: A brilliant young scholar should get a better seat than an older person who is an average scholar; whereas at a banquet, you should show preference to age in the seating plan (*Bava Batra* 120a).

## JOSHUA CHOSEN AS MOSES' SUCCESSOR

**(27:18) God said to Moses, "Take Joshua son of Nun, a man of spirit, and lay your hand on him."**

### ✖ *The Talmud Teaches*
**and lay your hand on him** Rava said: What verse supports the popular saying: "Although the wine belongs to the owner, the drinkers thank the waiter"? The verse "God said to Moses: Lay your hand on Joshua . . . so that the entire Israelite community will obey him." And it also says "Joshua, son of Nun was filled with a spirit of wisdom, because Moses had laid his hands on him. The Israelites therefore listened to him"

(Deuteronomy 34:19). Although wisdom comes from God, Moses is given the credit (*Bava Kamma* 92b).

**(27:20) Invest him with some of your splendor so that the entire community of Israel will obey him.**

⁂ *The Talmud Teaches*
**Invest him with some of your splendor** Give Joshua "*some* of your splendor" but not *all* of your splendor. The elders of that generation said: The face of Moses is like the sun; the face of Joshua is like the moon. Joshua's radiance was of a lower intensity than that of Moses; he was not as magnificent a personality as Moses (*Bava Batra* 75a).

**(27:21) Let him stand before Elazar the priest, who shall inquire for him the decision of the *Urim* before God. By his word, according to Elazar's declaration, they shall go out, and by his word they shall come in, he Joshua along with all the Israelites and the entire community.**

⁂ *The Talmud Teaches*
***Elazar the priest shall inquire for him the decision of the Urim*** How were the *Urim* and *Tumim* consulted? The questioner, that is, the king, should not speak in a loud voice, for it says "He shall inquire for him," alone, so that only the high priest wearing the breastplate can hear it. On the other hand, he should not just mentally reflect on the question either, for it says "He shall inquire for him," that is, he should articulate the question, for example, whether or not to go to war. He should put the question the way Hannah said her prayer, for it says "Now Hannah spoke in her heart, only her lips moved, but her voice could not be heard" (1 Samuel 1:13) (*Yoma* 73a).

NOTE: The *Urim* and *Tumim* was a slip of parchment on which the ineffable four-letter name of God was written. It was inserted in the fold of the high priest's breastplate. Twelve precious stones were attached to the front of the breastplate. When the *Urim* and *Tumin* were consulted, certain letters etched on the stones lit up. The high priest—with divine inspiration—was able to combine the letters and spell out the answer.

**(27:22) Moses then laid his hands on him and commissioned him. It was all done as God had commanded Moses.**

✖ *The Talmud Teaches*
*Moses then laid his hands on him* Moses placed both his hands on Joshua, although God had commanded him "place your *hand* on him" (27:18). R. Yose b. R. Choni said: The fact that Moses placed *both* his hands on Joshua, bestowing all his prophetic powers on him, exceeding God's instructions in favor of his disciple, proves that a man is jealous of everyone except his son and his disciple (*Yoma* 105b).

## OFFERINGS

**(28:4) For the daily sacrifice: Prepare one sheep in the morning, and the second sheep in the afternoon.**

✖ *The Jerusalem Talmud Teaches*
*Prepare one sheep in the . . . morning* The prayers were derived from the daily sacrifices: the morning prayer from the morning sacrifice, as it says "Prepare one sheep in the morning." The afternoon prayer from the afternoon sacrifice, as it says "the second sheep in the afternoon." The evening prayer has no explicit scriptural source. It relates to the limbs and the fat that burned on the altar all night (Jerusalem Talmud, *Berachot* 4:1).

**(28:15) On the new moon there shall also be one goat presented as a sin offering to God. All this shall be presented in addition to the regular daily burnt offering and its libation.**

✖ *The Talmud Teaches*
*as a sin offering to God* Resh Lakish said: Why is the goat that is offered on the new moon singled out in that it is described as a "sin offering *to God*"? The phrase *to God* does not occur in connection with the sacrifices of other festivals. Because God said: Let this goat be an atonement for Me for making the moon smaller. For when God created the sun and the moon, they were of equal size. The moon then said to God, "Is it possible for two kings to wear the same crown? I should be larger than the sun." God answered, "Go and make yourself smaller." The moon

pleaded, "Why should I make myself smaller just because I made a legitimate suggestion?" When God saw that the moon could not be placated, God said to the Jewish people, "Bring an atonement for Me, for making the moon smaller" (*Chullin* 60b).

**(28:30) On Shavuot you shall bring one male goat to atone for you.**

### ▓ *The Jerusalem Talmud Teaches*
*one male goat to atone for you* R. Mesharshiya said: In connection with the offerings of all the other festivals, it says "a male goat *as a sin offering*"; but with respect to Shavuot, it does not say "as a sin offering." How can this inconsistency be reconciled? God, in effect, is saying to Israel: Because you have accepted on yourselves the yoke of the Torah, I consider it as if you had never sinned (Jerusalem Talmud, *Rosh Hashanah* 4:8).

NOTE: The festival of Shavuot commemorates the giving of the Torah, which took place on that day.

**(29:1) The first day of the serene month [this is Tishri, which is Rosh Hashanah, the Hebrew new year] shall be a sacred holiday to you when you may not do any mundane work. It shall be of teruah, sounding the [ram's] horn.**

### ▓ *The Talmud Teaches*
*A day of teruah, sounding the ram's horn* In one verse, it says "a remembrance of *teruah*" (Leviticus 23:24), and here it says "a day of *teruah*." How can these verses be reconciled? R. Pappa explained: The first verse refers to the case when Rosh Hashanah falls on Shabbat, in which case the shofar is not blown, because of the concern that one may carry the shofar in a public domain, which is forbidden on Shabbat. So the shofar is just "remembered." The second verse applies to a Rosh Hashanah that falls on a weekday, in which case the shofar is sounded (*Rosh Hashanah* 29b).

**(29:2) As an appeasing fragrance to God, you must make a burnt offering consisting of one young bull, one ram, and seven yearling sheep all without blemish.**

### ❈ *The Jerusalem Talmud Teaches*

***You must make [va'asitem] a burnt offering***  R. Yose said:
With regard to all offerings, it says *vehikravtem* "you must *offer*
a burnt offering"; but with regard to Rosh Hashanah, it says
*va'asitem,* "you must *make* a burnt offering." How can this
inconsistency be reconciled? In effect, God is saying to Israel:
Because you have come to Me for judgment on Rosh Hashanah
and have gone forth in peace, I consider it as if you have been
*made* [into] a new creation (Jerusalem Talmud, *Rosh Hashanah*
4:8).

42

# Torah Portion

# Matot

### Numbers 30:2–32:42

## VOWS

**(30:3) If a man makes a vow to God, or makes an oath to establish a prohibition on himself, he must not break his word. He must do all that he expressed verbally.**

✳ *The Midrash Teaches*
*An oath to establish a prohibition on himself* I might think that even when he took an oath to eat carcass and *treifah*, "forbidden animals," and reptiles, the command of "he must do all that he expressed verbally" applies to him, and he has to eat these forbidden things. Therefore, it says "to establish a prohibition on himself," which means: to prohibit on himself something that is permitted but not to permit something that is prohibited; thus, he may not fulfill his oath of eating forbidden things *(Sifrei)*.

*He must do all that he expressed verbally* This tells me only that he must do the things he articulated with his mouth. But from where do I know that he must do the things he vowed or swore in his thoughts? From "to establish a prohibition on himself," literally, "on his soul" *(Sifrei)*.

**(30:13) However, if a husband annuls his wife's vows on the day he hears them, then all her verbally expressed vows and**

254

self-imposed obligations need not be kept. Since her husband
has annulled them, God will forgive her.

### ※ The Talmud Teaches

*God will forgive her* The verse is speaking about a woman
who made a Nazirite vow and then drank wine, thereby breaking her vow. However, her husband earlier had nullified her
vow without her knowledge; but she thinks that by drinking
wine, she broke her vow. The verse implies that she needs
atonement and forgiveness although, because her husband had
annulled her vow, she did not really break it. When R. Akiva
came to this verse, he cried: If a person who intended to eat
swine's meat but by chance ate lamb's meat needs atonement
and forgiveness, like the woman who intended to break her
Nazirite vow by drinking wine, when in reality she was not a Nazirite, surely a person who intended to eat swine's meat and actually ate it needs atonement and forgiveness! (*Nazir* 23a).

## THE WAR AGAINST MIDIAN

**(31:6) In the war against Midian, Moses dispatched a thou-
sand men from each tribe as an army, them and Pinchas son
of Elazar the priest, who was in charge of the sacred articles
and signal trumpets.**

### ✳ The Midrash Teaches

*them and Pinchas* The twelve tribes mustered altogether
twelve thousand men. The phrase "them and Pinchas" teaches
us that the twelve thousand men were equivalent to Pinchas,
and Pinchas was equivalent to all of them *(Sifrei)*.

**(31:8) Along with the other victims, they also killed the five
kings of Midian: Evi, Rekem, Tzur, Chur, and Reva, the five
Midianite kings. They also killed Balaam son of Beor by the
sword.**

### ※ The Talmud Teaches

*They also killed Balaam son of Beor* What was Balaam doing
in Midian when he lived in Aram (23:7)? R. Yochanan said: He

had gone to Midian to collect a reward for the twenty-four thousand Israelites whose death he had caused. Rav said: People have a saying for that: The camel went to demand horns, so they cut off the ears he had. [Balaam's desire for a reward led to his death] (*Sanhedrin* 106a).

NOTE: Balaam advised Moab and Midian to allow their daughters to seduce the Israelites. As a result of their immorality, twenty-four thousand Jews died in a plague (Numbers 25:9).

**(31:14) Moses was angry with the commanders of the army, the officers of the thousands and the officers of the hundreds, returning from the military campaign.**

### ※ *The Talmud Teaches*
*Moses was angry* Because the officers had allowed their troops to spare women who were known to have participated in the orgies. Moses said to Israel, "Have you backslid to your earlier sin of behaving immorally with the Moabite girls?" (25:1). They answered, "Not a single man is missing" (31:49), implying, not one has behaved promiscuously. Said Moses, "If so, why do you seek atonement by offering the gold ornaments you captured?" (31:50). They replied, "Although we escaped from the sin itself, we did not escape thinking about it, and for this we seek atonement" (*Shabbat* 64a).

**(31:50) [The generals and captains said to Moses:] We therefore want to bring an offering to God. Every man who found any gold article such as an arm band, an anklet, a ring, an earring, or a body ornament wants to bring it to atone for our souls before God.**

### ※ *The Talmud Teaches*
*a ring, an earring, or a body ornament* R. Sheshet said: Why does the Torah list the women's jewelry that is worn outside along with jewelry that is worn inwardly? To teach you that whoever gazes at a woman's little finger is as though he gazed upon her private parts (*Shabbat* 64b).

*to atone for our souls* In the yeshiva of R. Yishmael, it was taught: Why did the Jews of that generation need atonement?

Because they gratified their eyes looking at nakedness (*Shabbat* 64b).

## THE REQUEST OF REUBEN AND GAD

**(32:22) When the land is conquered before God, you may return home, and you shall be guiltless toward God and toward Israel. This land will then be yours as your permanent property before God.**

※ *The Talmud Teaches*
***You shall be guiltless toward God and toward Israel*** Which means that you should not act in a way that arouses suspicion. For example: It was taught: The family of Garmu were proficient in making the showbread for the Temple. The Sages praised them because their children were never found to have white bread, so that no one should suspect them and say, "They are taking from the flour of the showbreads for themselves." The Garmu family did this to comply with the command, "You shall be guiltless toward God and toward Israel," that is, you should avoid doing anything—even when acting rightly—that might arouse suspicion (*Yoma* 38a).

NOTE: Twelve loaves of *lechem hapanim*, "showbreads," were arranged every Shabbat in two stacks on the table in the sanctuary and eaten by the *kohanim* on the following Shabbat. Because the loaves were thin and fragile, preparing and baking them required great skill (Exodus 25:30 and Leviticus 24:5–9).

***You shall be guiltless toward God and toward Israel*** The Rabbis taught: The Avtinas family were proficient in preparing the incense for the Temple. The Sages praised them because it never happened that a bride in their family went out wearing perfume; and when they married a woman from someplace else, they stipulated that she should not wear perfume, so that no one should say, "The fragrance they are wearing is from the ingredients of the incense of the Temple." They did this in compliance of the command, "You shall be guiltless toward God and toward Israel" (*Yoma* 38a).

***You shall be guiltless toward God and toward Israel*** When the administrators of a charity fund have no poor people to whom to distribute their cash, they must exchange their copper coins, which become tarnished and depreciate with time, for silver coins of others, not for silver coins of their own, so that people will not suspect them of shortchanging the charity treasury. They did this because it says "You shall be guiltless toward God and toward Israel" (*Pesachim* 13a).

***You shall be guiltless toward God and toward Israel*** The shekel coins that were contributed by the people were deposited in a treasury chamber in the Temple. The money was used to buy the communal sacrifices. The person who entered the chamber to withdraw money to buy animals for the sacrifices did not wear a garment with a doubled-over hem, shoes, sandals, tefillin, or an amulet, so that people should not say that he hid in the hem money he stole. And so that if he became poor, people should not say that his poverty was his punishment for stealing money from the treasury and hiding it in these articles; and if he became rich, people should not say his wealth came from money he stole from the treasury. But if he did not wear any of these articles, people had no reason to be suspicious, for he had no way of hiding the money, because ancient robes had no pockets. Because you have to be careful to keep your good name in the eyes of people just as you must in the eyes of God, as it says "You shall be guiltless toward men and toward God" (*Shekalim* 3:2).

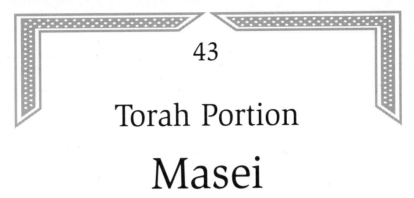

# 43

## Torah Portion

# Masei

### Numbers 33:1–36:13

## AARON'S DEATH

**(33:38) Aaron the priest climbed Hor Mountain at God's command, and he died there on the first day of the fifth month, in the fortieth year of the Israelites' Exodus from Egypt.**

⁂ *The Talmud Teaches*
*at God's command . . . he died* And not through the Angel of Death. From here, we derive that the Angel of Death did not hold sway over Aaron and that worms and maggots had no power over him (*Bava Batra* 17a).

## ACTS OF MURDER

**(35:11) You must designate cities which shall serve as refuge cities to which a murderer who killed a person accidentally can flee.**

⁂ *The Talmud Teaches*
*to which a murderer . . . can flee* From where do we infer that if the accused leaves the court convicted and someone says, "I have something to say in his defense," that he is brought back for a retrial? For it says "Do not execute the innocent" (Exodus 23:7), which means that it is forbidden to impose the death penalty as long as anyone has evidence to present in the accused's favor.

And from where do we infer that if the accused leaves the court not guilty and someone says, "I have something to say against him," that he may not be retried? From the verse, "Do not execute . . . the righteous" (Exodus 23:7). Once a suspect has been acquitted, the death penalty cannot be imposed, no matter how much evidence against him is found (*Sanhedrin* 33b).

**(35:12) These cities shall serve you as a refuge from the avenger, so that a murderer not die until he can stand trial before the courts.**

*The Talmud Teaches*

***until he can stand trial*** What does this teach us? Because it says "If the blood avenger finds the accidental murderer outside the borders of his refuge city, and the blood avenger puts the killer to death, it is not an act of murder" (35:27), I might think that the avenger might kill him right away; therefore, it says "until he can stand trial before the courts" and is sentenced to exile. Consequently, if the avenger kills the accidental murderer before he appeared in court, the avenger is executed (*Makkot* 12a).

**(35:16) If he had struck his victim purposely with an iron weapon, killing him, then he is a murderer, and he must be put to death.**

*The Talmud Teaches*

***If he had struck . . . with an iron weapon*** Rebbi said: It is well known to God that iron, no matter what its size, can kill; even a needle can kill, if it is thrust into the heart or the brain. Therefore, the Torah prescribed no size for an iron weapon (*Sanhedrin* 76a).

***The murderer must be put to death*** From where do we know the rabbinic principle: "Follow the majority"? R. Kahana said: It is derived from the case of the murderer, on whom the Torah imposes the death penalty. Now, why don't we fear that the murder victim may have been suffering from a fatal disease, in which case the murderer is not liable to the death penalty, because he killed a "dead" man? But the murderer is nevertheless executed, which proves that we follow the majority, and the majority of people are not afflicted with a fatal disease (*Chullin* 11b).

**(35:18) Likewise, if he strikes him with a deadly wooden hand weapon, and the victim dies, he is a murderer and must be put to death for murder.**

✳ *The Midrash Teaches*
*If he strikes him with a wooden hand weapon* The Torah mentions weapons made of iron, stone, and wood. Stone is not like wood in some respects; wood is not like stone in other respects; and both are not like iron. What they all have in common is that they are used as weapons by the murderer and cause the death of the victim. This comes to exclude the cases where the victim dies because he is pushed into a fire or into water or because a dog or a snake were stirred up against him, in which case the killer's judgment is turned over to the heavenly tribunal *(Sifrei)*.

NOTE: Or other indirect ways of causing death, such as pushing the victim into a pit and removing the ladder, or tying him up and leaving him to die of starvation, heat, or cold.

**(35:20) The avenger shall kill the murderer if the killer pushes down his victim or throws something down on him out of hatred, causing the victim to die.**

✳ *The Midrash Teaches*
*If the killer pushes down his victim or throws something down on him* This tells me only that the killer is liable to the death penalty if he killed the victim with an iron, stone, or wooden weapon. From where do we derive that if he killed the victim by pushing him off a roof, he is also liable? Because it says "If he pushes down his victim . . . out of hatred," killing him by any and all means *(Sifrei)*.

**(35:24) The assembly, that is, the court, shall judge between the killer and the blood avenger, according to these ordinances.**

### ❋ *The Talmud Teaches*

***The assembly . . . shall judge*** R. Yehudah said: A blind person is exempt from all the laws of the Torah. For it says "The assembly shall judge between the killer and the blood avenger, according to these ordinances." Whoever is subject to the law of the "killer" and the "blood avenger" is subject to "these ordinances," in general, that is, the mitzvoth of the Torah, and whoever is not subject to the law of the "killer" and the "blood avenger," for example, a blind person, is not subject to "these ordinances," that is, the mitzvoth (*Bava Kamma* 87a).

NOTE: The previous verse (35:23) speaks of a case in which someone unintentionally killed a person "without having seen him"; so in order to be subject to these laws, the killer must be able to see.

**(35:25) The court shall rescue the murderer from the hand of the blood avenger, and the court shall return him to the city of refuge where he had fled. The murderer must live there until the death of the high priest anointed with the sacred oil.**

### ❋ *The Talmud Teaches*

***The court shall rescue*** R. Akiva said: If the members of the Sanhedrin saw a man kill someone, they all become witnesses; and a witness cannot act as a judge. For it . . . says "The court shall judge. . . . and the court shall rescue" (35:25, 26), and because they have seen him kill a person, they cannot find any defense for him and "rescue" him (*Rosh Hashanah* 26a).

***the city of refuge where he had fled*** The inadvertent killer may not leave the city of refuge to testify with regard to a mitzvah, such as to report to the Sanhedrin the first sighting of the new moon, to be a witness in a monetary lawsuit, to testify in a capital case—even if all Israel needs him; even if he is an army commander like Joab ben Tzeruiah (2 Kings 2:5), for it says "where he had fled"—literally: he had fled there—to indicate that "there" shall be his permanent dwelling; "there" shall he die; "there" shall he be buried (*Makkot* 11b).

**(35:31) Do not take ransom for the life of a murderer who is condemned to die, since he must be put to death.**

❋ *The Midrash Teaches*
*who is condemned to die* Therefore, if someone is taken out to be executed after his trial and others wound or kill him, they are not liable, because after the trial has ended, the verdict cannot be overturned, so they wounded or killed a person who is technically "dead" *(Sifrei)*.

**(35:33) Do not pollute the land in which you live; it is blood that pollutes the land. When blood is shed in the land, it cannot be atoned for except through the blood of the person who shed it.**

❈ *The Jerusalem Talmud Teaches*
*blood pollutes the land* Because of the sin of spilling blood, the rains are withheld. For it says "It is blood that pollutes, *yachnif,* 'the land'"; *yachnif* can be read as a combination of *yichan af,* which means "God's anger will come to rest [on the land]" and it will manifest itself in the rains being withheld (Jerusalem Talmud, *Taanit* 3:3).

**(36:6) This is the thing that God has commanded regarding Tzelofchad's daughters: You may marry anyone you wish as long as you marry within your father's tribe.**

❊ *The Talmud Teaches*
*This is the thing* R. Shimon b. Gamliel said: On the fifteenth of Av, the tribes were permitted to intermarry with one another. From what passage did the Sages derive this? They expounded the phrase, "This is the thing," saying that the word *this* implies that the prohibition of intermarriage among the tribes shall be limited to *this* generation only *(Taanit* 30b).

NOTE: The Torah (Numbers 36:6, 7) states that a woman of the generation that entered the Land of Israel under Joshua and who had inherited property was forbidden to marry out of her tribe to prevent her inherited property from being transferred to her husband's tribe upon her death. This prohibition applied only to the generation that entered Eretz Yisrael, and it was left to the Sages to determine when it was no longer in force.

# Deuteronomy

# 44

## Torah Portion

# Devarim

### Deuteronomy 1:1–3:2

## HISTORICAL REVIEW OF THE WANDERINGS

(1:7) God said to us at Horeb, "Turn around and head toward the Amorite highland and all its neighboring territory, in the Aravah, the hill country, the lowlands, the Negev, the seashore, the Canaanite territory, as far as the great river, the Euphrates River."

✷ *The Talmud Teaches*
*the great river, the Euphrates River* Shimon b. Tarfon said: This is an example of the popular saying: Touch a person who is smeared with oil, and some of it will rub off on you (Rashi on *Shevuot* 47b, entry for *kerav*).

NOTE: The Euphrates is really the smallest of the four rivers listed in Genesis 2:14, but this verse calls it "the great river" because it is mentioned in connection with the Land of Israel; and anything connected with the Land of Israel is great.

## INSTRUCTIONS TO JUDGES

(1:16) Moses said, "I then gave instructions to your judges, saying, 'Listen to every dispute among your brethren, and judge honestly between each man and his brother, especially when a proselyte is concerned.'"

### ✳ *The Talmud Teaches*

*I then gave instructions to your judges*  R. Yochanan said: This is a warning to judges to use the rod and the strap with caution, only for the sake of carrying out justice but not as a display of power (*Sanhedrin* 7b).

NOTE: The rod is for beating a person who refuses to obey a court order; the strap is for administering the thirty-nine lashes (Deuteronomy 25:3).

*Listen [shamo'a] to every dispute among your brethren, and judge*  R. Chanina said: This is a warning to the court not to listen to the claims of one litigant in the absence of his opponent and a warning to the litigant not to present his case to the judge before his opponent shows up. It says *shamo'a,* "listen," which can be read also as *shamei'a,* "make your words heard among your brethren," implying that the litigants should explain their side of the argument only when both are present (*Sanhedrin* 7b).

*Judge honestly . . . when a proselyte is concerned*  R. Yehudah derives from the fact that a convert is mentioned in connection with "judging" that a person who converted in a lawful court is a legitimate convert, but one who converted privately, on his own, is not a convert (*Yevamot* 47a).

NOTE: Just as a judicial matter requires a *bet din* (rabbinic court) of three qualified persons, so does the conversion of a proselyte require a *bet din* that follows all the laws prescribed by Halachah (Torah law).

**(1:17) Do not give anyone special consideration in judgment. Listen to great and small alike, and do not be intimidated by any man, since judgment belongs to God. If any case is too difficult, bring it to me, and I will hear it.**

### ✳ *The Midrash Teaches*

*Do not give anyone special consideration in judgment*  Literally: "Do not recognize a face in judgment." This applies to the one who appoints judges. If he says: This man is handsome, so I will appoint him as a judge; this man is strong; this man speaks many languages, so I will appoint him as a judge—he indirectly causes a guilty person to be acquitted and an innocent one to be charged with a crime; not that the judge is an evil person, but because he is ignorant of the law. In such a case, Scripture considers the one who appointed the incompetent judge as having been "partial in judgment" *(Sifrei)*.

### ✄ *The Talmud Teaches*
**Listen to small and great alike** Resh Lakish said: This teaches us that you should treat a lawsuit involving one *perutah*—a small coin—with the same seriousness as you would a case involving a hundred *maneh* (a gold or silver coin worth one hundred shekels, as respectable a sum as $100). What are the practical ramifications of this rule? Do you think that it tells us to consider and investigate disputes about small and large amounts with equal care? That is obvious! It tells the judge to assign priority to whichever case comes first, even if the first case on the docket involves only a *perutah* (*Sanhedrin* 8a).

**Do not be intimidated by any man** Resh Lakish said: When two litigants appear before you in court, one mild-mannered, the other tough, then, before you have heard their case—or even after—so long as you are in doubt as to who is right, you may tell them, "I don't want to hear your case," for perhaps the tough one will be found guilty and cause you untold trouble. But once you have heard their claims and know who is guilty, you cannot withdraw and say, out of fear of antagonizing the tough one, "I don't want to get involved in your dispute." For it says "Do not be intimidated by any man" (*Sanhedrin* 6b).

**Do not be intimidated by any man** R. Yehoshua b. Korchah said: If a student is present when his master is judging a dispute [between a poor and a rich litigant], and he sees a point of defense for the poor litigant and against his rich opponent, from where do we know that he should not keep quiet? Because it says "Do not be intimidated *[taguru]* by any man." R. Chanin said: This means: Do not hold back your words because of anyone [he sees *taguru* as cognate with *agar*, "to collect, withhold"] (*Sanhedrin* 6b).

*Since judgment belongs to God* R. Chama b. R. Chanina said: God said: It is not bad enough for the wicked judges that they take away money from one person and give it to another unjustly, but they inconvenience Me to return it to the owner, that is, the judgment belongs to God to set the wrong judgment right (*Sanhedrin* 8a).

**(2:6) You may purchase from the descendants of Esau with money food to eat and drinking water.**

### ❖ The Jerusalem Talmud Teaches
*You may purchase* [tishberu] The word *tishberu* is related to *shavar*, "to break." This gives rise to the saying: If you can break, that is, appease your enemy with food, feed him; if not, load him up with money. This was what R. Yonatan used to do. When the governor would come to the city, he would send him expensive gifts, reasoning: If a case against an orphan or widow is brought before him, his anger will be soothed by the gifts, and he will be placated (Jerusalem Talmud, *Shabbat* 1:4).

**(2:9) God said to me, "Do not attack Moab and do not provoke them to fight. I will not give you their land as an inheritance, since I have given Ar to Lot's descendants as their heritage."**

### ❖ The Talmud Teaches
*Do not attack Moab* Now, you may well ask, could it have entered Moses' mind to wage war without God's approval, that God should have to warn him against it? We must assume therefore that Moses drew the following logical inference: If in the case of the Midianites who came only to assist the Moabites, the Torah commanded, "Attack the Midianites and kill them" (Numbers 25:17), should not the same apply even more so to the Moabites themselves? Therefore, God had to warn Moses explicitly not to attack Moab (*Bava Kamma* 38a, b).

NOTE: Ar is the name of the area where Moab was situated. Moab was Lot's son, born of his incestuous union with his daughter (Genesis 19:37). The Gemara explains the reason that the Moabites had to be spared was that Ruth the Moabitess, the ancestor of David and Mashiach, was destined to descend from them.

**(2:16, 17) When all the warriors among the people had died off, God spoke to me, saying . . .**

### *The Talmud Teaches*

***When all the warriors . . . had died off*** We have learned that as long as those destined to perish in the wilderness had not yet died, God did not speak directly to Moses, for it says "When all of the warriors had died off . . . God spoke to me, . . . saying." It was only then that God resumed speaking lovingly to Moses, as He used to. God did command many mitzvoth to Moses during that time, but He did not speak lovingly to him (*Taanit* 30b).

### *The Jerusalem Talmud Teaches*

***When all the warriors had died off*** R. Ze'ira said: What can the great men of the generation do, if the community is judged only according to the majority! For we find that all of the thirty-eight years that the children of Israel were out of favor, God did not speak with Moses, as it says "When all the warriors had died off, *then* God spoke to me, saying . . ." It was because the majority of the people had sinned that God withheld His favor from Moses (Jerusalem Talmud, *Taanit* 3:4).

NOTE: After the spies returned from their expedition to the Land of Israel and discouraged the people from entering the Land, God swore that all the men between the ages of twenty and sixty had to die during the wandering in the wilderness.

**(2:23) As for the Avvim who dwell in the open cities as far as Gaza, the Kaftorim came from Kaftor and defeated them, occupying their territory.**

### *The Talmud Teaches*

***As for the Avvim*** R. Shimon b. Levi said: There are many verses in the Torah that at first glance seem to be pointless, so that the casual reader might think that they should be deleted. Yet these verses are vital elements of the Torah. For example, it says "As for the Avvim who dwell in the open cities as far as Gaza." Who cares where the Avvim lived? It is important, because Avimelech, king of the Philistines, had bound Abraham by an oath, saying, "that you will not deal falsely with me, with my children, or with my grandchildren" (Genesis 21:23). Thus, Abraham swore not to take possession of the land of the Philistines. So God said: Let the Kaftorim come and take the land from the Avvim—who were Philistines—and then let Israel come and take it away from the Kaftorim, who are not Philistines. That way, the children of Israel were able to gain possession of the land without violating the oath Abraham made to Avimelech (*Chullin* 60b).

**(2:26) I sent emissaries from the Kedemot Desert to Sichon king of Cheshbon with a peaceful message, saying, "We wish to pass through your land."**

***The Talmud Teaches***

***From the Kedemot Desert*** The Kedemot Desert and the Sinai Desert are one and the same. Then why is it called *Kedemot?* Because it is the place where Israel's preeminence, *kadmut,* was established by their acceptance of the Torah (*Shabbat* 89a).

NOTE: Another reason may be because the Torah establishes *kadmut ha'olam,* the principle that the universe had a beginning with Creation, negating the erroneous Aristotelian theory that the world always existed.

# 45

## Torah Portion

# Va'etchanan

Deuteronomy 3:23–7:11

### MOSES' PRAYER

**(3:25) Please let me cross the Jordan. Let me see the good land across the Jordan, this good mountain, and the Lebanon.**

�֎ *The Talmud Teaches*
*Please let me cross the Jordan* R. Simla'i expounded: Why did Moses our teacher desire to enter the Land of Israel? Did he want to eat of its fruits or be satiated with its goodness? Certainly not. But this is what Moses said: The Jews were given many commandments that can only be fulfilled in the Land of Israel. I want to enter the Land of Israel so that I should be able to fulfill all of them (*Sotah* 14a).

**(3:26) But God was angry with me because of you, and He would not listen to me. God said to me, "Enough! Do not speak to Me any more about this!"**

✷ *The Talmud Teaches*
*Enough!* R. Levi said: Moses used the term *Enough!* in addressing the rebellious Korach and his party, saying, "Enough! you sons of Levi!" (Numbers 16:7). And with the same *Enough!*, he was addressed when God said to him, "Enough! Do not speak to Me any more about this!" God used Moses' own phrase, indicating that His decision was final (*Sotah* 13b).

**(3:27) Climb to the top of the cliff, and gaze to the west, the east, the north, and the south. Let your eyes feast on it, since you will not cross the Jordan.**

### ※ *The Talmud Teaches*
*Climb to the top of the cliff*  R. Elazar said: Prayer is more effective even than good deeds, for no one was greater in good deeds than Moses our teacher, and yet he was answered and granted a glimpse of the Land of Israel only after he prayed, as it says "Do not speak, that is, pray, to me about this any more"; and immediately after this, it says "Climb to the top of the cliff" (3:27) and view the land, for your prayer has appeased Me (*Berachot* 32b).

## BASIC BELIEFS

**(4:4) But you, who are attached to God your Lord, are all alive today.**

### ※ *The Talmud Teaches*
*But you, who are attached to God your Lord, are all alive today*  How is it possible to attach yourself to God about whom it says "For God your Lord is like a consuming fire" (4:24)? This is what the text means: Anyone who gives his daughter in marriage to a Torah scholar, or who does business in partnership with a Torah scholar, and gives him a share of the profits, so that the scholar can devote his time to Torah study, or who lets Torah scholars derive benefit from his resources, Scripture considers it as though he attached himself to the Shechinah, and in that merit, "you are all alive today"—you will be revived to eternal life; and not just scholars but whoever assists Torah scholars will be resurrected (*Ketubot* 111b).

*But you who are attached to God your Lord are all alive today*  Why the superfluous word *today*? It tells us: Even when all others are dead, you are alive. Just as you are all alive today, so will you be alive in the world to come, which provides an allusion to the resurrection of the dead in the Torah (*Sanhedrin* 90b).

**(4:6) Safeguard and keep these rules since this is your wisdom and understanding in the eyes of the nations. They will hear all these rules, and say, "This great nation is certainly a wise and understanding people."**

### ※ The Talmud Teaches
*This is your wisdom and understanding* R. Shmuel b. Nachmani said: From where do we know that it is a mitzvah to calculate the cycles of the seasons and the constellations? Because it says "Since this is your wisdom and understanding in the eyes of the nations." What kind of wisdom is recognized by the nations of the world? The science of astronomical cycles and the stellar constellations (*Shabbat* 75a).

**(4:7) What nation is so great that they have God close to it, as God our Lord is, whenever we call Him?**

### ※ The Jerusalem Talmud Teaches
*close to it* R. Levi said: From earth to heaven is a distance of five hundred years, that is, an unfathomable distance, yet you can enter a house of prayer and pray in a whisper, and the Holy One, blessed be He, hears your prayer (Jerusalem Talmud, *Berachot* 9:1).

**(4:8) What nation is so great that they have such righteous rules and laws, like this entire Torah that I am presenting to you today?**

### ※ The Jerusalem Talmud Teaches
*What nation is so great* R. Simon said: Normally, when a person knows that he is going to be judged, he puts on black clothes and goes around unkempt. He is worried sick, because he does not know how his judgment will come out. But on Rosh Hashanah, the Day of Judgment, Jews do not act like this. Instead they dress in white clothes, groom themselves, and eat and drink and rejoice, knowing that God will deal wondrously with them even if they do not deserve it (Jerusalem Talmud, *Rosh Hashanah* 1:3).

**(4:9) Only take heed and watch yourself very carefully, so that you do not forget the things that your eyes saw. Do not let this memory leave your hearts, all the days of your lives. Teach them to your children and grandchildren.**

### ※ *The Talmud Teaches*

*Watch yourself carefully* The story is told that once a pious man was praying on the road when a general passed by and greeted him. Because he was in the middle of *Shemoneh esrei* (Amidah), the pious man did not return the greeting. When he finished his prayer, the general said to him, "Don't you know that it says in your Torah, 'Watch yourself very carefully'?, meaning, 'Don't put your life in danger'? Why didn't you return my greeting? If I had cut off your head, who would have taken me to court for shedding your blood?" The pious man replied, "Suppose you were standing before a king of flesh and blood, and someone came by and greeted you, would you have turned away from the king and answered him?" "No," replied the general. The pious man continued, "You yourself admit that you would not have turned away from a king of flesh and blood, a man who is here today and tomorrow in the grave; surely, I cannot turn away when standing before the supreme King of kings, the Holy One, blessed be He, Who lives and endures for all eternity." Immediately, the general was placated and let the pious man go home in peace (*Berachot* 32b, 33a).

*Teach them to your children and grandchildren* R. Chiya b. Abba encountered R. Yehoshua b. Levi walking down the street, taking a child to the house of study. Instead of a formal turban, he was wearing a cloth casually thrown over his head. R. Chiya b. Abba asked him, "What's the rush, that you walked out without wearing the headgear befitting someone of your stature?" R. Yehoshua replied, "Is it then a small thing when it says 'Teach your children' followed by 'The day that you stood before God your Lord at Horeb?' Taking my grandson to his Torah class is as though I were standing at Sinai!" (*Kiddushin* 30a).

**(4:24) God your Lord is like a consuming fire, a jealous God.**

## ※ *The Talmud Teaches*

*a jealous God* A philosopher asked R. Gamliel: "It says in your Torah, 'God is like a consuming fire, a jealous God.' Why is He jealous of the worshippers of idols and not of the idol itself?" R. Gamliel replied, "You can compare it to a king who had a son. The son had a dog that he named after his father, and whenever he took an oath, he would swear, 'By the life of this dog, my father!' When the king hears of this, with whom will he be angry—with the son or the dog? Of course, he will be angry with the son!" (*Avodah Zarah* 54b).

## EXILE AND REPENTANCE

**(4:25) When you have children and grandchildren, and you will have been long in the land, you might become corrupt and make a statue of some image, committing an evil act in the eyes of God your Lord and making Him angry.**

## ※ *The Talmud Teaches*

*you will have been long [venoshantem] in the land* Mereimar expounded: What is meant by the passage "God hastened the calamity and brought it upon us; for God our Lord is *tzaddik*, 'righteous'" (Daniel 9:14)? Is it because God is righteous that He hurried to bring the calamity on us? He explained that the text means: God did a great kindness, *tzedakah*, by causing Israel to be sent into exile two years before the numerical value of *venoshantem* was reached, thus sparing them from the complete destruction that would have befallen them if their sins had "matured" another two years. From the phrase "that you will then quickly be destroyed" (4:26), which follows *venoshantem*, we see that the "quickly" of God is 852 [years] (*Gittin* 88a).

NOTE: The numerical value of *venoshantem* is 852 (*vav* = 6; *nun* = 50; *shin* = 300; *nun* = 50; *tav* = 400; *mem* = 40). The first Temple was destroyed 850 years after the Jews crossed the Jordan into the Land of Israel, two years before 852. Because of these two years, the prophecy of *venoshantem*—that is, 852, "you will have been long in the land"—was not fulfilled. As a consequence, the prophecy of the next verse, "you will be destroyed" (4:26) was not fulfilled either.

**(4:32) You might inquire about times long past, going back to the time that God created man on earth, and from one end of heaven to the other end. Has there ever been anything as great as this, or has anything like it been heard?**

### ※ *The Talmud Teaches*

*man on earth* R. Elazar said: Adam's height reached from earth all the way to heaven, for it says "going back to the time that God who is in heaven created man on earth." R. Yehudah said: Adam stretched from one side of the world to the other side of the world; that is, when lying down, he extended from the extreme east to the extreme west. For it says "from one end of heaven to the other end." If so, the verses seem to contradict each other! One verse says that he reached from earth to heaven; the other, that he extended from east to west. There is no contradiction. They both are the same distance, the distance from east to west is the same as from earth to heaven (*Chagigah* 12a).

NOTE: The *Nefesh Hachayim* by R. Chaim Volozhiner explains that this *Aggadah* should not be taken literally. It means that Adam's intellect was so clear and all-encompassing that he could comprehend the actions and processes of the entire universe.

## THE FIFTH COMMANDMENT

**(5:16) Honor your father and mother as God your Lord commanded you. You will then live long and have it well on the land that God your Lord is giving you.**

### ※ *The Talmud Teaches*

*You will then live long* R. Yaakov said: There is no reward given for mitzvoth in this world; the reward for mitzvoth is reserved exclusively for the world to come, for R. Yaakov said: There is not a single mitzvah in the Torah together with its reward, where this reward does not pertain to the world to come. For example, regarding honoring one's father and mother, it says "You will then live long and have it well." Regarding the mitzvah of sending away the mother bird, it says "If you do this, you will have it good and live long" (22:7). The promise of "you will live long" cannot refer to this world, for if a father tells his son, "Climb up that tall building and bring down little birds for me," and he climbs up, thereby fulfilling the mitzvah of honoring his father, takes the little birds, and first sends the mother away, thereby fulfilling the mitzvah of sending away the mother bird, and on his way down falls off the building and dies, where is his promise of long life? It must be therefore that the promise of "you will have it good" refers to the world that is completely good, that is, the world to come, and "you will live long" refers to the world that lasts forever (*Kiddushin* 39b).

## THE SHEMA

**(6:3) Listen, Israel, God is our Lord, God is the One and Only.**

### ※ *The Talmud Teaches*
**Listen Israel** The Rabbis taught: We know that God has greater love for Israel than for the ministering angels, for Israel mentions the name of God in the Shema after two words, for it says "Listen Israel, God," while the ministering angels mention His name only after three words, as it says "Holy, holy, holy [is] God, Master of Legions!" (*Chullin* 91b).

**(6:5) Love God your Lord with all your heart, with all your soul, and with all your resources.**

### ※ *The Talmud Teaches*
**Love God** This means that you should cause the name of heaven to be beloved. A person should study the Chumash, the Mishnah, and the Gemara; he should be honest in business and speak gently to people. What do people say about such a person? "Fortunate is the father who taught him Torah. Fortunate is the teacher who taught him Torah. Look how refined are his ways, look how correct are his deeds!" (*Yoma* 86a).

**with all your resources** R. Eliezer said: Because it says "with all your soul," why does it have to say, "with all your resources"? And because it says "with all your resources," why does it have to say "with all your soul"? For the person who values his life more than his money, it says "with all your soul," that is, even if you have to give up your life for the sake of God. And for the person who values his money more than his life, it says "with all your resources" (*Berachot* 61b).

**(6:7) Teach the Torah thoroughly to your children and speak of them when you are at home, when traveling on the road, when you lie down, and when you get up.**

### ✳ *The Talmud Teaches*
**Teach the Torah thoroughly [veshinnantam]** *Veshinnantam* is from the root *shanan*, "to be keen." This means that the words of the Torah should be clear in your mind, so that if a person asks you something, you should not hesitate but answer him on the spot. As it says "Say to wisdom, 'You are my sister,' and call understanding a friend" (Proverbs 7:4) (*Kiddushin* 30a).

NOTE: Rashi explains: A person should be as well versed in the Torah as he is familiar with the law that his sister is forbidden to him.

**(6:8) Bind these words as a sign on your hand, and let them be an emblem in the center of your head.**

### ✳ *The Talmud Teaches*
**Bind these words** It was taught: When you put on the tefillin, you should put on first the hand-tefillin and then the head-tefillin, for it says "Bind these words as a sign on your hand," and then it says "and let them be an emblem in the center of your head." But from where do we know that when you take them off, you should first take off the head-tefillin and then the arm-tefillin? Rabbah said: It says "and let them be an emblem in the center of your head;" that is to say, as long as they are "in the center of your head," both shall be there. "And let *them* be in the center of the head," which is plural, implies that the head-tefillin must never be alone on you; therefore, you should put it on last and take it off first (*Menachot* 36a).

**(6:9) Also write them on parchments affixed to the doorposts of your houses and gates.**

### ※ *The Talmud Teaches*

*Also write them*  It was taught: It is a mitzvah to place the mezuzah at the upper third of the doorpost. For it says "Bind them" and "Write them." Just as the binding of the tefillin is on the upper part of the arm, so too the writing, that is, the mezuzah, must be placed on the upper third part of the doorpost (*Menachot* 33a).

NOTE: The parchment on the doorpost is called mezuzah. Both the Shema and Deuteronomy 1:13–21 are written on the parchment in the mezuzah. When entering or leaving your house, the mezuzah reminds you of the Divine Presence and of your duty to keep the laws of the Torah.

**(7:4) Do not intermarry [with the Gentiles], for he will lead your child away from Me, causing him to worship other gods. God will then display His anger against you, and you will quickly be destroyed.**

### ※ *The Talmud Teaches*

*your child*  The child of a Gentile mother and a Jewish father is considered a Gentile, like the mother. For it says "For *he,* the Gentile father, will lead your son away from Me." If the father is a Gentile, he will lead the Jewish mother's son away, because the son is Jewish. This does not apply in the case when the mother is a Gentile. In that case, neither she nor the father can lead their son away from Judaism, because the son is not Jewish to begin with. Your son by a Jewish woman is called your son; but your son by a Gentile woman is not called your son but her son (*Kiddushin* 68b).

**(7:11) So observe the commandments, the rules and laws that I command you today by performing them.**

### ※ *The Talmud Teaches*

*today to perform them*  Today in this world, you have the opportunity to do them, but you cannot wait until tomorrow in the world to come to do them. Today in this world, you can fulfill the mitzvoth, but tomorrow, the world to come is set aside for you to receive the reward for doing them (*Eruvin* 22a).

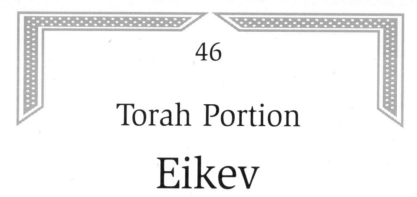

46

# Torah Portion

# Eikev

Deuteronomy 7:12–11:25

## REWARDS AND ADMONITIONS

**(7:26) Do not bring any abomination [that is, idolatry] into your house, since you may become just like it. Shun it totally and consider it absolutely offensive, since it is banned.**

�֎ *The Talmud Teaches*
*Do not bring any abomination into your house* R. Yochanan said: A person who is conceited is as though he worshiped idols, for it says "Every haughty person is an abomination to God" (Proverbs 16:5), and "abomination" signifies idol worship (*Sotah* 4b).

**(8:9) It is a land where you will eat bread without poverty, and you will not lack anything—a land whose stones are iron, and from whose mountains you will mine copper.**

✷ *The Talmud Teaches*
*a land whose stones are iron* R. Abba said: A Torah scholar who is not as hard and unyielding as iron is not a true Torah scholar, as it says "A land whose stones, *avaneha,* are iron." Don't read *avaneha,* "stones"; read instead *boneha,* "its builders." Torah scholars are the builders of the future of the Jewish people. They must be unyielding and steadfast in deciding the Halachah. Ravin said: Despite that, a Torah scholar must train himself to be gentle, for it says "Banish anger from your

282

heart, and remove evil from your flesh" (Ecclesiastes 11:10) (*Taanit* 4a).

**(8:10) When you eat and are satisfied, you must bless God your Lord for the good land that He has given you.**

### ✳ The Talmud Teaches
**When you eat and are satisfied, you must bless**  That is, recite Grace after Meals. God said to the angels: Why shouldn't I show favor to Israel! Look, I wrote in the Torah, "When you eat and are satisfied, you must bless God your Lord." I said they should bless only when they are satiated, but they are so stringent that even when they eat a piece of bread as small as the size of an olive or an egg, they recite Birkat Hamazon, Grace after Meals (*Berachot* 20b).

NOTE: You are required to say Birkat Hamazon after eating a piece of bread the quantity of an olive, according to R. Meir, and the quantity of an egg, according to R. Yehudah (*Berachot* 45a).

**(8:14) . . . and everything you own may increase. But your heart may then grow haughty, and you may forget God your Lord, the One who brought you out of the slave house that was Egypt.**

### ✳ The Talmud Teaches
**But your heart may then grow haughty**  R. Nachman said: This bears out the popular saying: "A full stomach leads to all kinds of sin." When all of a person's needs are met, he tends to forget God (*Berachot* 32a).

**(8:16) In the desert He fed you manna, which was something your ancestors never knew, in order to send you hardship, and in order to test you, but it was so He would eventually do all the more good for you.**

### ✳ The Talmud Teaches
**in order to send you hardship**  What kind of hardship was eating the good-tasting manna? R. Ammi and R. Assi each offered a different explanation. One said: You cannot compare a person

who eats and has bread in his basket to eat the next day to one who eats but has no bread in his basket. Because the manna that came down was enough only for that day, and none was left for the next day, it was a hardship of sorts. The other said: You cannot compare a person who sees what he is eating to one who does not see what he is eating. The manna tasted like whatever a person wished, but he could not see the dish he was tasting; he only saw manna. And therein lay the hardship (*Yoma* 74b).

## BREAKING THE TABLETS

**(9:14) God said to Moses, "Just leave Me alone, and I will destroy them, obliterating their name from under the heavens. I will then make you into a nation greater and more numerous than they."**

### ✳ *The Talmud Teaches*
*Just leave Me alone*  When Israel sinned with the golden calf, Moses became unnerved to the point that he lacked the strength to speak. However, when God said to him, "Just leave Me alone, and I will destroy them," giving him a hint that by praying he could stave off their destruction, Moses said to himself: I see, it's up to me. And he instantly stood up, praying fervently and pleading for mercy (*Berachot* 32a).

**(9:17) Moses said, "I grasped the two tablets, and threw them down from my two hands, breaking them before your eyes."**

### ✳ *The Talmud Teaches*
*breaking them before your eyes*  Before your eyes suggests that they saw something miraculous happen in front of their eyes. What did they see? The tablets were broken, but the letters flew upward toward heaven (*Pesachim* 87b).

**(9:25) I threw myself down before God and lay prostrate for forty days and forty nights, for God had intended to destroy you.**

### ✳ *The Talmud Teaches*
*for forty days*  It once happened that a student who officiated at prayer in the presence of R. Eliezer drew out his *Shemoneh*

*esrei* (Amidah) a long time. The other students complained: Rabbi, look how he is dragging out his prayer! He replied: Is he drawing it out any longer than our teacher Moses did, saying, "I threw myself down before God and lay prostrate for forty days and forty nights" (*Berachot* 34a)?

**(10:2) I will write on the tablets the words which were written on the first tablets that you broke, and you shall place them in the ark.**

✴ *The Talmud Teaches*
*the tablets that you broke, and you shall place them in the ark* R. Yosef taught: This teaches us that the second tablets and the broken pieces of the first tablets were deposited in the ark. From this, we derive that a Torah scholar who forgot his learning through no fault of his own should not be treated disdainfully; he is compared to the broken tablets, which were treated with respect by being placed in the ark (*Menachot* 99a).

## WHAT DOES GOD WANT OF YOU?

**(10:12) And now, Israel, what does God want of you? Only that you fear God your Lord, so that you will follow all His paths and love Him, serving God your Lord with all your heart and with all your soul.**

✴ *The Talmud Teaches*
*Only that you fear God your Lord* The Gemara asks: Is the fear of God such a small thing? The verse makes it sound as though the fear of God is only a minor matter. The Gemara answers: Yes! But look who is saying this verse? Moses. Well, for Moses it was a small thing. For R. Chanina said: You can compare it to the case of a person who is asked for a big article, and he has it. Because he has it, it seems like a small article to him. If he is asked for a small article, and he does not have it, it seems like a big article to him (*Berachot* 33b).

**(10:17) God your Lord is the God of the powers and the Lord of the lords. He is the great, mighty, and awesome God, Who does not give special consideration or take bribes.**

### ✻ *The Talmud Teaches*

***God of the powers*** R. Yochanan said: Wherever you find the power of God mentioned in Scripture, you also find His humility mentioned. For it says "God your Lord is the God of the powers and the Lord of lords." Immediately following this, it says "He brings justice to the orphan and the widow, and He loves the stranger" (*Megillah* 13a).

**(11:12) It is therefore a land constantly under God your Lord's scrutiny; the eyes of God your Lord are on it at all times, from the beginning of the year until the end of the year.**

### ✻ *The Talmud Teaches*

***The eyes of God your Lord are on it*** Sometimes for the people's benefit and sometimes to their detriment. How can it be sometimes for their benefit? Let's say that on Rosh Hashanah the Jewish people were in the category of the totally wicked, and heaven decreed that very little rain should fall that year; but later they repented. What should be done? God cannot increase the rainfall allotted for that year, because the decree has already been made. Therefore, God makes the little rain fall at the right time on the land that needs it, fields, vineyards, and gardens.

How can it be sometimes to the people's detriment? Let's say that on Rosh Hashanah the Jewish people were in the category of the completely righteous, and heaven decreed abundant rainfall for that year; but later on, they fell into error. To reduce the total amount of rainfall is impossible, because the decree has already been made. Therefore, God makes it rain not in the proper season and on land that does not require rain, on forests and deserts (*Rosh Hashanah* 17b).

## THE SECOND SECTION OF THE SHEMA

**(11:13) It will be that if you hearken to My commandments that I am prescribing to you today, and if you love God your Lord and serve Him with all your heart and . . . soul.**

### ✻ *The Midrash Teaches*

***if you hearken*** Literally, "If hearken you will hearken." What is the meaning of the redundant expression, "If hearken you will hearken"? If a person begins to hearken to one mitzvah, heaven enables him to hearken to many mitzvoth (*Mechilta Beshalach* 15:26).

**(11:14) I will provide rain for your land in its proper time, the early and late rains, and you will gather in your grain, your wine, and your oil.**

✳ *The Talmud Teaches*
*and you will gather in your grain*  R. Yishmael said: What does the Torah want to teach us by mentioning the gathering of the grain? Because it says "Let not this book of the Torah cease from your lips" (Joshua 1:8), I might think that this is to be taken literally, and a person should do nothing but learn Torah. That's why it says "that you may gather in your grain," which implies that you should combine Torah study with earning a livelihood, and the verse in Joshua 1:8 is not meant to be taken literally (*Berachot* 35b).

*and you will gather in your grain*  R. Shimon b. Yochai said: Is that possible? If a person plows in the plowing season, reaps in the harvest season, threshes in the threshing season, and winnows when the wind blows, what is to become of the Torah? When will he find time to learn Torah? Impossible! But when the Jewish people are doing God's will, their work is done by others, as it says "Strangers shall stand and feed your sheep, aliens shall be your plowmen and vine-trimmers" (Isaiah 61:5). But when the Jewish people are not doing God's will, they will have to do their work themselves, as it says "And *you* will gather in your grain" (*Berachot* 35b).

**(11:15) I will provide grass in your field for your cattle, and you will eat and be satisfied.**

✳ *The Talmud Teaches*
*for your cattle*  R. Yehudah said in the name of Rav: You are forbidden to eat anything before you feed your animals, because it says "I will provide grass in your field for your cattle" and then, "and you will eat and be satisfied" (*Berachot* 40a).

**(11:18) Place these words of Mine upon your heart and soul. Bind them as a sign on your arm, and let them be an ornament between your eyes in the center of your head.**

### *The Talmud Teaches*

***Place [vesamtem] these words*** The Rabbis taught: The word *vesamtem* sounds like *sam tam,* "a perfect remedy." The words of the Torah are "a perfect remedy." They are a life-giving elixir. God said to Israel: My children! I created the *yetzer hara,* "the evil impulse," and I created the Torah as its antidote. If you study the Torah, the *yetzer hara* will not be able to snatch you (*Kiddushin* 30b).

***Place these words on your heart. . . . Bind them . . . on your arm*** This teaches us that the tefillin should be placed opposite the heart, which means on the upper part of the left arm on the elevated part of the biceps and slightly inclined toward the side, so that when you let your arm down, the tefillin would be on a level with the heart (*Menachot* 37b).

**(11:18) Teach your children to speak of them when you are at home, when traveling on the road, when you lie down, and when you get up.**

### *The Talmud Teaches*

***Teach your children to speak of them*** Rav Yehudah said: In earlier times—because the Torah makes fathers responsible to teach their own children—children without fathers, or whose fathers were unlearned, went without education. Until R. Yehoshua b. Gamla introduced a new plan, the first system of comprehensive education in history. He arranged for teachers to be placed in every district and every town and for children to be taught from the age of six or seven (*Bava Batra* 21a).

**(11:21) In order to prolong your life and the lives of your children on the land that God swore to your ancestors, promising that He would give it to them as long as the heavens are above the earth.**

### ※ *The Talmud Teaches*

**on the land**  They told R. Yochanan, who lived in the Land of
Israel, that there were old men in Babylonia. Surprised to hear
that, he exclaimed: It says "In order to prolong your life and the
lives of your children *on the land,*" but not outside the Land of
Israel! When they explained to him that the old men in Babylonia come early to the synagogue and leave late, he said: That
is what helps them to live long (*Berachot* 8a).

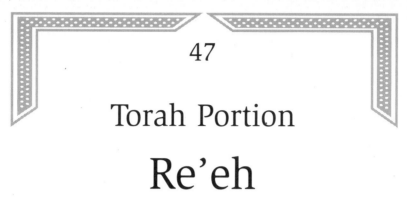

# 47

# Torah Portion

# Re'eh

### Deuteronomy 11:26–16:17

## SANCTITY OF THE LAND

**(11:31) For you are crossing the Jordan to come and possess the land that God your Lord gives you; you shall possess it, and you shall settle it.**

✳ *The Talmud Teaches*
*You shall possess it, and you shall settle it* It was taught in the yeshiva of R. Yishmael: "You shall possess it, and you shall settle it." How will you gain possession of the land? By settling it. From here, we know that land is acquired by *chazakah*— occupying it for a fixed period of time—or by means of a formal act of acquisition, like digging or fencing (*Kiddushin* 26a).

**(12:19) As long as you are in the land, you must be careful not to abandon the Levite.**

✳ *The Midrash Teaches*
*You must be careful not . . . to* This constitutes a negative commandment, in other words, "Do not abandon the Levite." "As long as you are in the land"—to include Sabbatical and Jubilee Years, meaning, the Levites must be provided for during those years, although the tithes are not separated then. Unlike the rest of the people, the Levites do not own land, so they cannot store produce in advance of the Sabbatical and

Jubilee Years when the land must remain untilled; "in the land"—but not in the exile *(Sifrei).*

**(12:21) If the place chosen by God, your Lord, to be dedicated to His Name is far off, you shall slaughter your cattle and your flocks that God will have given you, in the manner that I have prescribed. You may then eat them in your settlements in any manner you desire.**

❋ *The Talmud Teaches*
*in the manner that I have prescribed* Rebbi said: The verse, "You shall slaughter . . . in the manner that I have prescribed" teaches us that Moses was instructed that in *shechitah*, "ritual slaughter," the gullet and the windpipe must be cut. In the case of birds, the greater part of only one of these organs must be cut; and in the case of cattle, the greater part of both the gullet and the windpipe must be cut *(Chullin* 28a).

NOTE: The laws of *shechitah* that are referred to in the words "in the manner that I have prescribed" are not found in the written Torah. These laws were prescribed in the *Torah sheb'al peh,* the Oral Torah, which was verbally communicated to Moses on Mount Sinai.

**(12:23) Only be strong not to eat the blood—for the blood is the life-force—and do not eat flesh with the life in it.**

❋ *The Talmud Teaches*
*Do not eat* The Rabbis taught: "Do not eat flesh with the life in it." What is flesh still connected to life? A limb severed from the body of a living animal, *ever min hachai.* This is one of the seven Noahide laws that are binding on all mankind *(Chullin* 102b).

**(12:25) If you do not eat blood, you and your descendants will have a good life, since you will be doing what is right in God's eyes.**

❋ *The Talmud Teaches*
*If you do not eat blood, you and your descendants will have a good life* R. Shimon b. Rebbi said: Now, if a person is rewarded

for rejecting something as loathful as blood, then surely one who refrains from theft and immorality—which people desire and crave—will gain merit for himself, his children, and his grand-children until the end of all generations (*Makkot* 23b).

**(12:28) Be careful and listen to all these words that I pre-scribe to you, so that you and your descendants will have a good life forever, when you do what is good and right in the eyes of God your Lord.**

✳ *The Midrash Teaches*
**Be careful and listen** This teaches us that if you are careful to listen just a little, you will end up listening to much; and if you observe what you have heard, in the end you will observe things you have not heard, meaning, you will observe pre-cautionary rules that are designed to safeguard against trans-gression of the laws of the Torah itself *(Sifrei).*

NOTE: For example: The Rabbis prohibited the handling of any items whose use is forbidden on Shabbat, such as tools, money, writing equipment, candles, and matches. All such items are known as *muktzeh,* that is, set aside or excluded from Shabbat use or handling, for fear that they may be put to unlawful use.

**all of these words** What is meant by "*all* of these words"? It teaches us that you should cherish a "slight" mitzvah as much as a "weighty" one *(Sifrei).*

**what is good and right** What is "what is good," and what is "what is right"? R. Akiva said: What is good in the eyes of God and what is right in the eyes of man *(Sifrei).*

**(12:29) When God your Lord will cut down the nations to which you are coming and drives them away before you, you shall expel them and live in their land.**

✳ *The Midrash Teaches*
**and live in their land** The previous verse says "Be careful and listen to all these words." From the closeness of these two pas-

sages, we learn that the mitzvah of living in the Land of Israel is equivalent to all the mitzvoth in the Torah *(Sifrei)*.

**(13:5) Walk after God your Lord, remain in awe of Him, keep His commandments, obey Him and serve Him, and cling to Him.**

※ *The Talmud Teaches*
**Walk after God your Lord**  R. Chama b. R. Chanina said: What is meant by the passage, "Walk after God your Lord"? How is it possible for a human being to walk after the Shechinah? Doesn't it say "For the Lord your God is a consuming fire" (4:24)? This is what it means: You should follow the attributes of God: Just as He clothes the naked, so should you clothe the naked. Just as He visits the sick, so should you also visit the sick. Just as He comforts the mourners, so should you comfort the mourners. Just as He buries the dead, so should you too bury the dead (*Sotah* 14a).

NOTE: God clothed Adam and Eve (Genesis 3:21), and He buried Moses (Deuteronomy 34:6).

**Walk after God your Lord**  R. Tanchum said in the name of R. Yehoshua b. Levi: The congregation is not allowed to leave the synagogue until the Torah scroll has been returned to its place. Rava said: Ahina explained to me that this is based on the verse, "Walk *after* God your Lord," that is, you may walk out only *after* the Torah has been returned to the ark (*Sotah* 39b).

## THE WAYWARD CITY

**(13:18) Let nothing that has been banned remain in your hands, so that God will turn back from His burning wrath. He will then give you mercy and be merciful to you and multiply you, just as He promised your fathers.**

※ *The Talmud Teaches*
**Let nothing that has been banned remain in your hands**  Poriclos the son of Palospos asked R. Gamliel: Why are you bathing in the bath of Aphrodite? Doesn't it say "Let nothing that has been banned remain in your hands"? He replied: I did not come

into Aphrodite's domain; she has come into mine. The bath existed before the statue of Aphrodite was set up in it, and the bath was built for public use (*Avodah Zarah* 44b).

**He will then give you mercy** There are three characteristics by which the nation of Israel is known: Jews are merciful, modest, and benevolent. "Merciful" for it says "He will give you mercy, and be merciful to you" (*Yevamot* 79a).

NOTE: This is the section of the *ir hanidachat,* "the wayward city." Such a city must be completely destroyed. No kindness or pity—our basic character traits—may be shown the people of this city. But once national justice has performed its distasteful duty, God allows the people to resume their inherited tendency to kindness and mercy.

## PERMITTED AND FORBIDDEN FOODS

**(14:7) However, among the animals that bring up their cud or have cloven hoofs, there are some that you may not eat. These include the *shesuah,* the hare, and the hyrax, for they bring up their cud but their hoof is not split—they are unclean to you.**

### ※ *The Talmud Teaches*
**the shesuah** R. Chanan b. Rava said: The *shesuah* is a specific animal that has two backs and two spinal columns. Was Moses then a hunter or an archer that he would know the characteristics of such a rare animal? This gives the lie to those who maintain that the Torah was not divinely inspired, for Moses could not have known the identity and anatomy of all the animals mentioned in the Torah. Only God knows this, and it is He who enumerated the permitted and forbidden animals (*Chullin* 60b).

**(14:21) Since you are a holy nation to God your Lord, you may not eat any animal or bird that has not been properly slaughtered. You may give it to the resident alien in your settlements so that he can eat it, or you may sell it to a foreigner. Do not cook a kid in its mother's milk.**

✳ *The Talmud Teaches*
**Since you are a holy nation**  It was taught: From where do we derive that it is forbidden to eat meat and milk together? It says here, "Since you are a *holy* nation . . . Do not cook a kid in its mother's milk"; and elsewhere it says "Be a *holy* people to Me. Do not eat flesh torn off [a living animal] in the field" (Exodus 22:30). [Because the term *holy* occurs in both verses, we infer that] just as eating flesh torn off a living animal is forbidden, so too eating meat and milk together is forbidden (*Chullin* 115b).

## BE KIND TO YOUR FELLOW

**(15:9) In the year of release of all debts, be very careful that you do not have a lawless thought in your heart and say to yourself, "The seventh year is approaching, and it will be the remission year." You may then look unkindly at your impoverished kinsman, and not give him anything. If he then complains to God about you, you will have a sin.**

✳ *The Talmud Teaches*
**a lawless thought**  R. Yehoshua b. Korchah said: Whoever turns a deaf ear to a request for *tzedakah* (charity) is considered as though he worshiped idols, for concerning *tzedakah* it says "Be very careful that you do not have a lawless—*beliya'al*—thought in your . . . heart. . . . You may then look unkindly at your impoverished kinsman and not give him anything." And in connection with idolatry, it says "Lawless—*beliyaal*—men have emerged from your midst" (13:14). The word *beliya'al*, "lawless," occurs in the context of withholding *tzedakah* and in connection with idolatry. Thus, withholding charity is equated with idolatry (*Ketubot* 68a).

**You will have a sin**  R. Elazar said: Come, let's be grateful to the people who deceive us, pretending to be needy. For if not for the cheats, we who do not always respond to every request for *tzedakah* would be sinning every day. For it says about people who turn their back on a poor man, "If he then complains about you to God, you will have a sin" (*Ketubot* 68a).

NOTE: Rashi explains: But thanks to the swindlers who collect charity under false pretenses, we have an excuse for not responding to every request for *tzedakah.*

**(15:10) Therefore, make every effort to give him, and do not feel bad about giving it, for in return of this matter God your Lord will then bless you in all your endeavors, and in your every undertaking.**

✳ *The Talmud Teaches*
*For in return [biglal] of this matter* In the yeshiva of R. Yishmael, they expounded the word *biglal* as being related to *galgal*, "wheel," and they said that poverty is like a wheel that rolls around in the world, eventually striking all people or their descendants. This prompted R. Elazar Hakappar to say: A person should always pray for mercy to be spared from the hardship of poverty, for if he himself does not become poor, his son will; and if his son does not become poor, his grandson will (*Shabbat* 151b).

**(15:11) The poor will never cease to exist in the land, so I am commanding you to open your hand generously to your poor and destitute brother in your land.**

✳ *The Talmud Teaches*
*The poor will never cease to exist in the land* Shmuel said: The only difference between this world and the messianic era is that in the messianic era the Jewish people will be no longer under the domination of other nations; but even in messianic times, there will be needy people, as it says "The poor will never cease to exist in the land" (*Shabbat* 151b).

**(15:16) If the Jewish slave likes you and your family, and has it so good with you that he says "I do not want to leave you" . . .**

✳ *The Talmud Teaches*
*and he has it so good with you* What is implied by "with you [imach]"? *Imach* denotes a close affinity, as opposed to *itach*, which signifies a loose association. He must be with you,

*imach,* that is, equal to you, in food and drink; that you should not eat white bread and he black bread; you not drink old wine and he new wine; you sleep on a feather bed and he on straw. That's why people say: Whoever buys a Hebrew slave acquires a master for himself (*Kiddushin* 22a).

## THE FESTIVALS

**(16:1) Observe the month of springtime and perform the *pesach*-offering for God your Lord, since it was in the month of springtime that God your Lord brought you out of Egypt at night.**

✳ *The Talmud Teaches*
**Observe the month of springtime**  See to it that the earlier half of the month of Nisan should be when spring begins by adjusting the lunar calendar, declaring a leap year, and inserting a second month of Adar, so that Nisan remains in the spring (*Rosh Hashanah* 21a).

NOTE: The duration of a lunar month is about 29 ½ days; thus, the lunar year is twelve months times 29.5 days, or about 354 days. The solar year, the period of time in which the earth completes one revolution around the sun, has 365 days. So the lunar year is about eleven days shorter than the solar year. This means that if in a given year Passover falls in April, then the next year it falls eleven days earlier. If nothing were done to correct the situation, Passover and all the other holidays would be moving through the four seasons of the year. The Torah demands that Passover be in the spring. Therefore, a thirteenth month is inserted in seven years out of a nineteen-year cycle, so that Nisan remains in the spring.

**(16:3) Do not eat any *chametz* [leavened bread] with it; for seven days you shall eat matzo because of it, bread of affliction, for you departed from Egypt in a rush—so that you will remember the day you left Egypt all the days of your life.**

✳ *The Talmud Teaches*
**You shall eat matzo because of it**  This is preceded by "Do not eat any *chametz* [leavened bread] with it." This teaches us that

whoever is subject to the prohibition against eating *chametz* is subject to the mitzvah of eating matzos. Because women are subject to the prohibition of eating *chametz,* they are included in the obligation of eating matzos (*Pesachim* 43b).

NOTE: Eating matzos on Passover is a mitzvah that must be fulfilled at a fixed time—on Passover. Because women are exempt from all time-related mitzvoth, you might think that they are exempt from eating matzos. That's why this exposition is needed: to tell us that women *are* included in the mitzvah of eating matzos.

**(16:11) You shall rejoice on your festival along with your son and daughter, your male and female slave, and the Levite, the proselyte, orphan, and widow from your settlements.**

***The Talmud Teaches***

***along with your son and daughter*** The Rabbis taught: You should make your children and the members of your household rejoice on the Yom Tov, for it says "You shall rejoice on your festival along with your son and . . . daughter." How do you make them rejoice? Men with wine, and women with new clothes (*Pesachim* 109a).

48

# Torah Portion

# Shofetim

Deuteronomy 16:18–21:9

## JUDGES AND JUSTICE

**(16:19) Do not bend justice, and do not give special consideration to anyone. Do not take bribes, since bribery makes the wise blind and distorts the words of the righteous.**

✺ *The Talmud Teaches*
*makes blind . . . and distorts* The Rabbis taught: "Bribery makes the wise blind"—even a great sage who takes bribes will end up suffering from numbness of the mind. "It distorts the words of the righteous"—even a perfect *tzaddik* who takes bribes will end up suffering confusion of the mind (*Ketubot* 105a).

**(16:20) Righteousness, righteousness shall you pursue, so that you will live and possess the land that God your Lord is giving you.**

✺ *The Talmud Teaches*
*Righteousness, righteousness shall you pursue* Why the redundance? The first mention of righteousness refers to a decision based on strict law; the second, to a compromise. How so? For example: Two boats sailing on a river meet at a narrow strait in the river; if both try to pass simultaneously, they will collide and sink; whereas if one makes way for the other, both can pass without mishap. How should this case be decided? Who goes

first? If one is laden and the other unladen, the unladen one gives way to the laden one. If one is nearer to its destination than the other, the one nearer gives way to the other. If both are equally near or far from their destination, they should make a compromise and let the one that moves forward compensate the other for any loss incurred by allowing him to proceed (*Sanhedrin* 32b).

**(17:6) The accused shall be put to death only through the testimony of two or three witnesses. He shall not be put to death through the testimony of one witness.**

### ✼ *The Talmud Teaches*

*only through the testimony of two or three witnesses* It says "Kohelet sought to find words of delight" (Ecclesiastes 12:10). Kohelet, that is, Solomon, tried to reach legal decisions by intuition, without witnesses or warning, whereupon a heavenly voice went forth and said: It says in the Torah "The accused shall be put to death only through the testimony of two or three witnesses"; and no matter how wise you are, you cannot judge on the basis of intuition or hunches (*Rosh Hashanah* 21b).

*only through the testimony of two witnesses* R. Shimon b. Shetach said: "I swear that I saw a person chasing after a man into a ruin. When I ran after him, I saw him holding in his hand a sword dripping with blood, and the victim struggling in the throes of death. I called out to him, 'You wicked man! Who killed this man; either I or you!' Obviously, you are the murderer. But what can I do, because your life is not in my hands, for it says in the Torah, 'The accused shall be put to death only on the testimony of two witnesses'—circumstantial evidence is not admissible in a Jewish court—May God, Who knows the thoughts of man exact retribution on the one who killed his neighbor!" The Sages said that before the two left that spot, a snake came and bit the murderer, killing him (*Sanhedrin* 37b).

*The accused shall be put to death* Literally: "The dead one shall be put to death." The Gemara asks: Now, is the accused then dead? Isn't he alive? The Gemara answers: No, he is already counted as dead. From here, it is derived that the wicked, even in their lifetime, are called "dead" (*Berachot* 18b).

**(17:9) You shall come to the *kohanim,* to the Levites, and to the judge who will be in those days. When you make inquiry, they will tell you a legal decision.**

※ *The Talmud Teaches*
*who will be in those days* Can you imagine a person going to a judge who does not live in his days? The intention is that you must be satisfied to go to the judge who officiates in your days. Don't hold off going to court with the excuse that present-day judges are not as astute as earlier ones. God will lead them on the right path, so that they will render the right decision (*Rosh Hashanah* 25b).

**(17:11) You must keep the Torah as they interpret it for you, and follow the laws that they legislate for you. Do not stray to the right or left from the word that they declare to you.**

※ *The Jerusalem Talmud Teaches*
*You must keep the Torah as they interpret it for you* A prophet and an elder, that is, a member of the Sanhedrin, to what may they be compared? Suppose a king sent two emissaries to a province. In the credentials of one, he wrote: Do not trust him unless he shows my signature and seal; in the credentials of the other, he wrote: You can trust him even if he does not present my signature and seal. Similarly, with respect to a prophet, it says "He will present you with a sign or a wonder" (13:2); whereas here, regarding the elders, it says "You must keep the Torah as they interpret it for you." A prophet has to authenticate his pronouncement through a sign or wonder, whereas a ruling of the Sanhedrin must be obeyed without verification (Jerusalem Talmud, *Berachot* 1:4).

## THE KING

**(17:15) You shall surely set over yourself a king whom God your Lord shall choose; from among your brothers shall you set a king over yourself; you cannot place over yourself a foreign man, who is not your brother.**

### ※ *The Talmud Teaches*
*from among your brothers* It was taught: If his mother is Jewish, he is considered "from among your brothers," that is, a Jew (*Kiddushin* 76b).

*You cannot place over yourself a foreign man* King Agrippa, a descendant of Herod the Edomite, was reading in the Torah; and coming upon the verse "You cannot place over yourself a foreign man as king," he wept, because this verse disqualified him to be king. However, the people called out to him, "Do not fear, Agrippa! You are our brother; you are our brother!" because his mother was Jewish (*Sotah* 41a).

**(17:17) The king must not have too many wives, so that they do not make his heart go astray. He shall likewise not accumulate very much silver and gold for himself.**

### ※ *The Talmud Says*
*so that they not make his heart go astray* R. Yitzchak said: Why doesn't the Torah give reasons for all the mitzvoth? Because in the case of two laws, the reasons were revealed, and the great Solomon stumbled over them. Namely, it says "The king must not have too many wives—and the Torah gives the reason—so that they not make his heart go astray." But King Solomon said: I will take many wives, and I will not let my heart go astray. Yet we read, "So it was when Solomon grew old, his wives swayed his heart after the gods of others" (1 Kings 11:4). It also says "[The king] should not accumulate many horses—the reason being so as not to bring the people back to Egypt to get more horses" (17:16). But Solomon said: I will accumulate many horses, and I will not cause Israel to return to Egypt. Yet we read "A chariot could be brought out of Egypt for six hundred pieces of silver" (1 Kings 10:29), for Jewish traders went back and forth trading with Egypt (*Sanhedrin* 21b).

**(19:10) Innocent blood shall not be shed in the midst of your land that God your Lord gives as an inheritance, for then blood will be upon you.**

### ※ *The Talmud Teaches*

*for then blood will be upon you* From where do we know that if the aides of the court did not go out to clear the roads of thorns, to repair the avenues and the main highways, then if any blood is shed through this neglect, Scripture blames them for it, as if they themselves had shed it? From "then blood will be upon you" (*Mo'ed Katan* 5a).

## THE PLOTTING WITNESSES

**(19:17) The two men who have testimony to refute the plotting witnesses shall stand before God, before the priests and judges who will be in those days.**

### ※ *The Talmud Teaches*

*before God* The witnesses must bear in mind before whom they are testifying, and who will call them to account in the event they give false evidence (*Sanhedrin* 6b).

*before God* When King Yannai was on trial before the court, he came and sat down. Shimon b. Shetach then told him: King Yannai, stand on your feet, and let the witnesses testify against you. For it is not before us that you are standing, but before God, as it says "Then the two men . . . shall stand before God" (*Sanhedrin* 19a).

**(19:19) You must do the same to the plotting witnesses as they plotted to do to their brother, thus removing evil from your midst.**

### ※ *The Talmud Teaches*

*as they plotted* As they *plotted* to do but not as they actually have done. The plotting witnesses receive the penalty they planned to bring on someone else, but they are penalized only when the sentence has *not* been carried out. Based on this passage, the Rabbis said: If the plotting witnesses *already* killed, that is, if the accused was executed on the basis of their false testimony, then the plotting witnesses are not killed; but God will not let them go free. However, if the accused was not killed, they are killed (*Makkot* 5b).

## LAWS OF WARFARE

**(20:3) The priest anointed for battle shall say to the people, "Hear, O Israel, today you are about to wage war against your enemies. Do not be faint-hearted, do not be afraid, do not panic, and do not break ranks before them."**

### ※ *The Talmud Teaches*
*Hear, O Israel [Shema Yisrael]* Why does he begin with these words? R. Yochanan said: God said to Israel: Even if you fulfilled only the mitzvah of reading the Shema which begins with "*Shema Yisrael*," you will not be delivered into your enemies' hands (*Sotah* 42a).

**(20:7) And who is the man who has betrothed a woman and not married her? Let him go and return to his house, lest he die in the war and another man will marry her.**

### ※ *The Talmud Teaches*
*who has betrothed a woman* Before the army went into battle, an announcement was made that anyone who had built a new house, planted a vineyard, or betrothed a woman should go home.

The Rabbis taught: The text mentions first "who has built"; then "who has planted"; and then "who has betrothed." The Torah thereby teaches you how you should conduct yourself: first build a house, then plant a vineyard to have an income, and then get married (*Sotah* 44a).

**(20:19) When you lay siege to a city and wage war against it a long time to capture it, you must not destroy its trees, wielding an ax against it, for from it you will eat, and you shall not cut it down. Is the tree of the field a man who confronts you in the siege?**

### ※ *The Talmud Teaches*
*Is the tree of the field a man who confronts you in the siege?* R. Yochanan said: The verse compares man to a tree. It says about trees, "from it you will eat, and you shall not cut it

down"; but it also says about trees that do not bear fruit, "you may destroy it and cut it down" (20:20). How does this apply to a human being? The Gemara offers a metaphoric interpretation: If you have a Torah teacher who is a God-fearing person, eat from him and don't cut him down, meaning, learn from him and don't reject him; but if he is not God-fearing, destroy him and cut him down, meaning, reject him and turn your back on him (*Taanit* 7a).

## THE UNSOLVED MURDER

**(21:7) [If a corpse is found in a field between two cities, the elders of the city closest to the corpse must bring a female calf to a barren valley, ax the back of its head, and make a solemn declaration.] The elders shall speak up and say, "Our hands have not spilled this blood, and our eyes did not see it."**

※ *The Talmud Teaches*
*Our hands have not spilled this blood* Now, would it enter our mind that the elders of the court are murderers? What they meant to say is: The man found dead did not come to us for help, and we sent him away without food; we did not in any way indirectly cause his death by sending him away without food, so that he was too weak to fight off his attacker. We did not see him leave and let him go without escort (*Sotah* 45b).

49

# Torah Portion

# Ki Teitzei

Deuteronomy 21:10–25:19

## THE BEAUTIFUL FEMALE CAPTIVE

**(21:11) When you wage war against your enemies, and you see a beautiful woman among the prisoners and desire her, you may take her as a wife. When you bring her into your home, she must shave her head and let her fingernails grow.**

*The Talmud Teaches*

***she must shave her head and let her fingernails grow*** Literally: "she shall do her nails." What is meant by "She shall do her nails"? R. Akiva said: She should let them grow. From where does he derive that? He explains: An action—that is, the act of shaving her hair—was mentioned regarding the head, and an action—"doing something"—was mentioned regarding the nails. Just as the purpose of shaving her hair is to make her unattractive, so that the soldier gives up the idea of marrying her, so too the purpose of "doing" her nails is to make her unattractive, for ungroomed nails are distasteful (*Yevamot* 48a).

**(21:13) She must take off her captive's garb and remain in your house a full month, mourning for her father and her mother. Only then may you be intimate with her and possess her, making her your wife.**

*The Midrash Teaches*

***her captive's garb*** This teaches us that she takes off her fine clothing and puts on a widow's dress. The Canaanite girls used

to wear pretty clothes in war to tempt enemy soldiers to engage in promiscuity with them *(Sifrei).*

***mourning her father and her mother*** Why all this? In order to create a contrast, that although the captor's Jewish wife is cheerful, she should be depressed; although his Jewish wife grooms herself, this one should look unkempt *(Sifrei).*

**(21:14) But it shall be that if you do not desire her, you must send her away free. Since you have afflicted her, you may not sell her for money or keep her as a servant.**

✻ *The Midrash Teaches*
***But it shall be that if you do not desire her*** After you have taken her as a wife. The phrase "it shall be" tells him that he will end up hating her *(Sifrei).*

## FAMILY LAWS

**(21:15) If a man has two wives, one of whom he loves, and one of whom he dislikes, and both the loved and unloved wives bear him sons, but the firstborn is that of the unloved one . . .**

✻ *The Talmud Teaches*
***both the loved and the unloved bear him sons*** A cesarean birth is not considered firstborn for purposes of inheritance. From where is this derived? From "and they bear," implying a normal birth (*Bechorot* 47b).

✻ *The Midrash Teaches*
***and they bear him sons*** A person whose children belong to *him,* to exclude the children of a maidservant or a Gentile woman, whose children are not his *(Sifrei).*

***The firstborn is that of the unloved one*** The Torah predicts that the firstborn will be the unloved one's *(Sifrei).*

**(21:17) Rather, he must recognize the firstborn, the son of the hated wife, to give him the double portion in all that is**

**found with him; for he is his initial vigor, to him is the right of the firstborn.**

※ *The Talmud Teaches*
*he must recognize* Mar the son of R. Yosef said: A firstborn who was born after the death of his father does not receive a double portion. Why not? For it says "he must recognize the firstborn," and surely he is not alive to recognize him (*Bava Batra* 142b).

NOTE: Rashi explains that it is possible for a firstborn who was born after the death of his father to have siblings if his widow gave birth to twins or he left two widows and both gave birth to sons, one of whom was firstborn.

*in all that is found with him* From here, the Rabbis derive the law that the firstborn does not receive a double share of what is due to come after the death of the father, for example, a debt or an inheritance that is payable to the father; but the father dies before it becomes due. He receives a double share only of what was actually held in possession by the father (*Bechorot* 51b).

**(21:18) When a man has a wayward, rebellious son, who does not obey his father and mother, and they discipline him, but he does not listen to them . . .**

※ *The Talmud Teaches*
*When a man has a wayward, rebellious son* This follows immediately after the section of the beautiful captive woman. It teaches us that whoever marries a beautiful woman captured in battle will have a wayward and rebellious son (*Sanhedrin* 107a).

## LAWS OF BENEVOLENCE

**(22:1) You shall not see the ox of your brother or his sheep going astray, you must not ignore them. You must return them to your brother.**

✳ *The Midrash Teaches*
*the ox of your brother* This tells me only "the ox of your brother." From where do I derive that included in this mitzvah

is the ox of your enemy? From "If you come across your enemy's
ox or donkey going astray, bring it back to him" (Exodus 23:4).
If so, why does it say here, "the ox of your brother"? The Torah
addresses man's evil impulse, saying: Return not only your
brother's ox, but quell your evil impulse and return even
your enemy's ox *(Sifrei)*.

### ※ *The Talmud Teaches*
***You must return them to your brother*** Literally, "Return shall
you return them." Why the repetitive phrase? If you returned
the animal and it ran away—even four or five times—you must
continue returning it. For it says "Return shall you return
them"—signifying even a hundred times *(Bava Metzia* 30b).

**(22:2) If your brother is not near you, or you do not know
who the owner is, you must bring the animal home and keep
it until your brother seeks it, whereupon you must return it
to him.**

### ※ *The Talmud Teaches*
***until your brother seeks it*** Literally: "until you seek out your
brother." If he named the lost object but not its identifying sign,
it should not be returned to him. And if he is known to be a
fraud, even if he does give its sign, it should not be returned to
him. For it says "until you seek out your brother"—to determine
whether or not he is a cheat *(Bava Metzia* 28b).

***whereupon you must return it to him*** There has to be something worth returning—meaning, an animal that works for its
keep must be kept by the finder and earn its keep, but an animal that does not work for its keep must be sold, for it says
"you must return it to him." But if the finder keeps it and then
charges the loser with its keep, the keep may exceed its actual
worth, and so the return will be a loss and not something worth
returning *(Bava Metzia* 28b).

**(22:4) If you see your brother's donkey or ox fallen under its
load on the road, you must not ignore it. You must pick up
the load with him.**

✻ *The Talmud Teaches:*
**You must pick up the load with him** That is, together with the
owner. But if the owner leaves his fallen animal and sits down
and says to the passerby, "Because you are commanded to
unload it, go ahead and unload it. I am not commanded to do
it," the passerby is exempt from the obligation. For it says "with
him," that is, together with the owner. But if the owner is old
or sick, the passerby is required to unload it himself (*Bava Metzia* 32a).

**(22:6) If you come across a bird's nest on any tree or on the
ground, and it contains baby birds or eggs, if the mother is
sitting on the chicks or eggs, you must not take the mother
along with her young.**

✻ *The Talmud Teaches*
**If you come across a bird's nest** What is the Torah teaching us?
Because it says in the next verse, "You must first chase away
the mother, and only then may you take the young," I might
think that a person must go searching over mountains and hills
to find a nest with which to perform the mitzvah of chasing
away the mother bird; that's why it says "If you come across,"
that is, only if you happen to come upon it must you chase the
mother if you want to take the young (*Chullin* 139b).

**(22:8) When you build a new house, you must place a guard-
rail around your roof. Do not allow a dangerous situation to
remain in your house, since someone can fall from an unen-
closed roof.**

✻ *The Talmud Teaches*
**Do not allow a dangerous situation to remain in your house**
R. Natan said: From where do we know that you should not
raise a vicious dog in your house or place a rickety ladder in
your house? Because it says "Do not allow a dangerous situation to remain in your house" (*Ketubot* 41b).

**(22:12) Make yourself twisted threads—zizith—on the four
corners of your garment with which you cover yourself.**

## ⁂ *The Talmud Teaches*

*twisted threads* A "twisted thread" in the singular implies two threads, for you cannot make a twisted thread with less than two threads, and so "twisted threads" in the plural implies four threads. Then how should the zizith be made? Make a tassel out of four threads and twist it (*Yevamot* 5b).

NOTE: The four threads are inserted into the corner of the garment and folded to form a tassel of eight threads. The threads are joined by winding one of the eight threads around the others.

**(22:23) This is the law where a virgin girl is betrothed to one man, and another man comes across her in the city and has intercourse with her.**

## ✳ *The Midrash Teaches*

*another man comes across her in the city* The implication is that if she had not gone prancing around in the city but stayed at home and behaved modestly, this would not have happened. As the adage has it: The breach in the wall invites the thief *(Sifrei)*.

**(22:27) If a man raped a betrothed girl out in the field, only the rapist shall be put to death. After all, the man attacked her in the field; and even if the betrothed girl had screamed out, there would have been no one to come to her aid.**

## ⁂ *The Talmud Teaches*

*there would have been no one to come to her aid* It was taught in the yeshiva of R. Yishmael: From where do we know that it is permitted to save a betrothed girl by killing her attacker? For it says "there would have been no one to come to her aid," which implies that if there is a rescuer, he must save her by all possible means, including killing the attacker (*Sanhedrin* 73a).

## AMMONITES AND MOABITES

**(23:3) An Ammonite or Moabite may not enter the congregation of God, even after the tenth generation.**

### ✳ The Talmud Teaches

*An Ammonite . . . may not enter* Yehudah, an Ammonite convert, appeared in the study hall and asked the Sages: Am I permitted to enter into the community of Israel and marry a Jewish woman? R. Yehoshua said: You are allowed to marry a Jewish woman. R. Gamliel said: But doesn't it say explicitly, "An Ammonite or Moabite may not enter the congregation of God"? To which R. Yehoshua retorted: Do the original nations of Ammon and Moab still live in their native countries? Surely, Sancheriv, king of Assyria, came long ago and mixed up all the nations under his domain. Therefore, today we don't know who is a descendant of the original Ammonites. And we have a principle that when in doubt we follow the majority, and the majority of the world population are not Ammonites. Therefore, even though this convert Yehudah comes from the country of Ammon, he is part of the majority and is not an Ammonite. Hence, he is permitted to marry a Jewish woman (*Berachot* 28a).

**(23:5) Because of the fact that they did not greet you with bread and water on the road when you were on the way out of Egypt, and also because they hired Balaam, son of Beor, of Petor in Aram Naharayim, to curse you.**

### ✳ The Talmud Teaches

*Because of the fact that they did not greet you* R. Yochanan said: Giving a mouthful of food to wayfarers is of great importance, for the failure to do so alienated two families from Israel, that is, the nations of Ammon and Moab. For it says Ammon and Moab are forbidden to Israel, although they are related to Israel, as descendants of Lot, Abraham's nephew, "because of the fact that they did not greet you with bread and water" (*Sanhedrin* 103b).

**(23:9) Children who are born to the Edomites and the Egyptians in the third generation after becoming proselytes may enter the congregation of God.**

### ✳ The Midrash Teaches

*the third generation* R. Shimon said: The Egyptians who drowned Jewish children in the Nile and the Edomites who attacked

Israel with the sword (Numbers 20:18) were forbidden to marry Jews only until the third generation. On the other hand, the Ammonites and Moabites, who caused Israel to sin by seducing them to behave immorally with the Moabite girls (Numbers 25:1–3), were forbidden forever to marry Jews. To teach you that causing a person to sin is worse than killing him. For the one who kills him removes him only from this world, whereas he who makes him sin removes him even from the world to come *(Sifrei)*.

**(23:14) When you go out to fight against your enemies you shall have a shovel along with your weapons, so that when you have to sit down to relieve yourself, you will first dig a hole with it, and then sit down, and finally, cover your excrement.**

### ✸ *The Talmud Teaches*
**along with your weapons** Bar Kappara expounded: What is alluded to by the verse, "You shall have a shovel in addition to your weapons—*al azeinecha*"? Don't read *al azeinecha,* "along with your weapons," but *al oznecha,* "on your ear." Which means: If you hear something improper, you should use your fingers to stop up your ears *(Ketubot* 5a).

**(23:24) When you have spoken, be careful of your word and keep the pledge that you have vowed to God your Lord.**

### ✸ *The Talmud Teaches*
**When you have spoken** This tells me only that you must keep a pledge you uttered with your lips. From where do we derive the same law for things you resolved in your heart? Because it says "everyone whose heart motivates him shall bring it" (Exodus 35:5) *(Shevuot* 26b).

**(24:1) When a man takes a wife and lives with her, if she is displeasing to him or he has evidence of sexual misconduct on her part, he shall write her a bill of divorce and place it in her hand, thus releasing her from his household.**

※ *The Talmud Teaches*
**When a man takes a wife** R. Shimon said: Why does the Torah say "When a man takes a wife" and not "When a woman is taken by a man"? Because it is the way of a man to look for a wife, and she is passive; but it is not the way of a woman to look for a husband. You can compare it to a person who lost an article: Who goes looking for the lost item? Surely, the loser will go looking for the thing he has lost. Ever since Adam lost his rib, every man has been trying to retrieve it by looking for a wife (*Kiddushin* 2b).

**(24:9) Remember what God did to Miriam on your way out of Egypt.**

✳ *The Midrash Teaches*
**Remember** The previous verse deals with the disease of *tzaraas* (leprosy). What does Miriam have to do with the preceding verse? To teach that leprous marks come only because of slander. Miriam maligned Moses regarding the "Kushite woman" he had married. In the wake of her slander, she was stricken with leprosy (Numbers 12:1) *(Sifrei)*.

**(24:13) If you took a garment as a security from a poor man, return it to him at sundown, so that he will be able to sleep in his garment and bless you. You will then have charitable merit before God your Lord.**

※ *The Talmud Teaches*
**You will then have charitable merit before God your Lord** It was taught: King Monobaz of Adiabene, a vassal state of the Parthian empire, spent his own fortune and that of his forebears to feed the hungry in the years of drought. His brothers and his family scolded him, "Your father saved and added to the treasures, while you squander them." He replied, "My father gathered for others—his heirs—but I have gathered for myself, as it says '*You* will then have charitable merit before God your Lord'" (*Bava Batra* 11a).

**(24:15) You must give a laborer his wage on the day it is due, and not let the sun set, with him waiting for it. Since he is a**

**poor man, and his life depends on it, do not let him call out to God, causing you to have a sin.**

### ✳ *The Talmud Teaches*
*his life depends on it* This teaches us that if a person holds back a laborer's wages, it is as if he takes his life. Why did the laborer climb the ladder or suspend himself from a tree, risking his life, if not for his wages, so that for withholding a laborer's pay a person is punished as for taking his life *(Bava Metzia* 112a).

**(25:15) You must have a full honest weight and a full honest measure. If you do, you will long endure on the land that God your Lord is giving you.**

### ✳ *The Talmud Teaches*
*You must have a full honest weight* From where do we know that you may not give a leveled measure where the custom is to heap it up and that you may not give a heaped-up measure where the practice is to level it? Because it says "You must have a full honest measure." And from where do we know that where the practice is to heap it up, if someone says: I will give level measure and reduce the price; or where the practice is to give a level measure, if someone says: I will heap up and raise the price, that we should not listen to him? Because it says "You must have a full honest measure" *(Bava Batra* 88b).

# 50

## Torah Portion

# Ki Tavo

### Deuteronomy 26:1–29:8

## FIRSTFRUITS

**(26:1) It will be when you enter the land that God your Lord is giving you as a heritage, occupying and settling it.**

✳ *The Midrash Teaches*
**It will be when you enter the land** Perform the mitzvah of *bikkurim*, "firstfruits," mentioned in this portion. In its merit, you will enter the land *(Sifrei).*

**(26:3) You shall come to the priest officiating at the time, and say to him: Today I am affirming to God your Lord that I have come to the land that God swore to our forefathers to give to us.**

▨ *The Jerusalem Talmud Teaches*
**to our forefathers** A convert brings *bikkurim*, "firstfruits," but he does not recite the formula, for the phrase "that God swore to our forefathers" does not apply to him (Jerusalem Talmud, *Bikkurim* 1:4).

**(26:6) You shall then call out and say before God your Lord: An Aramaean tried to destroy my forefather [that is, Laban deceived and pursued our forefather Jacob]. He went to Egypt with a small number of men and lived there as an**

**immigrant, but it was there that he became a great, powerful, and populous nation.**

### ▓ The Jerusalem Talmud Teaches
**You shall then call out and say** In the beginning, whoever could recite the declaration by himself did so; whoever could not recited after another. Thereupon, people stopped bringing *bikkurim* to avoid embarrassment. It was therefore instituted that everyone should recite after another, based on "You shall then call out *[ve'anita]* and say," for *ve'anita* also means "you shall answer"; and "answering" implies repeating after someone else (Jerusalem Talmud, *Bikkurim* 3:4).

**(26:15) Look down from Your holy habitation in heaven, and bless Your people Israel, and the land that You have given us, the land flowing with milk and honey that You swore to our forefathers.**

### ▓ The Jerusalem Talmud Teaches
**Look down [hashkifah]** R. Huna b. R. Achah said: Let me show you how much power you have when you do a mitzvah. For whenever the word *hashkifah*, "look down," occurs in Scripture, it foreshadows curses, but the *hashkifah* in this verse that follows after the mitzvah of *bikkurim* portends blessing; and what's more, the first word in the next verse is "today," indicating that the blessing will come right away (Jerusalem Talmud, *Maaser Sheini* 5:5).

**(26:17) You have singled out God today to be a God for you, and to walk in His ways, and to observe His decrees, His commandments, and His statutes, and to listen to His voice.**

### ▒ The Talmud Teaches
**You have singled out God today** The next verse says "God has similarly singled you out, making you His treasured nation." God said to Israel: You have made Me a unique essence in the world, meaning, Israel acknowledges that there is only one source of existence in the universe, the Creator. And I will make you a unique entity in the world. You have made Me a

unique essence in the world, for it says "Hear, O Israel, the Lord our God, the Lord is One" (6:4). And I will make you a unique entity in the world, for it says "Who is like Your people Israel, one nation in the world" (1 Chronicles 17:21) (*Berachot* 6a).

***You have singled out God today . . . God has similarly singled you out*** We hereby swore to God that we would not exchange Him for a different god; and He too swore to us that He would not exchange us for a different nation (*Gittin* 57b).

## BECOMING A NATION

**(27:9) Moses and the *kohanim*, the Levites, spoke to all Israel, saying, "Be attentive and listen, Israel! Today you have become a people to God your Lord."**

### ※ *The Talmud Teaches*
***Be attentive [haskeit]*** This is the only time the word *haskeit* occurs in all of Scripture. *Haskeit* is a combination of the words *hass,* "make," and *kitot,* "classes." It means: Form groups to study Torah, because the Torah can be acquired only if you learn with a study partner (*Berachot* 63b).

***Be attentive [haskeit]*** Another explanation of *haskeit* is: Cut yourself to pieces *(kittetu)* for the sake of Torah, meaning, be ready to suffer for the sake of Torah study. As Resh Lakish said: Torah endures only with a person who is willing to die for it, that is, to forgo the comforts of life, for it says "This is the Torah, when a person dies in a tent," that is, in a house of study (Numbers 19:14). How can you acquire Torah? When you are ready to give up luxuries and creature comforts (*Berachot* 63b).

***Today you have become a people to God*** How could Moses say "today"? Was the Torah then given to Israel on that day? After all, the day when he was speaking was at the end of the forty-year wandering through the desert, forty years after the giving of the Torah at Sinai! The verse comes to teach you that the Torah is as beloved to those who study it today as it was on the day it was given on Mount Sinai (*Berachot* 63b).

# BLESSINGS AND CURSES

**(27:26) "Cursed is he who does not uphold and keep this entire Torah." All the people shall say, "Amen."**

### ❈ *The Jerusalem Talmud Teaches*
*who does not uphold [yakim]* Literally, "cause to stand." R. Acha says: If a person learned and taught, observed and did, and was in a position to strengthen the Torah by supporting Torah scholars and did not do so, he is included in "Cursed is he who does not uphold and keep this entire Torah." If he did not learn, teach, observe, or do; and he was not in a position to strengthen the Torah but nevertheless did so through self-sacrifice, he is included in "Blessed is he who upholds . . ." (Jerusalem Talmud, *Sotah* 7:4).

**(28:1) If you listen diligently to the voice of God your Lord, carefully keeping all His commandments as I am prescribing them to you today, then God will make you highest of all nations on earth.**

### ❈ *The Talmud Teaches*
*If you listen diligently* Literally: "If listening, you will listen." R. Zeira said: Come and see what a difference there is between the norms of mortal man and the norms of God. By the norms of mortal man, an empty vessel holds what is put into it, and a full vessel cannot hold anything that is added to it. But by the norms of God, a full vessel holds whatever is added to it, while an empty vessel cannot hold what is put into it. For it says "It shall be if listening, you will listen," which means: If you listen and learn, you will continue to listen; your mind, "a full vessel," will be able to absorb more and more knowledge—but if you do not make it a practice to listen and learn, then you will not listen; in other words, a person who was not trained in his youth to study Torah, "an empty vessel," will not be able to grasp it later in life (*Sukkah* 46b).

**(28:10) All the nations of the world will realize that God's name is associated with you, and they will be in awe of you.**

✳ *The Talmud Teaches*
*that God's name is associated with you* R. Eliezer the Great
said: This refers to the tefillin of the head. The letter *shin* is
embossed on the sides of the head-tefillin, and the knot of the
head-tefillin is shaped like a *dalet*. Thus, the letters *shin* and
*dalet*—the greater part of the divine name *Shaddai* (Almighty)—
are contained in the head-tefillin. Seeing God's name on your
tefillin, the Gentiles will be in awe of you (*Menachot* 35b).

(28:29) **You will grope about in broad daylight just like a
blind man gropes in the darkness, and you will have no success in any of your ways. You will be constantly cheated and
robbed, and no one will help you.**

✳ *The Talmud Teaches*
*like a blind man gropes in the darkness* R. Yose said: All my
days, I was troubled over the meaning of the verse, "You will
grope in broad daylight just like a blind man gropes in the darkness." Now, I wondered, what difference is there between
darkness and light to a blind man? Why does he grope more
in darkness than in daylight, as Scripture implies? Until I wit-
nessed the following incident, which explained the verse for
me: One time, I was walking in the darkness of night, and I saw
a blind man who was walking along the road holding a torch in
his hand. I said to him: My son, why do you need this torch? He
answered: As long as I am carrying a torch, people see me and
save me from harming myself in ditches, thorns, and briers.
Thus, R. Yose interpreted this verse: "Just like a blind man
gropes in darkness," when no one can see him and help him
(*Megillah* 24b).

(28:66) **Your life will hang in the balance, and you will be
frightened night and day, and you will not be sure of your
livelihood.**

✳ *The Talmud Teaches*
*Your life will hang in the balance* R. Chanan said: The verse
"Your life will hang in the balance" refers to a person who buys
grain from year to year. He has no land of his own; therefore,

he worries whether he will have the wherewithal to buy grain the next year. "You will be frightened day and night" refers to a person who buys grain from week to week. "And you will not be sure of your livelihood" refers to a person who has to rely on the baker for his daily bread (*Menachot* 103b).

**(28:67) In the morning you will say, "If it were only night!" and in the evening you will say, "If it were only morning!" Such will be the internal terror that you will experience and the sights that you will see.**

### ※ The Talmud Teaches
*In the morning you will say* Rava said: From the day that the Temple was destroyed, each day's curse is more oppressive than that of the preceding day, as it says "In the morning you will say, 'If it were only night!' and in the evening you will say, 'If it were only morning!'" Which morning would they long for? If I say, the morning of the next day; nobody knows what it will be. It may be even worse. Therefore, it must be that they long for the morning of the previous day (*Sotah* 49a).

**(28:69) The above are the words of the covenant that God instructed Moses to make with the children of Israel in the land of Moab, besides the covenant that He sealed with them at Horeb.**

### ※ The Talmud Teaches
*The above are the words of the covenant* R. Shimon b. Lakish said: The word *brit,* "covenant," is mentioned in regard to salt, for it says "Do not leave out the salt of your God's *brit* [covenant] from your meal offerings" (Leviticus 2:13). The word *brit* is mentioned also in connection with suffering, as it says at the end of the *Tochachah,* the chapter of terrifying curses, "These are the words of the *brit.*" Just as with *brit* written in respect to salt, salt lends a taste to the meat and improves it; so also with *brit* that is mentioned in regard to suffering, the sufferings wash away a person's transgressions and turn them into merits (*Berachot* 5a).

## MOSES' FINAL ADDRESS TO THE PEOPLE

**(29:3) But until this day, God did not give you a heart to know, eyes to see, and ears to hear.**

### ❊ The Talmud Teaches
**God did not give you** Moses gave this admonition only at the end of the forty years of wandering in the wilderness. For Moses said in the next verse, "I led you through the desert for forty years" (29:4). Said Rabbah: From this, you can learn that it may take forty years for a student to fathom the mind of his master (*Avodah Zarah* 5b).

**(29:8) If you preserve the words of this covenant and keep them, you will be successful in all that you do.**

### ❊ The Talmud Teaches
**If you preserve the words of this covenant and keep them** The Sages interpret this verse to mean: "If you preserve the words of this covenant, you will make them." R. Elazar said: Whoever teaches his neighbor's son Torah is regarded by Scripture as if he "made" the words of the Torah. For it says "If you preserve the words of this covenant, you will make them." By teaching the words of the Torah to your neighbor's son, you will create new Torah insights. Rava said: He is regarded as if he "made"—that is, created—himself, for it says "You will make them—*otam.*" Do not read *otam,* "them," but *atem,* "you," meaning, you will make yourself. By teaching others, you yourself grow in wisdom (*Sanhedrin* 99b).

**you will be successful** R. Yehoshua b. Levi said: Whoever engages in Torah study will be successful in all his undertakings. For it says "If you observe the words of this covenant and keep them, you will be successful in all that you do" (*Avodah Zarah* 19b).

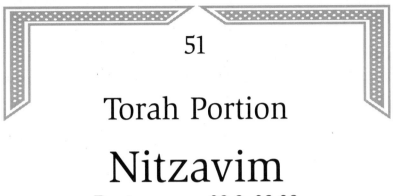

# 51

## Torah Portion

# Nitzavim

### Deuteronomy 29:9–30:20

## REAFFIRMATION OF THE COVENANT

**(29:9) You are standing today, all of you, before God, your Lord, the heads of your tribes, your elders, and your officers— all the men of Israel.**

※ *The Jerusalem Talmud Teaches*
*the heads of your tribes, your elders* "Elders" refers to Torah scholars; "heads of tribes" refers to communal leaders who are not necessarily Torah scholars.

    Moses placed "heads" before "elders," whereas "[Joshua] summoned the elders of Israel, their heads, and their officers" (Joshua 24:1), placing "elders" before "heads." The reason Moses placed heads before elders is that both the heads and the elders were his disciples, so that they were each other's colleagues. That's why the elders did not feel slighted being placed after the heads. By contrast, in the case of Joshua, the heads and the elders were not all his disciples; that's why Joshua placed the elders, who were greater scholars, before the heads of the tribes.

    Another reason: Moses did not need the elders for the conquest of the land, because he was to die before entering the Land of Israel. Therefore, he placed the heads before the elders. But Joshua needed the elders' support for the conquest; that's why he placed them before the heads of the tribes.

Another view: Because Moses was not exhausted by Torah study and did not need the advice of the elders, he placed heads before elders, but Joshua was exhausted and needed the advice of the elders, so he placed elders before heads.

Another opinion: Because Moses foresaw prophetically that Israel was destined to be subjugated by the nations, and that heads, that is, spokesmen, would be appointed over them to mediate with the kings of the nations in their behalf, he placed heads before elders. If the Jewish communal leaders do not appease hostile government officials, persuading them to cancel harsh decrees, Torah scholars have no peace of mind to learn (Jerusalem Talmud, *Horayot* 3:5).

**(29:13) But it is not with you alone that I am making this covenant and this oath.**

***The Talmud Teaches***

***But it is not with you alone*** When Moses our teacher placed Israel under oath, he said: You should be aware that I do not place you under oath according to the way you interpret the oath but according to God's and my understanding of it, as it says "But it is not with you alone that I am making this covenant and this oath, that is, not according to your understanding of the oath" (*Shevuot* 39a).

**(29:14) I am making this covenant both with those who are standing here today with us before God our Lord, and also with those who are not [yet] here with us today.**

***The Talmud Teaches***

***and also with those who are not [yet] here with us today*** How do we know that the coming generations and proselytes who are later to be converted were also placed under this oath? Because it says "and also with those who are not yet here with us today," meaning, future generations and converts. From here, we know that they were placed under oath for the commandments they received at Sinai.

How do we know that they were placed under oath for the commandments that were going to be given later, such as the reading of the *Megillah,* ordained by Mordechai, a thousand years after the giving of the Torah? Because it says regarding Purim, "The Jews undertook and obligated themselves" (Esther 9:27). They undertook to fulfill what they had long ago obligated themselves in principle to do (*Shevuot* 39a).

***and also with those who are not [yet] here with us today*** When the serpent came to Eve, enticing her to eat the forbidden fruit, it had sexual relations with her and infused her with sensuality. But when the Jewish people stood at Mount Sinai, their lustfulness left them.

R. Acha b. Rava asked R. Ashi: What about proselytes? Their ancestors were not at Mount Sinai—at what point did their sensuality depart? He replied: Although they themselves were not present at Sinai, their souls were there, as it says "Moses said, But it is not with you alone that I am making this covenant and this oath. I am making it both with those who are standing here today before God our Lord and with the souls of those who are not [yet] here with us today," so that the converts' sensuality left them also at Sinai (*Shabbat* 146a).

**(29:27) God drove them from their land with anger, rage, and great fury, and He exiled them to another land, where they remain even today.**

***The Talmud Teaches***

***God drove them from their land*** The ten tribes that were taken into exile in Assyria (2 Kings 17:16) have no share in the world to come, for it says "God drove them from their land"—in this world; "and He exiled them to another land"—banishing them from the world to come—so says R. Akiva. R. Shimon b. Yehudah said: If their deeds are like "today," that is, the day they were exiled, and they did not repent, they will not return; but if they do repent, they will return to the Land of Israel (*Sanhedrin* 110b).

**(29:28) Hidden things may pertain to God our Lord, but that which has been revealed applies to us and our children forever. We must therefore keep all the words of this Torah.**

✴ *The Maimonides Code of Law Teaches*
**forever** This teaches us that all the words of the Torah are binding on us forever (Rambam, *Yesodei Hatorah* 9:3).

## REPENTANCE AND REDEMPTION

**(30:5) God your Lord will then bring you to the land that your ancestors occupied, and you too will occupy it. God will then be good to you and make you flourish even more than your ancestors.**

❁ *The Jerusalem Talmud Teaches*
**and make you flourish even more than your ancestors** Your forefathers, although they were redeemed, were again subjugated; but you, once you have been redeemed, will be subjugated no more. Where is this alluded to? In the verse "Ask now and see if a male has ever given birth" (Jeremiah 30:6). Just as a male does not give birth, so you, once you are redeemed, will never again be subjugated (Jerusalem Talmud, *Kiddushin* 1:8).

**(30:12) This commandment that I command you today. It is not in heaven, for you to say, "Who shall go up to heaven and bring it to us so that we can hear it and keep it?"**

✻ *The Talmud Teaches*
**It is not in heaven** R. Avdimi b. Chama said: "It is not in heaven," for if it were in heaven, you would have to go up after it; and if it were over the sea, you would have to go across the sea to get it (*Eruvin* 55a).

**It is not in heaven** Rava said: This means that the Torah cannot be found in a person whose haughtiness is as high as the heavens. R. Yochanan said: "It is not in heaven" means the Torah cannot be found among the arrogant (*Eruvin* 55a).

**It is not in heaven** What is implied by "The Torah is not in heaven"? R. Yirmeyah explained: Because the Torah has already been given to us at Mount Sinai, we pay no attention to heavenly voices that support an individual over a majority halachic opinion, because God has already commanded us in the Torah, "follow the majority" (Exodus 23:2) (*Bava Metzia* 59b).

**It is not in heaven**  Rav Yehudah said: Three thousand halachas were forgotten during the period of mourning for Moses. They said to Joshua, "Ask that these forgotten halachas should be revealed to you from heaven." He replied, "'The Torah is not in heaven,' and from now on all doubts are to be resolved not by revelation but by majority vote" (*Temurah* 16a).

**(30:13) It is not across the sea that you should say, "Who will cross the sea and get it for us, so that we will be able to hear and keep it?"**

### ※ The Talmud Teaches
**It is not across the sea**  [This] means that the Torah cannot be found among merchants and traders who are too busy pursuing their business to study the Torah (*Eruvin* 55a).

**(30:14) It is something that is very close to you. It is in your mouth and in your heart, to perform it.**

### ※ The Talmud Teaches
**in your mouth and in your heart**  R. Yitzchak said: When is the Torah close to you? When it is in your mouth, when you articulate it clearly, and in your heart with the intent to keep it. It is not close to a person who studies Torah for purposes of scientific, linguistic, or archeological research, rather than with the intent to fulfill it (*Eruvin* 30:14).

**(30:17) But if your heart turns aside, and you do not listen, you will be led astray to bow down to foreign gods and worship them.**

### ※ The Talmud Teaches
**But if your heart turns aside**  This teaches you that if you turn your heart away, meaning, if you give up hope of ever grasping the Torah teachings and do not review your lessons, you will no longer listen, and you will gain no further knowledge (*Sukkah* 46b).

**(30:19) I call heaven and earth as witnesses! I have placed life and death, blessing and curse before you. You must choose life, so that you will live, you and your offspring.**

### ✵ *The Jerusalem Talmud Teaches*
**You must choose life** R. Yishmael taught: "You must choose life"—this refers to a profession. From here, the Sages ruled: A person is required to teach his son a profession. If he did not teach him, the son is required to teach himself. From where do we know this? Because it says "So that *you* will live." When you have a profession, you will earn a livelihood (Jerusalem Talmud, *Kiddushin* 1:7).

**You must choose life** From here, R. Akiva ruled: A person is required to teach his son how to swim. If he does not teach him, the son is required to teach himself. From where do we know this? Because it says "So that *you* will live." Knowing how to swim, he will be able to survive a shipwreck (Jerusalem Talmud, *Kiddushin* 1:7).

**(30:20) You must thus make the choice to love God your Lord, to obey Him and to attach yourself to Him, for the Torah is your life and the length of your days, to dwell in the land that God swore to your fathers, Abraham, Isaac, and Jacob, promising that He would give it to them.**

### ✳ *The Talmud Teaches*
**and to attach yourself to Him** Is it possible for a human being to "attach himself" to the Shechinah? What it means is this: If you marry off your daughter to a Torah scholar or do business on behalf of a Torah scholar or benefit a Torah scholar with your possessions, you are regarded by Scripture as if you attached yourself to the Shechinah (*Ketubot* 111b).

**the Torah is your life and the length of your days** Torah study is one of the mitzvoth whose fruits a person enjoys in this world but whose principal remains intact for the world to come, as it says "For the Torah is your life—in this world—and the length of your days—in the world to come" (*Kiddushin* 40a).

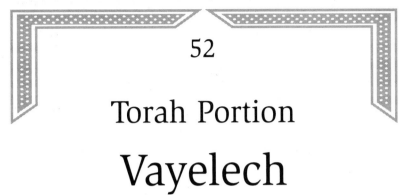

52

# Torah Portion

# Vayelech

Deuteronomy 31:1–31:30

## MOSES BIDS FAREWELL

**(31:2) Moses said to them, "Today I am 120 years old, and I can no longer go out and come in. God has also told me that I would not cross the Jordan."**

✳ *The Talmud Teaches*
*Today I am 120 years old* What is the intent of "today"? Moses meant to say: Today, the seventh of Adar, my days and years are complete, for Moses was born and died on the seventh of Adar. This teaches you that God rounds out the days of the righteous from day to day and from month to month, as it says "I will fill the number of your days" (Exodus 23:26) (*Sotah* 13b).

*I can no longer go out and come in* What did Moses mean by "go out and come in"? Do you think it should be taken literally, that he was physically weak? But it says "Moses was 120 years old when he died; his eye had not dimmed, and his vigor had not diminished" (34:7). And it also says that on his final day, "Moses ascended from the plains of Moab to Mount Nebo" (34:1); and we learned: There were twelve steps, and Moses bounded them with one leap! So it cannot mean that he was frail and infirm. R. Shmuel b. Nachmani said: It means that Moses was no longer able "to go out and come in" in the words of the Torah, implying that the gates of wisdom were closed to him (*Sotah* 13b).

**(31:8) Moses summoned Joshua, and in the presence of all Israel said to him, "Be strong and brave, since you will come along with this nation to the land that God swore to their fathers that he would give to them. You will be the one to parcel it out to them."**

### �֎ *The Talmud Teaches*
*since you will come along with this nation* Implying that Joshua is on the same level as the people. Yet further on, it says "You, Joshua, will *bring* the children of Israel to the land" (31:23), suggesting that he is their leader. How can this inconsistency be reconciled? R. Yochanan said: In the first verse, Moses said to Joshua: You will come along with the people. You should be together with the elders of the generation; listen to their advice, and do not order them around. But in the second verse, it was God who said to Joshua: Take a stick and hit them over the head, meaning: Assert your authority! There can be only one leader for a generation, not two (*Sanhedrin* 8a).

## THE KING READS DEUTERONOMY

**(31:11) On the festival of Sukkot, when all Israel comes to present themselves before God your Lord, in the place that He will choose, you must read this Torah before all Israel, so that they will be able to hear it.**

### ✴ *The Maimonides Code of Law Teaches*
*this Torah* He must read it in the holy tongue, for it says "You must read *this* Torah"—in the language in which it was written, even though there may be people in the audience who speak other languages (Rambam, Laws of *Chagigah* 3:5).

**(31:16) God said to Moses, "When you go and lie with your ancestors, this people will rise up and stray after the alien gods of the land into which they are coming. They will thus abandon Me and violate the covenant that I have made with them."**

### ✖ *The Talmud Teaches*
*will rise up* The Romans asked R. Yehoshua b. Chananiah: Where in Scripture does it say that God resurrects the dead and

that He knows what will happen in the future? He replied: Both concepts can be derived from the following verse, "God said to Moses, 'When you go and lie down with your ancestors and rise [proof of resurrection]; this people will go astray [proof of God's knowledge of the future].'"

The Romans countered: Perhaps the verse means only "and this people will rise and go astray" [not that Moses will rise from the dead], so that the verse does not prove resurrection. R. Yehoshua replied: Accept at least the proof for half of your question, namely, that God knows the future (*Sanhedrin* 90b)!

**(31:17) I will then display My anger against them and abandon them. I will hide My face from them, and they will be their enemies' prey. Beset by many evils and troubles, they will say, "It is because my God is no longer with me that these evils have befallen us."**

### *The Talmud Teaches*

***Beset by many evils and troubles*** What is the difference between *evils* and *troubles?* Isn't that redundant? Rav said: The Torah speaks about evils that clash with each other. For instance, if a person is stung at the same time by a wasp and a scorpion (*Chagigah* 5a).

NOTE: Rashi explains: The remedy for a wasp bite is hot water; and for a scorpion's bite, cold water. The reverse is dangerous. Therefore, when both happen simultaneously, there is no remedy.

**(31:18) On that day I will utterly hide My face because of all the evil that they have done in turning to foreign gods.**

### *The Talmud Teaches*

***On that day I will utterly hide My face*** Rava said: God says: Although I hide My face from them, I shall speak to them in a dream (*Chagigah* 5b).

NOTE: Rashi explains that Rava infers this from the words "on that day": God will hide His face during the day, but at night He will appear to them in a dream.

✦ *The Jerusalem Talmud Teaches*
*I will utterly hide My face*   R. Yaakov said: It says "I shall wait
for God Who has hidden His face from the house of Jacob, and
I will hope to Him" (Isaiah 8:17). There was never a worse mo-
ment in the world than when God said to Moses, "On that day
I will utterly hide My face," yet, says Isaiah, "I will hope to
Him," for He said in Sinai, "For the Torah will not be forgotten
by their descendants" (Jerusalem Talmud, *Sanhedrin* 10:2).

✦ *The Talmud Teaches*
*I will utterly hide My face*   Some Papunians [Papunia is a town
near Baghdad] asked R. Mattenah: Where is Esther alluded to
in the Torah? He replied: In the verse, "I will utterly hide *[astir]*
My face;" and "*astir*" sounds like Esther (*Chullin* 139b).

NOTE: This is not just a play on words. The meaning is: The
Jews in the days of Esther had turned their back on God, therefore, God hid *(astir)* His face and sent Haman, who sought to
destroy them (Book of Esther).

## THE TORAH AS TESTIMONY

**(31:19) Now write for yourselves this song, the Torah, and
teach it to the children of Israel, place it in their mouth, so
that this song shall be for Me a witness against the children
of Israel.**

✦ *The Talmud Teaches*
*Now write for yourselves*   Rabbah said: Even a person who
inherits a Torah scroll from his parents, it is a mitzvah for him
to write one of his own, for it says "Now write for yourselves
this song," and *song* refers to the Torah (*Sanhedrin* 21b).

NOTE: But if you buy a Torah scroll from a *sofer* (scribe) you also
fulfill the mitzvah of writing a *sefer Torah* (*Yoreh Dei'ah* 270).

*and teach it*   R. Akiva said: From where do we know that a
person must repeat the same lesson to a student until he
knows it? For it says "and teach it to the children of Israel."
And from where do we know that not only do they have to

know it, but that it has to be completely clear to them? For it says "Place it in their mouths," implying that they can repeat it fluently (*Eruvin* 54b).

**(31:20) When I bring them to the land flowing with milk and honey that I promised their ancestors, they will eat, be satisfied, and grow fat. They will then turn to foreign gods and worship them, despising Me and violating My covenant.**

### ※ *The Talmud Teaches*
*They will eat, be satisfied, and grow fat* This bears out the saying: A full stomach leads to all kinds of sin (*Berachot* 32a).

**(31:21) When they are then beset by many evils and troubles, this song shall speak up for them as a witness, for it shall not be forgotten by their descendants. I know their inclination through what they are doing right now, even before I have brought them to the promised land.**

### ※ *The Talmud Teaches*
*for it shall not be forgotten* R. Shimon b. Yochai said: God forbid that the Torah will be forgotten by the Jewish people, for it says "It shall not be forgotten by their descendants." What then is the meaning of the verse, "They will roam about to seek the word of God, but they will not find it" (Amos 8:12)? It means that nowhere will they find a clear-cut halachah and a lucid Mishnah, but every statement will be challenged and disputed, as is the case in the Talmud; but of course, the Torah will never be forgotten (*Shabbat* 138b).

**(31:26) Moses gave orders to the Levites, saying, "Take this Torah scroll and place it at the side of the ark of God your Lord's covenant, leaving it there as a witness."**

### ※ *The Talmud Teaches*
*Take this Torah scroll* R. Yochanan said: The Torah was transmitted in separate scrolls, and although it says "Take this Torah scroll," that is, one scroll, this refers to the time after the separate scrolls had been joined together (*Gittin* 60a).

NOTE: Each time Moses heard a pronouncement from God, he wrote it down on a separate scroll; and at the end of the forty-year wandering, he sewed the sections together.

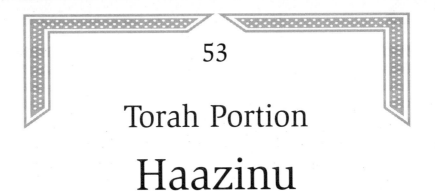

# 53

## Torah Portion

# Haazinu

### Deuteronomy 32:1–32:52

### THE SONG OF MOSES

**(32:1) Listen, heaven! I will speak! Earth! Hear the words of My mouth!**

✳ *The Midrash Teaches*

***Listen heaven . . .*** Why did Moses call heaven and earth to bear witness over Israel? He said to the children of Israel: Observe heaven and earth. Although they are not rewarded for obeying God's laws, the planets and stars do not deviate from their assigned paths. You, who are rewarded when you deserve it and punished if you sin, surely you should not deviate from your assigned path *(Sifrei)*!

***Listen, heaven . . .*** Why did Moses call heaven and earth to testify over Israel? Moses said: I am flesh and blood; tomorrow I will die. If they want to say: We never received the Torah, who shall refute them? Therefore, I call to testify over them two witnesses that will live forever *(Sifrei)*.

**(32:2) May my teaching drop like the rain, may my utterance flow like the dew; like storm winds upon vegetation and like raindrops upon blades of grass.**

### ✳ The Talmud Teaches

**May my teaching drop like rain** Here it says "May my teaching drop like rain." But this is followed by "May my utterance flow like dew." Why the different similes? If a scholar is a God-fearing person, then the Torah is to him like dew, which is always a blessing; if he is not, it destroys him, just as a powerful rainstorm crushes the crops (*Taanit* 7a).

**May my teaching drop like rain** Rav Yehudah said: The day when it rains is as great as the day when the Torah was given, for it says "May my teaching drop like rain." Rava said: It is even greater than the day when the Torah was given, for it says "May my teaching drop like rain." When you make an analogy, what is compared to what? Surely, the smaller thing—the teaching, that is, the Torah—is compared to the greater, the more obvious, that is, the rain (*Taanit* 7a).

NOTE: Maharsha explains: The underlying thought is: The Torah is as essential to a Jew's spiritual existence as rain is to his physical existence.

### ✳ The Midrash Teaches

**Like storm winds upon vegetation** Just as the winds descend on the vegetation and make it grow, producing all varieties—green, red, black, and white—so too the words of Torah produce all varieties of men: rabbis, pious laymen, sages, *tzaddikim* (righteous men), and *chasidim* (devout men) *(Sifrei)*.

**(32:4) The deeds of the Mighty One are perfect, for all His ways are just. He is a faithful God, never unfair, righteous and moral is He.**

### ✳ The Talmud Teaches

**The deeds of the Mighty One are perfect** When R. Chanina b. Teradyon and his wife and daughter were led away to be burned at the stake by the Romans, they accepted the righteousness of divine judgment. R. Chanina said, "The deeds of the Mighty One are perfect, for all His ways are just." His wife continued, "He is a faithful God, never unfair, righteous and moral is He." His daughter joined them, saying, "Great in counsel and mighty in deed, Your eyes observe all ways of mankind, so as to repay each man according to his ways and the consequences of his deeds" (Jeremiah 32:19) (*Avodah Zarah* 18a).

***He is a faithful God*** Just as the wicked are punished in the world to come even for the smallest transgression, so too the righteous are punished in *this* world for the slightest transgression. "Never unfair": Just as the righteous receive their reward in the world to come, even for a minor mitzvah, so too are the wicked rewarded in *this* world even for a minor mitzvah they performed (*Taanit* 11a).

***Righteous and moral is He*** The Sages said: When a person leaves this world, all his deeds are spelled out before him, and he is told: Did you do such and such a thing in such and such a place on such and such a day? He will answer: Yes. Then they tell him: Sign, and he signs. But not only that, the person acknowledges that the judgment is fair; and he says: You have judged me correctly, to fulfill the verse "You are justified when You speak" (Psalms 51:6) (*Taanit* 11a).

**(32:6) Is this the way you repay God, you ungrateful, unwise people? Is He not your Father, your Master? He created and established you.**

### *The Talmud Teaches*

***He created and established you*** R. Meir used to expound this verse as follows: "He created and established you"—the Jewish people are a community in which all classes are represented: From their own ranks, they produce priest, prophets, officers, and kings, as it says "From them shall come cornerstones, from them tent pegs, from them bows of combat, and every leader will also come from them" (Zechariah 10:4).

**(32:13) He carried them over the earth's high places, to feast on the crops of the field. He let them suckle honey from a stone, oil from a flinty rock.**

### *The Talmud Teaches*

***He let them suckle honey from a stone*** R. Avira expounded: In Egypt, when the women of Israel gave birth, God would send an angel from heaven who gave the babies two cakes, one of honey and one of oil. Because the women wanted to protect their babies from the Egyptians, they gave birth secretly and could not make any preparations, so the angel nourished them, "He let them suckle honey from a stone and oil from a flinty rock" (*Sotah* 11b).

**(32:14) Butter of cattle and milk of sheep with fat of lambs, rams born in Bashan and he-goats, with wheat as fat as kidneys; and you will drink blood of grapes like delicious wine.**

### ※ *The Talmud Teaches*

*wheat as fat as kidneys* This alludes to the fact that in time to come a kernel of wheat in the Land of Israel will be as large as the two kidneys of a big bull. And this should come as no surprise, for in the Land of Israel a fox once made his den inside a turnip, and what was left of the turnip weighed sixty Tzipori pounds (*Ketubot* 111b).

NOTE: Tzippori pounds are pound weights of Sepphoris, a town in the Upper Galilee.

*and you will drink blood of grapes* This indicates that the messianic age is not like this world. In this world, there is the toil of harvesting and pressing the grapes. But in the messianic age, a person will bring one grape on a wagon or a ship, put it in the corner of his house, and draw wine from the grape as if it were a large barrel. It does not need pressing, for it says "You will drink blood of grapes" (*Ketubot* 111b).

**(32:15) Jeshurun [a poetic name for Israel] thus became fat and rebelled. You grew fat, thick and gross. [The nation] abandoned the God who made it, and was contemptuous of the Rock who was its support.**

### ※ *The Talmud Teaches*

*Jeshurun thus became fat and rebelled* This ties in with the popular saying, "A full stomach is the source of all troubles," meaning: overindulgence leads to sin (*Berachot* 32a).

**(32:20) God said: I will hide My face from them, and see what will be their end. They are a generation that reverses itself, children that have no faith.**

### ※ The Talmud Teaches
*children that have no faith*  R. Meir said: Even when Israel does not do the will of God, they are still called His children, as it says "children that have no faith" (*Kiddushin* 36a).

**(32:24) They will be bloated by famine, consumed by fiery demonic fever, cut down by bitter plague. I will send against them fanged beasts, with venomous creatures that crawl in the dust.**

### ※ The Talmud Teaches
*consumed by fiery, demonic fever [reshef]*  R. Shimon b. Lakish said: If you study Torah, painful sufferings will leave you, as it says "And the sons of *reshef*, flaming demons, *uf*, fly upward" (Job 5:7). The word *uf* refers to Torah, for it says "If you close your eyes, *hata'if* [related to *uf*], it is gone" (Proverbs 23:5). And *reshef* refers to demons, for it says "they will be consumed by *reshef*, cut down by bitter plague." Thus, it is the *uf*, the Torah, that chases away *reshef*, the demons (*Berachot* 5a).

*the venomous creatures that crawl in the dust*  R. Yose said: Whoever challenges the sovereignty of the house of David deserves to be bitten by a snake. For it says "Adoniahu slaughtered sheep, cattle, and fat oxen at the Stone of Zochelet" (1 Kings 1:9), for a banquet at which he wanted to challenge David's monarchy and take power himself. And it . . . says "with venomous creatures that crawl [*zochalei*] in the dust" (*Sanhedrin* 110a).

NOTE: *Zochalei*, referring to snakes, is seen as cognate with *Zochelet*, the place where Adoniahu wanted to rebel against David.

**(32:36) God will take up the cause of His people and comfort His servants, when He sees that their power is gone, and there is no leader or helper.**

### ✳ *The Talmud Teaches*
**God will take up the cause of His people** It says "God will take
up the cause of His people, that is, He will redeem them, when
He sees that their power is gone, and there is no leader or
helper." Which means: Mashiach will not come until students
of the Torah become few. Another explanation: until the Jews
give up hope for the redemption, as it says "there is no leader
or helper," meaning, as if Israel had no Supporter or Helper
(*Sanhedrin* 97a).

**(32:39) But now see! It is I! I am the only One—There are no
other gods with Me! I kill and I give life! I wounded and I
will heal! But none can save from My hand!**

### ✳ *The Talmud Teaches*
**I kill and I give life** The Rabbis taught: It says "I kill and I give
life." You might say that this means, I kill one person and give life
to another person, in the way of the world where people die
and people are born. That's why it says "I wounded and I will
heal"; just as the wounding and healing obviously refer to the
same person, the wounded person is the one who will be
healed, so do death and life refer to the same person, the person who died will be revived. This verse is a conclusive answer
to those who claim that the resurrection of the dead is not mentioned in the Torah.

The passage can be interpreted a different way: Initially,
people will be resurrected with the disabilities they had in their
former life—blind, deaf, or lame—and then, "what I wounded I
will heal," meaning, after they are resurrected, I will heal them
of the physical impairments they had in their previous existence
(*Pesachim* 68a).

**but none can save from My hand** A righteous father cannot
earn merit for his wicked son, as it says "None can save from
My hand."

Abraham cannot save his wicked son Ishmael from God's
punishment; Isaac cannot save his wicked son Esau; and similarly, the righteous King Hezekiah cannot save his wicked son
Menashe (*Sanhedrin* 104a).

NOTE: But a righteous son can earn merit for a wicked father and mother, because a child receives his early education from his parents. And if the son is righteous, the parents deserve some of the credit.

**(32:43) Let the nations sing the praises of His people, for He will avenge the blood of His servants. He will bring retribution upon His foes, and His land will atone for His people.**

### ※ *The Talmud Teaches*
*His land will atone for His people*  R. Anan said: Whoever is buried in the Land of Israel is as if he were buried under the altar, for regarding the altar it says "Make an earthen *[adamah]* altar for Me" (Exodus 20:21); and it says here, "His land *[admato]* will atone for His people." Which shows that the entire territory of the Land of Israel has the same power of conferring atonement as the altar, which is the symbol for atonement (*Ketubot* 111a).

**(32:47) The Torah is not an empty thing from you. It is your life, and with it you will long endure on the land which you are crossing the Jordan to occupy.**

### ※ *The Jerusalem Talmud Teaches*
*The Torah is not an empty thing from you*  R. Manna said: "The Torah is not an empty thing." And if you think it is empty, it is "from *you*," that is, it is your fault. Why so? Because you do not try hard enough to study the Torah (Jerusalem Talmud, *Pe'ah* 1:1).

### ✳ *The Midrash Teaches*
*The Torah is not an empty thing . . .*  This teaches us that there is no empty thing in the Torah. In every word, you can find important truths that will have a bearing on your whole life in this world and a lasting principal in the world to come *(Sifrei)*.

**(32:48) God spoke to Moses in the middle of this day, saying . . .**

## ✳ *The Midrash Teaches*

*in the middle of this day*  Why in the middle of the day? Because Israel said: We won't let Moses die. God replied: I am going to bring him into the cave to die at midday; whoever wants to stop Me, let him try *(Sifrei)*!

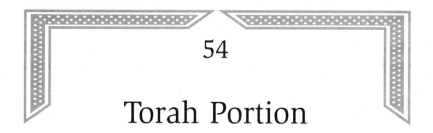

# 54

Torah Portion

# Vezot Haberachah

Deuteronomy 33:1–34:12

## THE BLESSING OF MOSES

(33:2) Moses said: God came from Sinai, shone forth to them from Seir, appeared from Mount Paran, and then approached with some of the holy myriads—from His right hand He presented the fiery Torah to them.

### ✖ *The Talmud Teaches*
*God came from Sinai, shone forth from Seir [that is, Esau and Rome], appeared from Mount Paran [that is, Ishmael and the Arabs]* What did God have to do in Seir and Mount Paran? R. Yochanan said: This teaches us that God offered the Torah to every nation and language group, but no one accepted it until He offered it to Israel, who accepted it (*Avodah Zarah* 2b).

*From His right hand He presented the fiery Torah to them* When you hand a Torah scroll to someone else, you should use your right hand; and similarly, the one who receives it should receive it with his right hand—as it was originally given. For it says "From His right hand He presented the fiery Torah to them" (*Soferim* 3:10).

*the fiery Torah* It was taught in the yeshiva of R. Yishmael: It says "From His right hand He presented the fiery Torah to them"—The Holy One, blessed be He, said: It is fitting that they be given the fiery Torah to subdue their bold personality. Some

343

say: The Jewish people are bold by nature, and if the Torah had not been given to them and weakened them, no nation could have resisted them (*Beitzah* 25b).

**(33:3) Although He shows love to the nations, all Your holy ones are in Your hand; They follow in Your footsteps and uphold Your word.**

### ✳ The Talmud Teaches
*They follow in Your footsteps* R. Yosef learned: This refers to the Torah scholars who bruise their feet going from town to town and from country to country to learn Torah. "And uphold Your word" means that they are constantly involved in discussing the words of God (*Bava Batra* 8a).

**(33:4) The Torah that Moses commanded to us is the heritage of the congregation of Jacob.**

### ✳ The Talmud Teaches
*The Torah that Moses commanded to us* The Rabbis taught: When a child begins to talk, his father should teach him Torah. What is meant by "teach him Torah"? R. Hamenuna said: He should teach him to recite the verse, "The Torah that Moses commanded to us is the heritage of the congregation of Jacob" (*Sukkah* 42a).

*the heritage of the congregation of Jacob* R. Yehudah said in the name of Rav: Whoever withholds a halachah from a student is as if he robbed him of his ancestral heritage, for it says "The Torah that Moses commanded to us is the heritage of the congregation of Jacob," which means that it is a heritage to all of Israel since the six days of Creation. Because God created heaven and earth for the sake of the people of Israel, who were destined to inherit the Torah (*Sanhedrin* 91b).

**(33:6) Reuben will live and not die, and may his population be included in the count.**

### ✳ The Talmud Teaches
*Reuben will live and not die* Rava said: Where do we find an allusion to the resurrection of the dead in the Torah? He an-

swered: In the verse "Reuben will live and not die"—He will live in this world and not die in the next world (*Sanhedrin* 92a).

**(33:9) He [Levi] was the one who said of his father and mother, "I did not see them," his brothers he does not recognize, and his children he does not know. Thus they kept Your word and safeguarded Your covenant.**

### ✵ The Talmud Teaches
*He was the one who said of his . . . father* Rav Yehudah said: The tribe of Levi did not take part in the worship of the golden calf, for it says "Moses stood at the camp's entrance and announced, 'Whoever is for God, join me!' All the Levites gathered around him" (Exodus 32:16). The sons of R. Abba b. Papa challenged him: It says concerning the Levites, "He was the one who said of his father and mother, 'I do not see them'; his brother he does not recognize, and his children he does not know."

NOTE: The verse refers to the sin of the golden calf, when the Levites avenged God and put to death those who worshipped the idol, even if they were their closest relatives. This is proof that there were Levites who did worship the golden calf.

The Gemara answers: When the verse speaks of "his father," it refers to his mother's father, who was a Yisrael, and when it says "his brother," it refers to a half-brother who has the same mother but a different father, who was a Yisrael; and when it says "his son," it means the son of his daughter, which she had from a Yisrael. Thus, the Levites themselves did not worship the golden calf (*Yoma* 66b).

**(33:12) To Benjamin he said: "God's beloved one shall dwell securely by Him. He hovers over him all day long; and shall dwell between his shoulders."**

### ✵ The Talmud Teaches
*He hovers over him all day long* R. Levi b. Chama said: A strip of the altar extended from Judah's portion, entering into Benjamin's territory. This was a strip of one cubit width on the east side and the south side of the altar. Benjamin lamented about this every day, wishing that the entire area of the altar would

be in his territory, for it says "He hovers over him all day long."
Therefore, Benjamin was privileged to become a host for the
Shechinah, as it says "He dwells between Benjamin's shoulders," for the Temple was built on the highest spot in Benjamin's territory (*Zevachim* 53b, 54a).

**He hovers over him**  R. Meir says: "He hovers over him" alludes
to the First Temple, which was destroyed; "all day long"
alludes to the Second Temple, which was destroyed also; "He
shall dwell between his shoulders" alludes to the days of
Mashiach, when the third Temple will be rebuilt and which will
last forever (*Zevachim* 118b).

**He longs for it**  R. Dimi said: The Shechinah rested on Israel
in three places, namely: In Shiloh, in Nob, and in the Temple in
Jerusalem; and all of these are situated in the territory of Benjamin. For it says "God hovers over Benjamin all day long," implying that all "hoverings" of the Shechinah will be only in the
portion of Benjamin (*Zevachim* 118b).

**He shall dwell between his shoulders**  R. Meir says: When the
children of Israel were standing by the Red Sea, the tribes were
fighting with each other, each wanting to be the first to enter
the sea. Then the tribe of Benjamin jumped ahead and went
first into the sea while the waters were still raging. Because of
that, the righteous Benjamin was worthy to become the host
of the Almighty, for the Holy of Holies was built in the territory of
the tribe of Benjamin. As it says in Moses' blessing to Benjamin,
"[God] dwells between his shoulders" (*Sotah* 37a).

**He shall dwell between his shoulders**  When David and Samuel
were trying to find a suitable site for the Temple, they thought
of building it at Ein Etam, for that is the highest spot. But they
reconsidered, saying: Let us build it on a slightly lower location
in Jerusalem, for it says "He dwells between his shoulders," and
the shoulders are lower than the head; thus, it should not be
built on the highest spot. Another reason why they did not
build it at Ein Etam is that there was a tradition that the Sanhedrin should be located in Judah's territory, whereas the Temple should be in Benjamin's portion. They reasoned: If we build

the Temple on the highest spot, the Temple and the Sanhedrin will be far apart. Let us build it a little lower, as it says "He dwells between his shoulders" (*Zevachim* 54b).

✳ *The Midrash Teaches*
*He shall dwell between his shoulders*  Why did Benjamin merit having the Temple built in his portion? Because all the tribes were born outside the Land of Israel; only Benjamin was born in the Land of Israel *(Sifrei)*.

**(33:18) To Zebulun he said: Rejoice Zebulun in your business journeys, and Issachar in your tents of study. The tribes will assemble at the mountain where they will slaughter offerings of righteousness, for by the riches of the sea they will be nourished and by the treasures concealed in the sand.**

✳ *The Talmud Teaches*
*The tribes will assemble at the mountain*  Zebulun said to God: Master of the universe: To my brothers, You gave fields and vineyards and land; but to me you gave mountains, hills, lakes, and rivers. God answered: All your brothers will need you for the *chilazon* [that] is found in your territory.

NOTE:  The *chilazon* is a creature that comes out of the sea near the territory of Zebulun and climbs up into the mountains. The blue *techeilet* dye needed for the zizith fringes is made from its blood.

For it says regarding Zebulun, "The tribes will assemble at the mountain of Zebulun, for that is where the *chilazon* is . . . found. . . . for by the riches of the sea they will be nourished, and by what is hidden in the secret treasures of the sand, that is, the *chilazon.*" Zebulun then said to God: Master of the universe: Who will inform me if anyone tries to take the precious *chilazon* without paying for it? God replied: "There, they will slaughter offerings of righteousness." This will be a sign for you; just as a sacrifice is invalid if it is stolen, so too if anyone finds a *chilazon* and takes it without payment, it will not benefit his business at all; the color produced by the dye of the stolen *chilazon* will be ruined (*Megillah* 6a).

**(33:21) Of Gad he said: He chose the first portion for himself, for that is where the lawgiver's [Moses'] plot is hidden; he came at the head of the nation. He carried out God's justice and His ordinances together with Israel.**

### ※ The Talmud Teaches
*He carried out God's justice and His ordinances together with Israel* It was taught: Moses died in the portion of Reuben and was buried in the portion of Gad. The distance between the two portions is about four miles. Who carried him those four miles? He was placed on the wings of the Shechinah, and the ministering angels declared, "He carried out God's justice and His ordinances together with Israel" (*Sotah* 13b).

**(33:24) To Asher he said: The most blessed of children is Asher, and filled with God's blessing, he will be desired by his brothers and dip his foot in oil.**

### ※ The Talmud Teaches
*and dip his foot in oil* This refers to the territory of Asher, which gushes forth olive oil like a well. The story has been told that once the people of Ludkia needed oil. They appointed a non-Jewish agent and instructed him to buy a hundred myriad *maneh* worth of oil. He went, and finding a farmer digging up the earth around olive trees, he waited until he finished and went with him. As soon as the farmer got into town, his maidservant brought out a bowl of hot water and washed his hands and his feet. She then brought out to him a golden bowl filled with oil and dipped his hands and feet in it, thereby fulfilling the verse, "He shall dip his foot in oil" (*Menachot* 85b).

NOTE: Applying oil to the body of a person was practiced by wealthy, luxury-loving people of the Greek empire where Ludkia was located. Ludkia (Laodicea), a city in Syria, was founded by the Seleucids and probably is the same as today's Latakia, Syria, a Mediterranean port city.

**(33:27) The eternal God is a shelter above, and below are the arms of the world. He drove out the enemy before you, by His command: "Destroy!"**

### ※ The Talmud Teaches
*and below are the arms of the world*   R. Abbahu said: The world continues to exist only in the merit of a person who considers himself as nonexistent, for it says "Below are the arms of the world." Meaning: The lowly and humble are the pillars that hold up the world (*Chullin* 89a).

**(33:28) Israel shall dwell in safety, alone, at the fountain of Jacob, in a land of grain and wine. Your heavens also drip with dew.**

### ※ The Talmud Teaches
*Israel will dwell in safety, alone*   R. Yose b. R. Chanina said: Moses pronounced a harmful decree on Israel, but a prophet came and called it off. Moses said, "Israel shall dwell in safety, alone, at the fountain of Jacob."

NOTE: Rashi explains this to mean that Israel will dwell securely only when they are as righteous as Jacob.

But Amos came and canceled it, saying, "And I said, 'Lord God, please refrain! How will Jacob survive, for he is small!'" meaning: How can the people of Israel be as righteous as Jacob? "So God relented concerning this: 'It too shall not be,' said the Lord God" (Amos 7:5, 6) (*Makkot* 24a).

**(33:29) Happy are you, Israel! Who is like you? You are a nation delivered by God, the Shield who helps you, and your triumphant Sword. Your enemies will try to deceive you, but you will trample on their high places.**

### ※ The Talmud Teaches
*but you will trample on their high places*   R. Nachman b. Yitzchak said: Whoever takes delight in Shabbat is saved from the subjugation by the nations of the exile. It says "If you proclaim the Sabbath a delight . . . then I will set you astride *the heights* of the earth" (Isaiah 58:13); and it says "You will trample on their the nations' *high places*," which Rashi interprets to mean that you will tread on the necks of your enemies (*Shabbat* 118b).

*you will trample on their high places* When Haman was brought down by Mordechai, he said to him: Doesn't it say "If your enemy falls, don't rejoice?" (Proverbs 24:17). Mordechai answered: Villain! That refers to a Jewish enemy, but about your kind it says "And you shall trample on their high places," that is, on their backs (*Megillah* 16a).

**(34:5) It was there in the land of Moab that God's servant Moses died by the mouth of God.**

### ❋ The Talmud Teaches
*Moses died* Is it possible that after Moses was dead he wrote the words, "Moses died"? That would not be true! So how could he have written this verse? We must say therefore that up to this point Moses wrote the text; from this point on, Joshua wrote (*Bava Batra* 15a).

### ✳ The Midrash Teaches
*by the mouth of God* From here, we know that when God takes the soul of the righteous, He does so gently with a "kiss," without suffering *(Sifrei)*.

**(34:6) God buried him in the valley, in the land of Moab, opposite Bet Peor. No one knows his burial place to this day.**

### ❋ The Talmud Teaches
*God buried him* The principle of measure for measure applies also in connection with the good. Moses earned merit by attending to the bones of Joseph for burial, as it says "Moses took Joseph's remains with him" (Exodus 13:19), and there was none greater than Moses. Therefore, he too merited that God Himself took care of his burial, as it says *"He* buried him" (*Sotah* 9b).

*God buried him* R. Simla'i expounded: The Torah begins with an act of kindness and ends with an act of kindness. It begins with the act of kindness of clothing the naked, for it says "God made garments of skin for Adam and his wife." It ends with an act of kindness, for it says "God buried him in the valley"; and attending to the dead is the most selfless act of kindness there is, for the dead cannot thank you (*Sotah* 14a).

*in the valley, in the land of Moab, opposite Bet Peor*  R. Berechiah said: The Torah gives us hint after hint at the location of the grave, yet "no one knows his burial place to this day" (*Sotah* 13b).

*opposite Bet Peor*  R. Chama b. R. Chanina said: Why was Moses buried opposite Bet Peor? Why was he not buried in the Land of Israel, as Joseph was? To atone for the episode at Peor where the Israelites behaved immorally with the daughters of Moab who seduced them to worship idols (Numbers 25:1–9) (*Sotah* 14a).

*no one knows his burial place*  The wicked Roman government once sent the following message to the governor of Bet Peor: Show us where Moses is buried. An expedition was sent to search for the site. When they stood above the location, his grave seemed to be below; when they stood below, it seemed to be above. They then split up into two groups; to those that went to the top, it seemed to be on the bottom; to those that went below, it seemed to be on top. This bears out the passage, "No one knows his burial place" (*Sotah* 13b).

*no one knows his burial place*  R. Chama b. R. Chanina said: Why was Moses' grave hidden from the view of flesh and blood? Because, foreseeing that the Temple would be destroyed and that Israel would be exiled from their land, God wanted it that way; otherwise people would come to Moses' grave weeping and imploring, and Moses would arise and annul the decree—for the righteous are even more beloved by God in their deaths than in their lives (*Sotah* 13a in *Ein Yaakov*).

**(34:8) The children of Israel bewailed Moses in the plains of Moab for thirty days; then the days of tearful mourning for Moses ended.**

### ※ *The Talmud Teaches*
*for thirty days*  Before his death, Rebbi instructed: Open the yeshiva after thirty days of mourning. Rebbi gave this order

because he said: I am not greater than Moses our teacher, about whom it says "The children of Israel mourned Moses in the plains of Moab for thirty days" (*Ketubot* 103b).

**(34:9) Joshua son of Nun was filled with a spirit of wisdom, because Moses had laid his hands on him, so the children of Israel obeyed him and did as God had commanded Moses.**

### ※ *The Talmud Teaches*
**his hands** Rava asked Rabbah b. Mari: What is the scriptural basis for the familiar saying, "Although the wine belongs to the owner, the waiter gets the thanks"? For it says "God said to Moses, 'Lay your hand on [Joshua] . . . so that the entire Israelite community will obey him'" (Numbers 27:18, 20). And it says also "Joshua son of Nun was filled with a spirit of wisdom, because Moses had laid his hands on him, so the children of Israel obeyed him." Although the spirit of wisdom comes from God, Moses is given all the credit (*Bava Kamma* 92b).

**(34:10) Never again will there arise in Israel a prophet like Moses whom God knew face to face.**

### ※ *The Talmud Teaches*
***Never again will there arise in Israel a prophet*** Kohelet, that is, Solomon, tried to be like Moses, as it says "Kohelet sought to find words of delight" (Ecclesiastes 12:10); but a heavenly voice went forth and said to him, "Words of truth have been recorded properly in the Torah (12:10), stating, 'Never again will there arise in Israel a prophet like Moses'; thus, you should not aspire to become like him" (*Rosh Hashanah* 21b).

### ✳ *The Midrash Teaches*
***will there arise in Israel a prophet like Moses*** In Israel, there will not arise; but among the nations, there did arise. And who was that? Balaam. The prophecy of Balaam can be compared to the knowledge of the king's cook. The cook has an exact knowledge of the expenditures of the king's table but no knowledge of the king himself *(Sifrei)*.

NOTE: The underlying idea is that Balaam's knowledge was limited to crude, mundane matters. Moses, on the other hand, was close to God and familiar with the deepest mysteries.

**(34:12) [No one else could reproduce] the strong hand and awesome power that Moses displayed before the eyes of all Israel.**

### ▓ *The Jerusalem Talmud Teaches*
*the strong hand* How did Moses display "the strong hand and awesome power"? After all, it was God who performed the miracles, and Moses was only God's agent!

It was taught: When Moses went up on high to receive the tablets and Israel made the golden calf, God tried to take them from his hand. But the hand of Moses prevailed and seized them from Him. Thereupon, God said, "Peace to the hand that prevailed over Mine!" And so does Scripture praise him with the words "the strong hand." Thus, it was Moses' "strong hand and awesome power" that triumphed over God (Jerusalem Talmud, *Taanit* 4:5).

# Glossary

**Aggadah:** Ethical and inspirational teachings of the Talmud.

**Amidah:** Important part of daily prayer, also called *Shemoneh esrei*.

**B'nei Yisrael:** The children of Israel.

*baal teshuvah:* A newly observant Jew.

*berachah:* Blessing.

**Bet Hamikdash:** Temple.

*bet midrash:* House of study.

**brit:** Ritual circumcision.

*Chumash:* Five books of Moses.

*ephod:* The half cape worn by Aaron and later high priests when performing the service in the Tabernacle and Temple.

**Eretz Yisrael:** The Land of Israel.

*etrog: See* Sukkot.

**Gemara:** Talmud.

*haddasim: See* Sukkot.

**Halachah:** Torah and rabbinic law.

**Hallel:** meaning "praise"; a prayer consisting of Psalms 113–118 that is recited on festivals.

**kashruth:** Laws of kosher food.

*kedushah:* Holiness.

**Kiddush:** Blessing recited over wine before Sabbath or holiday meal.

*kohen* (**pl.** *kohanim*)**:** Priest(s), members of the priestly tribe.

**Kohen Gadol:** High priest.

*lulav: See* Sukkot.

**Mashiach:** Messiah.

**matzo, matzos (pl.):** Unleavened bread.

*Megillah:* Scroll of Esther, which is read on the Purim festival.

**menorah:** The seven-branched candelabrum used in the Temple and the eight-branched candelabrum used on Hanukkah.

**mezuzah:** Parchment scroll affixed to doorpost.

**Midrash:** Homiletic teachings of the Sages.

**Mishnah:** The teachings of the *Tannaim,* which form the basis of the Talmud.

**mitzvah (pl. mitzvoth):** Torah commandment(s).

*nazir:* Nazirite; person who vowed to abstain from wine and dedicated himself to God.

**Pesach:** Passover.

**Purim:** The Feast of Lots, commemorating the day on which the Jews were saved from their Persian oppressors.

**Rabbis:** Teachers of the Talmud and Midrash.

**Sages:** Teachers of the Talmud and Midrash.

**Sanhedrin:** Highest court of seventy-one sages that met in the Chamber of the Hewn Stones in the Jerusalem Temple. Instituted by Moses, it administered both criminal and capital cases. Decisions required a majority of the votes. It ceased to function after the destruction of the Temple by the Romans in 70 C.E.

**seder:** Passover service conducted in the home on first two nights of Passover.

*sefer Torah:* Torah scroll.

**Shabbat:** Sabbath.

**Shavuot:** Festival of Weeks, Pentecost.

**Shechinah:** Divine Presence.

*shechitah:* Ritual slaughter of animals.

**Shema Yisrael:** Literally: "Hear, O Israel," first words of fundamental prayer declaring faith in God.

*Shemoneh esrei:* Eighteen Blessings, or Amidah, important part of daily prayer.

*shochet:* Ritual slaughterer.

**Simchat Torah:** The Rejoicing of the Torah; last day of Sukkot, when the public Torah readings are completed annually.

*sotah:* Suspected adulteress.

*sukkah:* Booth covered with greenery in which the family gathers for meals during Sukkot.

**Sukkot:** Festival of Booths, Tabernacles. During the festival, the family gathers for meals in the *sukkah* (booth) erected for the occasion. Covered with greenery, the *sukkah* recalls the time when Israel wandered in the wilderness after the Exodus, protected by God's supervision. On Sukkot, we wave the *lulav* bundle comprising the "four species": the *lulav,* the *etrog* (citron), three myrtle twigs, and two willow sprigs.

*talmid chacham:* Torah scholar.

**Tanach:** Hebrew acronym for Torah, Prophets, and Writings.

**Tanna (pl. Tannaim):** Teacher of the Mishnah.

**tefillin:** Phylacteries.

*teshuvah:* Repentance.

*tzaddik* **(pl. *tzaddikim*):** Righteous man.

*tzedakah:* Charity.

**yeshiva:** Torah school.

*yetzer hara:* Evil impulse.

**Yom Tov:** Jewish holiday.

**zizith:** Tassels attached to the four corners of the tallith.

# Bibliography

*Arachin:* Talmudic tractate dealing with valuations of things dedicated to the Sanctuary.

*Avodah Zarah:* Talmudic tractate, dealing with idol worship.

Avot: Talmudic tractate, also known as Ethics of the Fathers.

Avot d'Rabbi Natan: A commentary on Avot by the Babylonian sage R. Natan (ca. 210 C.E.).

*Bach, Yoreh Dei'ah:* Commentary on a section of the Code of Jewish Law.

*Bava Batra:* Talmudic tractate dealing with the laws involving real property.

*Bava Kamma:* Talmudic tractate dealing with torts and damages.

*Bava Metzia:* Talmudic tractate dealing with movable property and wages.

*Bechorot:* Talmudic tractate dealing with first-born animals.

*Beitzah:* Talmudic tractate dealing with the festivals.

*Berachot:* Talmudic tractate dealing with prayers and blessings.

*Bereishit Rabbah:* The primary part of the Midrashic collection known as *Bereishit Rabbah,* a running commentary on Genesis.

*Bikkurim:* Talmudic tractate dealing with the first fruits.

*Chagigah:* Talmudic tractate dealing with festival offerings.

*Challah:* Talmudic tractate dealing with dough offerings.

*Chidushei Harim:* Commentary on the Talmud by R. Yitzchak Meir Alter, the first Gerer Rebbe.

*Chullin:* Talmudic tractate dealing with kashruth.

*Derech Eretz:* Talmudic tractate dealing with rules of ethical conduct.

Devarim Rabbah: A midrash on Deuteronomy, homiletic commentary.

*Eight Chapters:* Also known as *Shemonah Perakim,* it is the introduction to Maimonides' commentary on Tractate Avot ("Ethics of the Fathers"). A seminal work, it addresses such topics as the nature of the soul, prophecy, predestination, and man's freedom of will. First published in Mantua in 1560, and translated into English by Avraham Yaakov Finkel, Yeshivath Beth Moshe, 1994.

*Ein Yaakov:* The ethical and inspirational teachings of the Talmud, translated into English by Avraham Yaakov Finkel.

*Eruvin:* Talmudic tractate dealing with the various domains with regard to carrying on the Sabbath.

Etz Yosef: Commentary on *Ein Yaakov*; see above.

*Gittin:* Talmudic tractate dealing with divorce.

Hirsch, R. Samson Raphael (1808–1888): Eminent commentator on the Torah (first published in Frankfurt am Main 1867–1878).

*Horayot:* Talmudic tractate dealing with decisions of the Sanhedrin.

Jerusalem Talmud: Compiled by the Palestinian masters of the Talmud who remained in the Land of Israel after the Romans drove out most of the scholars. When we speak of the Talmud, we always mean the Babylonian Talmud, which is the more accepted. The Jerusalem Talmud was first printed in Venice in 1523.

*Keritot:* Talmudic tractate dealing with offenses that are punishable by excision or premature death.

*Ketubot:* Talmudic tractate dealing with marriage contracts.

*Kiddushin:* Talmudic tractate dealing with laws of marriage.

Kotzker Rebbe: Great Hasidic master, R. Menachem Mendel Mogenstern (1787–1859).

*Maaser Sheini:* Talmudic tractate dealing with the "second tithe."

Maharsha: Acronym of Rabbi Shmuel Eliezer Eidels, great talmudic commentator (1555–1631).

Maimonides: Better known as Rambam, the acronym of Rabbi Moshe ben Maimon (1135–1204). One of Judaism's leading Torah authorities.

*Makkot:* Talmudic tractate dealing with the penalty of lashes.

Mechilta: Midrashic commentary on Exodus by the school of R. Yishmael (ca. 120 C.E.), (first published in Constantinople, 1513).

*Menachot:* Talmudic tractate dealing with meal offerings.

*Midrash Rabbah:* Midrashic collection on the Torah (first published in Constantinople, 1512).

*Mishneh Torah:* The monumental, fourteen-volume, all-inclusive halachic body of law, written by Maimonides. It is the first comprehensive code of all Torah laws. First published in Rome, before 1480, and in Soncino in 1490.

*Mo'ed Katan:* Talmudic tractate dealing with the intermediate days of a festival.

*Nazir:* Talmudic tractate dealing with the Nazirite vow.

*Nedarim:* Talmudic tractate dealing with vows.

*Nega'im:* Talmudic tractate dealing with leprous marks.

*Niddah:* Talmudic tractate dealing with the laws concerning menstruation.

*Pe'ah:* Talmudic tractate dealing with the portions of the harvest that must be left over for the poor.

*Pesachim:* Talmudic tractate dealing with the Passover and its sacrifices.

*Pesikta Zutreta:* Also known as *Lekach Tov,* this is a Midrachic work by Rabbi Tovia ben Eliezer HaGadol (1036–1108). First printed in Venice in 1546, the work is a collection of midrashim on Leviticus, Numbers, and Deuteronomy. The author lived in Bulgaria and Serbia.

*Pirkei d'Rabbi Eliezer:* Midrashic work by the school of R. Eliezer HaGadol, first published in Constantinople in 1514.

Rambam: See Maimonides.

Rashi: Acronym of Rabbi Shlomoh ben Yitzchak (1040–1105), author of the most important commentary on the Bible and Talmud (first published in Rome, ca. 1470).

Rebbi: Rabbi Yehudah Hanasi, also known as Rabbeinu Hakadosh and Rebbe, compiler of the Mishnah.

*Rosh Hashanah:* Talmudic tractate dealing with the New Year and the calendar.

*Sanhedrin:* Talmudic tractate dealing with the judiciary system.

*Shabbat:* Talmudic tractate dealing with the Sabbath.

*Shekalim:* Talmudic tractate dealing with the half-shekel donations given to the Temple.

*Shevuot:* Talmudic tractate dealing with oaths.

*Sifra:* Midrashic commentary on Leviticus.

*Sifrei:* Midrashic commentary on Numbers and Deuteronomy.

*Sotah:* Talmudic tractate dealing with a suspected adulteress.

*Sukkah:* Talmudic tractate dealing with the festival of Sukkot.

*Taanit:* Talmudic tractate dealing with fasts.

Talmud: The Oral Torah as taught by the great masters, between 50 B.C.E. and 500 C.E. It is composed of the Mishnah and the discussions of the Mishnah in the great academies of Babylonia. Next to the Torah itself, the Talmud is the most important text for the Jew. Interspersed among the legal sections of the Talmud is a wealth of ethical and inspirational teachings called Aggadah. The entire Talmud was first printed in Venice in 1523, along with the commentaries of Rashi and Tosafot.

*Tanna debei Eliyahu:* An early Midrash attributed to the teachings of the prophet Elijah, first printed in Venice, 1598.

Targum: Aramaic translation of the Torah by the convert Onkelos (around 90 C.E.). Printed in most major editions.

*Temurah:* Talmudic tractate dealing with exchanged sacrifices.

*Terumah:* Talmudic tractate dealing with priestly offerings.

*Torah Temimah:* A comprehensive Torah commentary by Rabbi Baruch Epstein (1860–1942), first published in Vilna in 1904. The work quotes the main Talmudic references to a verse, offering commentaries on them.

*Torat Kohanim:* Also known as *Sifrei,* this is one of the earliest commentaries on Leviticus, written by the Talmudic sage Rav (about 220 C.E.) and often quoted in the Talmud. First published in Constantinople in 1530.

*Tosefta:* Additions to the Mishnah, often quoted in the Talmud.

Vayikra Rabbah: Midrash on Leviticus.

*Yesodei Hatorah:* Fundamentals of Torah, a section of Maimonides' Code of Law.

*Yevamot:* Talmudic tractate dealing with a widowed sister-in-law.

*Yoma:* Talmudic tractate dealing with Yom Kippur.

*Yoreh Dei'ah:* Section of the Code of Jewish Law by R. Yosef Caro, dealing with dietary laws.

*Zevachim:* Talmudic tractate dealing with sacrifices.

# The Author

Avraham Yaakov Finkel was born in Basel, Switzerland, and lived in the Hague, Netherlands, until 1942, when the Nazis deported him to Bergen-Belsen.

He is the author of such books as *The Essential Maimonides; In My Flesh I See God; Contemporary Sages; The Essence of the Holy Days; The Great Chasidic Masters; The Responsa Anthology; The Great Torah Commentators; Shabbos Secrets;* and most recently, *Kabbalah,* biographical sketches of the Kabbalistic masters, followed by excerpts from their works. He has also translated numerous works, including such monumental classics as *Ein Yaakov* by Rabbi Yaakov ibn Chaviv, *Kuzari* by Rabbi Yehudah Halevi, *Chovot Halevavot* (Duties of the Heart) by Rabbi Bachya ibn Pakuda, five volumes of Mishneh Torah, the compendium of all Jewish laws by Maimonides, and *Selected Letters* by Maimonides.

He resides in New York with his wife, Suri.

# Index

## T

**Temple Israel**
Minneapolis, Minnesota

IN HONOR OF THE BAT MITZVAH OF
COURTNEY ANN WOLD
FROM HER GRANDPARENTS,
DR. SANFORD & TONI RAIHILL

APRIL 24, 2004